CUMB[illegible] M
A SOC[illegible] IVE
[illegible] 4

IAN ASHBRIDGE

REDBURN PUBLISHING

First edition

Published in Great Britain

By Redburn Publishing 1999

A CIP catalogue record for this book is available from the British Library

ISBN 0 9536887 0 4

Redburn Publishing
PO Box 72
Cramlington
NE23 6YQ
Great Britain

Cover photograph courtesy of Carlisle Library

Printed and bound in Great Britain
By Ink Truck, Carlisle, Cumbria

CONTENTS

ACKNOWLEDGEMENTS

My thanks go to the Assistant County Archivist of Cumbria Records Office, Carlisle, who welcomed me there as long ago as 1989 when I was researching family history, and where the idea for this book first took shape. Subsequently I owe a debt of gratitude to the staff there and to those of Carlisle Library, most of whom assisted me with access to various local material relating to the period under scrutiny, available at one place or the other or both: census returns, maps, newspaper reports, articles, and a particularly interesting paper by D.R. Perriam on Carlisle Gaol.

I am indebted to the Head Librarian at Workington for similar assistance, to Harry Fancy, for his instructive information on Whitehaven, and to members of staff at Kew Public Records Office, where papers relating to several of the cases presented here are preserved. Nor can I forget the authors of the publications listed in the bibliography at the end of this work, whose own findings were such an invaluable source of background information, along with occasional material from other publications just too numerous to mention, several of the sociological publications listed being made available to me by the Literary and Philosophical Society of Newcastle upon Tyne, whose obliging staff I must also thank.

I spent an interesting and constructive day with David Garner, Curator of the Cumbria Police Museum at Penrith, who was also kind enough to photocopy a number of papers for me from his archives before I departed. It was he who imbued me with additional interest in Rudge, Martin and Baker. However, I must emphasise that the views expressed here in respect of the police manhunt for the infamous trio are mine and not his.

Many Cumbrian folk were exceedingly helpful during my field trips to Lanercost, Cockermouth, Workington and elsewhere, and here I am thinking especially of Rees Banton of Flimby. But I am indebted also to Bob Baker and Marie-Ann Casey for their artistic input, and to my nephew Andrew Richardson for taking several of the photographs in use here, complementing the material which Carlisle Library, H.M. Stationery Office, Cumbrian Newspapers Limited and Cumbria Police obligingly allowed me to reproduce. I also have my nephew as well as my friend Mary Signey to thank, for reading the original manuscript and encouraging me to try and get it published. And last but not least, my thanks are due to Adrienne Storey, who re-typed and amended the manuscript in her spare time, with her unfailing interest and patience.

BACKGROUND

Cumbria undoubtedly had a more violent history than many of our regions. As early as the second century A.D. there is mention of its Celtic tribesmen rising savagely against the Romans in the Lake District, presumably chaffing at the occupation, this proceeding decades of earlier struggle against the Scots and the Irish. The Romans were to keep the local inhabitants on a tight rein throughout most of their time in Britain, primarily for wider-reaching defensive reasons, but indications are that they also remained consistently wary of the natives themselves.

With the passing of the Romans came the Norse invasions, when at one stage Carlisle itself was left in total ruins following extensive slaughter. Gradually, given continuous incursions too, from Scotland and kingdoms to the east and south, the racial composition of the original Cumbrian in fact changed, to become a mixture of Celt, Pict, Angle, Dane, Saxon and others, much as it is today, leading to a race of shrewd, industrious, tenacious people, albeit well-attuned to violence too, as a result of their on-going environment, often leaving many with little choice but to fight or perish.

The situation changed to some degree with the advent of the Normans, who divided much of the region into Baronies, with the emphasis on masters and men, bringing peace of sorts for a time, but Cumberland, as it was now specifically known, was never entirely free from armed conflict, given the proximity of Scotland.

Continuing border warfare gave rise to the mafia-like activities of the Border Reivers, reaching their culmination in the sixteenth century, with several of the latter being eventually hanged at Carlisle and much of the countryside beyond becoming at times greatly impoverished. The Civil War brought further bloodshed, with especially heavy fighting around Cockermouth and the subsequent persecution of papists and Quakers throughout the county following the Restoration.

The 1715 rebellion led to trials at Carlisle though perhaps surprisingly, none of those sentenced to death appear to have been executed. It was a different state of affairs following the 1745 rebellion, affording perhaps the greatest stain on Cumberland's character, with more than three hundred prisoners being held in inhuman conditions in Carlisle Castle, barbaric executions ultimately taking place at Brampton, Penrith and Carlisle. The last were carried out on Harraby Hill, long the disposal site for most manner of local felons, one of the condemned men apparently taking bitter consolation at the fact that he wouldn't be tried by a Cumbrian jury in the next world.

Even before the coming of the eighteenth century however, the local scene was already beginning to change. Cumberland had now ceased to be a regular battleground and its people were no different to those anywhere else after all, in that the majority wished to live without the continuing threat of violence. The gibbet on

Harraby Hill for its part eventually fell into disuse and the county's execution site was transferred to the less commanding surroundings of Carlisle Sands, sometime in the late eighteenth century.

Nevertheless, there was still plenty of crime of all kinds in Cumberland as elsewhere, fuelled to some extent by the dismal social and economic conditions of the times, albeit with some felons remaining rather more colourful than others. One of the latter was John Hatfield of 'Mary of Buttermere' fame who was dispatched on the Sands for forgery in September 1803. But it was said too that the Cumbrian jury who decided against Hatfield were swayed primarily by his dishonourable conduct towards the maid of Buttermere, rather than his counterfeiting activities.

A much more ruthless individual, the double murderer, James Wood, went the same way as Hatfield on the Sands in 1808. The following year, two Whitehaven bank robbers, Edwards and Stock, were executed in the old city though the site of their execution is uncertain, as is that of Danny McCrory, who was turned off for multiple burglary in 1813.

Thereafter however, we know that the execution venue was in the area of the old Carlisle Gaol, situated between Blackfriars Street and West Walls and close to the court houses in English Street. Several felons were hanged publicly in that area over succeeding years on a scaffold erected temporarily for the purpose: John Donald for burglary in 1816, John Townsend and Christopher Gale for forgery and theft in 1819. And in August 1820, a twenty-one year old Wigton man, James Lightfoot, was hanged there for murder. Lightfoot protested his innocence to the end and was not without sympathisers, even while circumstantial evidence was strong against him. He was followed onto the scaffold the following month by an infamous trio, Little, Armstrong and Woof, who were all hanged together for a series of local robberies, Little threatening beforehand to break the neck of the hangman.

The new Carlisle Gaol opened officially in 1827, built next to the court houses in English Street, still there today after almost 200 years. Robert Fox and Philip Tinnaney were both hanged on the front wall of the goal that same year for the murder of wife and girlfriend respectively. Three years later, in 1830, two young teenagers, Robert Lamb and Joseph Furnace each had death sentences recorded against them for housebreaking. But the sentences were commuted to transportation and it seemed highly unlikely that the twosome would ever have been hanged.

Times were indeed changing, but it has to be said that many felons in the county of Cumberland were actually reprieved over preceding decades too, with transportation or imprisonment often being substituted for the original death sentences imposed, such a practice having became increasingly common throughout Britain. While contrary to popular belief, many had also been acquitted.

Cumberland's record was as good as any. By the time John Pearson was hanged for murder at Carlisle in March 1835, it was true to say that such an event was now fairly rare in the county while by 1837, a large number of offences previously punishable by hanging were deemed to no longer merit a death sentence country-wide. On the other hand, there were still to be a number of murder trials in Cumberland over ensuing years, several of these culminating in the death penalty. Between mid 1860 and early 1862 there were in fact no less than five such trials and two public executions.

But following this, the pattern of capital crime did become more staggered in Cumberland again, with only one execution for murder during the next twenty-four years, that of the tragic James Dalgleish in 1876. There were other trials for murder, or attempted murder, but these ended mainly in imprisonment, or acquittal, with unsoundness of mind being a prime consideration on at least three other occasions. A more persistent capital offence continued to be that of single girls charged with eliminating their illegitimate offspring at birth, though this very often reverted to a short term of imprisonment or acquittal for concealment of birth only. By and large however, most Cumbrians generally continued to draw back altogether from any senseless taking of life, even while a wide variety of other crimes continued, but were nevertheless increasingly contained by a young vigilant police force. Such was the general picture in Cumberland as the nineteenth century advanced against a backdrop of some economic and social progress nationally, though the county itself still had its share of people living in very poor circumstances and was from time to time too, still rocked by some especially unpleasant crime such as the sinister riddle of Lucy Sands in 1881, and the Rudge, Martin and Baker episode of 1885.

This book seeks to cover crime in Cumberland from 1834 to 1894 in tandem with the attendant social scene, which had to have some bearing on many of the crimes committed, though not all of them, the emphasis being on capital offending but with attention being afforded to other types of crime too. Though spanning just sixty years, this was an especially interesting period in Britain overall, with evidence of growing liberal thinking in respect of many social issues, particularly in the realms of crime, following upon winds of change which finally saw not only the end of hanging for any crime short of murder, but also transportation beyond the seas. Public hanging too became obsolete and there was a growing anti-hanging lobby. Even while paradoxically, a fourteen-year-old local boy could still be sentenced to be whipped two dozen times for theft in 1865, with the judge enquiring benignly as to whether the cat or the birch would be more effective? Cumbrian sentencing still had more than its share of contradictions, irrespective of the social scene, and these were to continue over the decades, as in many other regions.

But while there were undoubtedly innocents of a sort, there were certainly blackguards too in the Cumberland calendar, an interesting bunch nonetheless, be they murderers, thieves, or mere deviant misfits who did often steal just to survive and who could probably be termed victims of their environment, along with a whole range of other reprobates, the majority providing a quite fascinating insight into a side of local history all too often neglected or misrepresented by writers of books on Cumberland. This book seeks to make good that deficiency.

1: THE BEAST OF RANDYLANDS

Not all criminals are necessarily so unlikeable whatever their crimes and the reader will encounter a number in this book who had some redeeming qualities and others who were simply unfortunate. However, Cumberland threw up some particularly odious specimens too, during the period under scrutiny. We actually begin with a man who was of especially brutal disposition, who mounted the scaffold at Carlisle in March 1835 mumbling religious platitudes, but who was essentially concerned with his own immediate needs, with little mention to make at all of the defenceless woman whose life he had taken. We shall encounter others as callous and more cunning than John Pearson, but few to equal him for sheer persistent selfishness and cruelty.

For more than seven years, following the double execution in March 1827 of Robert Fox for poisoning his wife near Sellafield and of Philip Tinnaney, for battering out his girlfriend's brains in the St. Nicholas area of Carlisle, no one had been executed in Cumberland. This had to be something of a continuing tribute to the majority of law-abiding Cumbrians and those living among them, as well as to the forces of law and order in the county, gradually improved following the formation of Peel's police force in 1829, and to the more reasoned thinking already beginning to prevail in the local courts as elsewhere, at least in respect of what were still deemed more serious crimes. John Pearson was to change all that.

The story begins at an inn at Abbey Bridge in October, 1834, some two miles north of the small town of Brampton and half a mile from Lanercost and its beautiful priory church. There is still an inn at Abbey Bridge today and the church itself remains, semi-ruined but appealing as ever, with farms and houses situated discreetly about it. The surrounding countryside is itself unspoiled with narrow lanes and high hedges, meadows and woodland, the whole within fairly easy reach of Naworth Castle, the home of the Howard family. The immediate scene of the murder, a dwelling known as Randylands in a field above Lanercost is long gone, but the surrounding basic setting has altered little since John Pearson's crime.

During the early evening of 13th October, 1834, Pearson arrived at the Abbey Bridge Inn with his wife Jane. He was forty-seven years old and has been described as stout and middle-sized. Variously employed as a farm worker, drainer and mole catcher, he cut an unprepossessing figure in a dirty mole-skin jacket and tartan trousers. He had been married before and there were several children of the union but his first wife had died of consumption. He had married his second wife, Jane, only six weeks previously.

We know less of Jane Pearson than we know of her husband but given that he was soon to become so obsessed in his inebriated state over what he believed to be her infidelity, she was probably still quite attractive. We do know that she was only forty-four years old with a full head of black hair which is a pointer of sorts.

Impressions otherwise are of a quiet inoffensive woman, quite dutiful towards her partner.

Pearson drank steadily as the evening progressed but his wife was not observed to drink at all. Though merely a hired man he appears to have had ample money to spend on liquor but being well known as a poacher, may have had additional money available from this latter activity. Then finally the couple rose to go. Pearson would have drank on at the inn but his wife had suggested that he round off his day's drinking at home. In the light of events to come, she would probably have done much better to have left him to drink himself insensible where he was and gone on home alone but wasn't to know what lay in store. As it was, Pearson took with him a small portion of coals and his wife undertook to carry a gill of rum for her sire. It was noted in passing that he was already the worse for drink but not excessively so. In nineteenth century Britain, still as notorious in 1834 for heavy drinking as the century before it, a man had to be very drunk indeed to merit undue attention. The couple made their way over the bridge outside the pub and on through the darkness towards Randylands where they had a room.

We are dependent upon the word of Rachel Whitehead, a lodger in the same abode as the couple for what transpired over ensuing hours. Whitehead scarcely knew the Pearsons who had only moved in eleven days previously. Her husband had recently been forced to travel elsewhere to find work, a not uncommon occurrence then as now. She was currently living alone in a room next to that of a couple in a single storey building which appears to have been a kind of common lodging house with a communal kitchen. The rooms were divided by partitions without so much as a ceiling, a contrast indeed to the luxury of Naworth Castle not much more than a mile away. Britain was glaringly inequal in those days, in housing as in much else, and Cumberland was no different to other regions.

The landlady of the inn was sure that the Pearsons had departed at eight p.m. Whitehead had thought they arrived home around seven thirty p.m. This slight difference in timing was never fully queried but at least it was reasonably established that the couple arrived home together before the late evening. As it was, given the flimsy walls and lack of any ceiling, Whitehead soon became aware of Pearson's voice raised accusingly against his wife and the sound of repeated blows, though the victim herself remained docile and silent beyond a single cry of 'murder!' Whether such behaviour had already became common on the part of Pearson during the short marriage is unknown but on this occasion the rotund drunkard was clearly accusing his wife of infidelity and becoming ever increasingly violent.

Whitehead was too frightened to intervene but nor could she sleep as the beating continued intermittently for hours. Then there was silence. With the coming of daybreak, Pearson left the building. About eight thirty a.m. the victim cried out to Whitehead, requesting a cup of tea. Whitehead obliged, noting that Jane Pearson was lying on the bed naked and bloodied. But the neighbour was still too frightened to engage in any extended conversation, nor did the abused woman appear inclined to encourage her to speak a great deal at all, beyond asking for a cup of water after she had drank the tea, obvious evidence of persistent thirst after heavy loss of body fluid, in this instance, blood.

Pearson himself hadn't gone very far, merely back to the Abbey Bridge Inn where he advised the landlady that he couldn't recall taking away any coals the previous evening, though he now presented as reasonably sober. Did he recall the quart of rum taken away at the same time by his wife? We don't know for certain but he now returned the empty bottle, exchanging it for a further pint of the same. He made no mention of his wife at all at the inn but returning to Randylands, encountered Rachel Whitehead. According to the latter, he began almost at once to speak of Jane Pearson's infidelity, brandishing her gown and after striking his wife again, threatening to finish Whitehead also. It was now around eleven a.m. The frightened neighbour beat a hasty retreat and encountered another woman along the highway, Sarah Thirlwell, to whom she gave an account of recent events at Randylands.

Sarah Thirlwell was made of rather sterner stuff. She went along to the Pearsons' abode and peered inside, noting the inflamed husband wielding a huge rake shank but neither heard nor saw anyone else. Then her courage deserted her and she too hurried on her way. In those days, as now, few seemingly wished to interfere in domestic disputes, but the prospect of confronting someone like Pearson had to be an added deterrent. Fairly soon afterwards, a pedlar names James Barrett was passing the house and saw a naked woman lying on the ground outside. It was Jane Pearson. She got unsteadily to her feet and went back inside. Her husband appeared on the scene and followed her.

The pedlar went on to inform a local woman, Ann Thompson, of what he had seen. Thompson and others converged on Randylands but it was too late. It was now early afternoon and the pathetic woman could be seen through a window lying on the bed, partially covered with a quilt. Pearson stood nearby, swigging from his bottle, whistling and singing, and advising anyone prepared to listen that his wife was dead. Closer scrutiny by Thompson and others confirmed this to be the case. Beside the bed with its bloodstained linen and tragic occupant lay the rake shank covered with blood, and a lock of the victim's hair torn from her head. But even now, the drunken bully denied any part in the crime, saying that he had found his wife in her present state. Shortly afterwards he was taken into custody and lodged in Carlisle Gaol, insinuating that the bloodstains on his hands and clothing were the marks of clay from his employment as a drainer.

Thereafter, events moved quickly. A post mortem revealed bruises all over the body and face of the victim but death was deemed to have eventually occurred as a result of a violent blow to the back of the head. Everything pointed to John Pearson as the culprit though he continued to stubbornly maintain his innocence. On the other hand, gaol staff had at first been inclined to think that he had been simulating insanity when first brought in, possibly as a kind of last ditch defence to fall back on. He had been given to shaking fits and contortions and hallucinations. What appears to have been the real explanation in this instance is that Pearson had been suffering withdrawal symptoms given his long history of alcohol abuse. In sum, the man was probably a champion alcoholic, given the background information which was eventually to emerge and it seems rather surprising that the gaol authorities didn't comprehend this earlier. But be this as it may, the prisoner was quite lucid by the time of his trial at Cumberland Lent Assizes the following March before Baron James Parker, firmly pleading not guilty to murder.

Needless to say, given the number of witnesses ranged against him, his prospects of acquittal were slim. Bloodstained bedding and clothing produced in court damned him irrevocably, along with the rake shank, some five feet long and one and a half inches thick, all causing considerable excitement in the crowded court, for the majority of the public were as much taken with the trappings of macabre crime then as they are today, in Cumberland or anywhere else, as well as with the killer and the crime itself.

Pearson still obviously hoped he might extradite himself from his dangerous dilemma however. Being invited to speak up in his own defence he launched into a long garrulous account of how both he and his wife had been drunk the night before her death. He spoke of having lost her and of then finding a man with their basket in a local field. But there had still been no sign of Jane and she had the door key! He went to seek his wife but remembered nothing until the next morning when he woke up in bed with her, finding her all bloodied. She had spoken of a man having taken advantage of her. He took off to seek the culprit and arrived home again to find his wife dead. He had given her a kiss and informed those about him.

A lot of this had to be so much arrant nonsense and perhaps tells us something of the man's level of functioning. There were too many people who had already testified as to what had really occurred in their experience, certainly from the late evening onwards of 13th October 1834 until well into the following day, when Pearson must almost undoubtedly have recalled what he had been doing. Thereupon Baron Parker proceeded to sum up. His address to the jury need not concern us here in its entirety but he made some especial play on the fact that voluntary drunkenness was no excuse for what someone might do while under the influence; and Pearson had not been made deliberately drunk by anyone else, which told even further against him. His Lordship intoned that a blow struck in anger caused by provocation and leading to death could nevertheless result in such a crime being reduced to manslaughter. But such had scarcely been the case here for there was no evidence of any provocation. Likewise a man finding his wife actually committing adultery and killing her might also have his charge reduced to manslaughter, given the provocation involved, but there was no evidence that Jane Pearson had been untrue at all while the beating itself had gone on over an extended period and there had to be a question as to whether it arose from genuine anger or evil intent?

There was more in the same vein. All in all, the judge spoke for almost an hour, seeking to present a balanced picture for the benefit of the jury but the relentless beating of the unfortunate woman, the extent of her injuries and the final mortal wound had to be almost sufficient of themselves to damn her husband in the eyes of the twelve good men and true. They took but fifteen minutes to find him guilty. A hush fell upon those packed in the courtroom as sentence of death was pronounced. The person most unmoved appeared to be John Pearson. He asked for his hat, clapped it on his head and walked from the dock without a backward glance.

The man's apparent indifference to his fate confirmed his villainy insofar as the public were concerned. There had never been much sympathy for him in any case. He had taken his wife's life in a most brutal way, there could be no doubting that; it was felt that he deserved to be found guilty. Yet the poor victim herself was already slipping into obscurity and there was no one else around to cover the missing gaps in the tragic saga, primarily concerning her alleged infidelity. In sum, could she have been involved with another man on that fatal night, during the very short space of time actually unaccounted for?

That does seem highly unlikely, nor was she drunk as her husband stated, there having been no evidence of this whatsoever. She may have became impatient and abandoned Pearson along the short stretch of dark road winding upwards towards Randylands, but it couldn't have been for long for Rachel Whitehead heard them both return home together. This at a time when the landlady was sure they were in fact still at the inn, but Whitehead's clock might have been wrong, presuming she possessed one, or she could have merely guessed the time. The fact remained that they were both heard arriving home, certainly before nine p.m. as that was the time another neighbour, Harry Hewer, and his son, claimed to have discovered a small basket below a hedge close to Randylands. They heard raised voices and then Pearson virtually fell through the hedge, took the basket and mouthed a few drunken words of thanks before staggering off again. This must have been the episode the murderer referred to in his defence statement but both he and his wife had been heard by Rachel Whitehead prior to this; indeed, the beating already seems to have commenced, though there was no evidence at all that anyone else had been abroad earlier on the dark road to proposition Jane Pearson or take advantage of her and there was very little time available for this in any case.

What seems most likely is that her husband stumbled drunkenly away on his own, rendered the more incapable by the cold air, and couldn't find his wife for a time. However, they must have soon came together again for Whitehead heard them both arrive home, contrary to what Pearson had said. But the basket was missing, which either he or his partner had set down and lost in the darkness. He presently recovered it from another man, drawing all the wrong conclusions again and then may have had difficulty getting back into the house, further inflaming him, his wife having the key and perhaps reluctant to readmit him given his aggressive state. What is more certain is that shortly afterwards he embarked fully upon an orgy of drunken intermittent violence which continued until his wife was dead, punctuated noticeably by a visit to the inn for more drink. What happened to the coals he had been carrying the evening before we don't know. He may have lost those also but irrespective of anything else, Jane Pearson had to deserve much better from a man who only six weeks previously had promised to love and cherish her.

While Pearson had been in Carlisle Gaol awaiting trail, all kinds of stories were circulating about him. For instance, it was put about that he had also murdered his first wife, and a young girl he had fished out dead from the Tyne. There was no truth in either of these rumours or any others like them but after the trial and execution, what emerged were more authentic details of a totally self-centred individual who had dedicated his life to drink and petty crime, neglected those close to him, thrown away all his chances, and ignored the recent advice of a very considerate employer.

John Pearson, it transpired, had been born in 1788 near Haltwhistle in Northumberland, close to the border with Cumberland. His father had died while he was still a child and there had obviously been little firm guidance from anyone else or he had preferred to ignore such. He had taken early to poaching and drinking and was firmly set on a course of self-destruction before he was out of his teens. Though he was to obtain a number of good situations in the north as a gamekeeper and agricultural worker over ensuing years, he lost most of these through drinking. Nor could he refrain from poaching but was almost invariably caught eventually and sentenced to hard labour or fined. At one stage he tried the army but after a few years, took his discharge. The discipline of soldiering was seemingly not his forte either.

During much of this time he had a wife and eventually five children, but totally neglected them, usually in favour of drink or womanising. His wife eventually dying of consumption, his children appear to have disowned him which was scarcely surprising. He came to the Brampton area and found a good situation with a farmer, Thomas Taylor. The Taylor family attempted to guide him and show him every example but he was imbibing harder than ever. In a society noted for its heavy drinking he appears to have gone well beyond the norms even accepted by the hardest drinkers and such was his state when he married Jane. What she saw in him no one will ever know but possibly she was poor and lonely and prepared to overlook his failings, presuming that she even knew of them initially. As it was, his drinking continued and the rest is history.

He was sentenced to death on Wednesday, 11th March, 1835 and scheduled to hang on the following Friday. Such was the speedy manner of dispatch in those days once the trial was over. Given the man's deplorable history, it may sound rather odd that he should subsequently have embraced religion but he did at least go through the motions while in gaol for the last time as indeed others like him had done before, which is perhaps not too surprising after all with the hangman's noose a distinct possibility almost from the time of his arrest.

But during his last few hours on earth, John Pearson seemed much more concerned to find a suitable burial place in the prison yard. The story goes that he finally settled upon a place near the pump and his wish to lie there was granted. Just before the execution itself he did admit to having knowingly beaten his wife in his drunken passion and to perhaps having inflicted the fatal wound, albeit with no intention of taking her life, but with no real expression of regret or sympathy. Immediately prior to being turned off on the front wall of the gaol before a huge crowd, his main concern was to eschew the blindfold for as long as possible, that he might continue to see the world about him to the end.

He was hanged in his clogs which were buried with him and there is a final ironic twist to the sorry tale. Years later, workmen were digging the foundations for a new building within the gaol confines on a piece of ground which took in Pearson's grave. Of the beast of Randylands not a great deal remained but the clogs were recovered in a reasonable state of preservation. However, no one really knows what became of them afterwards.

2: DEATH OF A CHILD

Following the Pearson trial and its outcome, the Cumbrian court scene reverted back to its rather monotonous pattern. Not for a further twelve years would there be another hanging in the county. It is interesting to note how carefully the British courts as a whole continued to go about the business of trying potential gallows birds with a mind to avoiding the supreme penalty if possible, as indeed they had done for some decades now.

The courts also remained considerate in the trying of crimes committed by the criminal rank and file: the burglar, the petty thief, the forger, and others of similar ilk. Many of the foregoing offenders would almost inevitably have ended on the scaffold in the not too distant past, come what may. This was definitely no longer the norm. On the other hand, there were still plenty of alternatives to hanging at the disposal of the courts and these continued to be used with unremitting harshness once the verdict of guilty had been reached as it often was, in Cumberland as anywhere else.

One consistent means of disposal in the 1830s and 1840s was still transportation and this was especially well favoured in the land of the lakes. Let any criminal re-offend but once, or possibly twice, and he or she could quickly be en route from Carlisle to the prison hulks at Portsmouth, Deptford or Woolwich, there to await passage to Australia or Van Diemen's Land.

Most were sentenced to seven years initially, but not inevitably. There were those with a meagre record who went for ten years, and fourteen years and others for life. Nor was age or category of crime any greater barrier. Thus in 1841, twenty-three year-old Isaac Milburn was sentenced to ten years transportation for stealing a coat valued at two shillings. In 1844, twenty-nine-year-old John Sewell received fourteen years for stealing two sheep. The following year, twenty-year-old John Gillespie was transported for the remainder of his natural life for burglary at Wigton. And not too long afterwards, twelve-year-old Thomas Rudd was transported for ten years for stealing a comb, a tin box and other assorted articles. Apparently his parents had been unable to reform him. It is probably worthy of mention too that irrespective of sentence, few ever returned from down under.

Other sentences in Cumberland about this time ranged from nine months imprisonment inclusive of three weeks solitary confinement for a fifty-five year old woman for stealing a petticoat, an apron and a handkerchief, to six calendar months hard labour for twelve-year-old Thomas Drewery for theft at Workington, with the added recommendation by his Lordship that the boy's father should whip him well upon his release.

Hard times undoubtedly, though clearly the emphasis was on the protection of property, with a fifty-three-year-old man receiving only twelve months for raping a nine year old girl during the same period. And when thirty-six-year-old Frank Wardrop stabbed and wounded another man in Longtown, he received a mere one week's imprisonment.

Most crimes of theft at least were committed by those of limited education and meagre prospects who were generally offending because they were so desperately poor. Cumberland was no exception in this respect. But most of the offenders still had their lives at the end of it all. A woman in a rather different category who might just have added to the Cumbrian hanging statistics of the 1840s was Jane Crosby, taken into custody and eventually brought to court following a horrendous episode which became known as the Lamonby child roasting case.

Crosby was a thirty-year-old Scot, married to a Cumbrian, William Crosby. The couple had been domiciled for some time in the small rural community of Lamonby, nine miles from Penrith. The husband however was often absent. He was the tenant of the local inn, the Blue Miller, but normally left his wife in charge of it from weekend to weekend while he worked on a distant farm. Such seems to have been a quite regular pattern by that time in many communities, the husband leaving his wife behind to seek a living elsewhere as indeed we have already noted in our encounter with Rachel Whitehead.

In this instance, however, the husband was leaving an obviously disturbed and complicated lady to watch the shop. More ominously still, she also had sole charge of their two children, ten-year-old Mary and seven-year-old Sarah Ann.

Jane Crosby was not only well known in the locality as a chronic drunkard. She was also known to physically abuse her children and to threaten her husband with violence. Only months before the tragedy which was soon to engulf the small family, he had been spending an extended period at home laid up in bed with a bad back. She had threatened to straighten his back with a poker then poison the 'bairns' and poison herself and had already made several attempts to harm herself prior to this. Well it might be asked in the light of the foregoing why such a woman was ever deemed fit to cope with two dependent children and a public house? And why her husband left her alone at all?

It was probably a case of needs must. The pub itself appears to have been no more than a pot house of which there were many in those days; a room in a dwelling house given over to the retailing of liquor, an activity which only just paid its way. The pittance William Crosby earned as a farm servant was probably the more tangible mainstay which he relied upon to feed and clothe the family at least reasonably adequately in those times known as the hungry forties. No great skill would be required otherwise on the part of his wife to serve a pint of ale or a glass of rum to the rural clientelle.

But what still of his wife's intemperate habits and her volatile state of mind? Ready access to alcohol obviously wouldn't incline her towards sobriety nor would enforced responsibility assist her mental condition. But again, to be charitable to her husband, he may have became resigned and accustomed to his wife's problems, with familiarity allaying overt concern. Children for their part were taken rather more for granted in an age of high mortality and speedy reproduction. Those who survived were generally expected to shift for themselves at a much younger age and to cope with many more privations than they are today.

Yet people still had feelings too and Cumbrians were no exception. Thus when Jane Crosby had been seen chasing her children and swinging them around by the hair during her husband's absence, such conduct did not go unremarked. Her drunkenness and pathetic suicide attempts were noted critically, even in an age when drunken parents and eccentric individuals were commonplace enough. Silent contempt was finally to spill over into fierce outrage following a terrible occurrence on the night of 28th January, 1845.

Late that evening, neighbours were roused by the older girl in a distraught state. She told the nearest neighbour the rather garbled story that her mother had been to Skelton village, two miles away, and that her sister had got burnt. To another she said that her sister's clothing was on fire and her mother couldn't put it out. They hurried to the inn which was devoid of clientelle. A horrifying sight met their eyes. The kitchen was full of smoke and there was Jane Crosby holding her younger daughter beside a blazing fire. The naked child was extensively burnt about the breast, hands and face with much of her hair singed off. And yet perhaps miraculously, the seven-year-old youngster was still alive.

First to challenge the mother was the local blacksmith, John Wilson, a comparative newcomer to the district and a not unkindly man who had came to know Jane Crosby fairly well. He recognised her failings but was still inclined to give her the benefit of the doubt. Wilson attempted to stifle his nausea and enquired as to what the hell had gone on? Meanwhile, young Mary busied herself remaking the tangled bed in an adjoining room.

The pathetic woman, now comparatively sober though she had been observed to be drunk earlier in the day, told a rambling tale of having set off earlier for Skelton to buy provisions. On the way back she had thought she smelt smoke and found her bed on fire and her youngest daughter lying outside by a stile badly burnt. But then she contradicted herself, speaking of having trodden on Sarah within the door upon her return, while saying she had been no further than some lime kilns a short way up the road. Possibly she was shocked but there appeared some indication too that she could be telling lies to exonerate herself.

By this time the place was crowded with people. The little victim cried out for water but was dead shortly afterwards, despite the efforts of a doctor to treat her. And several of those present had not failed to notice an ugly bruise on the older girl's head.

At the ensuing inquest, a more damning story was told by the older child. She spoke of her mother having been drinking on the day of the tragedy and of having gone early to bed without ever leaving the house afterwards, locking the outer door and leaving she and her sister by the fire in the kitchen. Sarah Ann's clothing had caught alight. Upon being awakened the mother had leapt from her bed and put out the flames with some bedclothes. But then she had taken Sarah close to the fire and held her over it. Mary was sure that this was what had caused her sister's death.

The mother was removed to Carlisle Gaol. Upon being taken away she threatened suicide, a not unfamiliar refrain, and spoke with some hostility of local witnesses and her eldest daughter: 'that little bugger will do for me'. She also dictated a statement emphasising her innocence but it did not take long for her to be indicted for the wilful murder of Sarah Ann on the strength of her elder daughter's testimony.

Word of 'the Lamonby child roasting' and the players involved had quickly found its way into the local press. There was no sympathy there for Jane Crosby. She was virtually deemed guilty before having ever been tried, with exaggerated reports of the tragic episode provided to titillate the public as a whole. Those who couldn't read had accounts read to them by those who could. By the time of the date set for the trial the following month, public interest was at fever pitch but was as quickly dampened. Given Mary Crosby's seemingly low emotional state and the fact that she was the key witness, the trial was adjourned until the next Assizes some six months hence.

In the meantime, the father had already sold up anything he had and moved away from Lamonby. Mary had remained in custody and it was suggested that she now be bailed back to him. But it being felt that she might be at some risk of contamination as a witness if this happened, she went into the care of the chief gaoler's wife at Carlisle instead. Her mother remained elsewhere in the gaol.

At the August Assizes the same feverish interest continued, with the crowded courtroom so hot that several panes of glass had to be broken to let in air. Mary looked much better for having been in the care of the gaoler's wife who had obviously looked after her better than her own mother had ever done. It quickly emerged however, that the fact of the girl having said different things before and during the inquest would be a key factor in the case.

Beginning to sob profusely, Mary stuck by her statement to the Coroner, that her mother had held Sarah over the open fire after extinguishing the original flames. Neighbours too told of the mother's contradictory utterances afterwards, of her mistreatment of her children and her desultory way of life. There was also the added factor of the dead child's clothing found at close hand. Medical opinion had it that the burning of the frock and slip alone would not have caused all the injuries found upon the body, the clothing still being comparatively intact and recognisable. What was the truth of the matter?

The defence put up a good case for the mother. Why should Sarah be found clinging to her parent after the event with the latter addressing her tenderly? The mother's contradictory talk afterwards might simply have been the result of shock. And what of Mary's evidence? First the child had said, in sum, that her sister's clothing had caught fire and that her mother couldn't put the flames out after coming from Skelton. But then following questioning by the Coroner she had taken a different line, that her mother had never left the home and deliberately held Sarah over the fire after smothering the blazing garments with bedclothes. But why should Jane Crosby burn the child so openly afterwards in front of her elder daughter and then send her to call the neighbours? And was it feasible that such a crime would actually be committed in a public house where anyone could normally walk in? Much play too was made upon the blacksmith's statement that he had never seen Jane Crosby abuse her children, though indeed, others had testified to the contrary. Couldn't Mary in fact have caused the tragedy herself then conveniently turned the blame upon her mother? The defence didn't spare itself, while eschewing any mention of the prisoner's disturbed personality or her persistent drinking or the state of the deceased child's remaining clothing.

The judge obviously inclined towards the thinking of the defence, feeling that there had to be improbability in Mary's story and summed up accordingly. Within ten minutes of the jury retiring they were back with a verdict of not guilty. The mother was discharged but with a warning to treat Mary kindly and forget the past and to bear in mind that she would remain under observation. However, she wasn't discharged immediately from the courthouse itself. There was a hostile mob outside and she was detained several hours more until all the angry sceptics had departed. Then presumably she and her husband and surviving daughter departed together, with Victorian justice having been seen to be done. The trial itself had continued for eight hours. But just how valid was the verdict?

We might do well to examine the statement the agitated semi-illiterate woman had originally dictated in a search for some kind of reasoned answer. It was short but afforded a number of possible clues, even while it received but cursory attention in the courtroom. It ran as follows:-

"As to anything I have to say either one way or the other, certainly she was an obstinate girl. The two girls agreed very badly, the greater was the master of the little one. Sarah sometimes ran away and I was harder on her on that account. I never knew or saw her burning until I found her. I have taken my foot and kicked them in my passion. I was quite innocent of her. I was on the road when the child was burnt. I left her sitting and found her burnt. When I returned I found the lower part of the bed burning. It was smouldering, the coat was the worst to put out. I found the child besideways of the pump. I cannot say there was anything upon her but her stockings when I lifted her; if there was it fell off before I took her into the house. I cannot say how the coat was lying on the bed that night, but I generally threw the upper part of the coat to the far side of the bed and the coat tails hung over the outside of the bed. I have nothing more to say but I'm quite innocent of the child."

In fact the mother was never able to prove categorically that she had been away from the Blue Miller immediately prior to the tragedy. And her story of the body by the stile was proved to be without foundation. But it was confirmed that she had been in a neighbour's house between 8.00 p.m. and 9.00 p.m. The alarm itself wasn't raised until shortly before 10.00 p.m. This still left at least an hour unaccounted for and brings us to the content of the short statement.

What is immediately apparent is that neither girl was easy to handle. Scarcely surprising, given their mother's emotional make-up and life-style and treatment of her offspring, leading perhaps to an element of disturbance in both children. Meanwhile, it was almost midweek. The mother was to say that the family had been without provisions for three days and it is not unreasonable to support that after visiting the neighbour's house, she decided to travel on to Skelton to the store there. However, Skelton was a very long walk, reached by roads much lonelier than they are today with only the hamlet of Ellonby en route. Nevertheless, though still probably under the influence of drink, the pathetic woman could well have set off to procure provisions, albeit leaving her two vulnerable children seated by an unguarded fire without any kind of supervision as she had probably done many times before, in an establishment which few patronised.

Thereafter we enter the realms of total supposition. But let us assume that the sisters fell to squabbling and that the younger girl was pushed accidentally onto the fire, her clothing quickly catching alight. In a state of panic, Mary then tried to put the flames out with her father's spare coat with some success. But Sarah had became so badly burnt that she stumbled blindly outside, tearing off most of her burnt clothing as she went. Mary then threw the smouldering coat onto the bed but ignited the blankets in the process. Meanwhile, the mother hadn't got very far along the road given that it was a cold snowy night and turned back to be met by smoke and tragedy. Though still not totally sober, she may well have attended to the smouldering bedding before picking Sarah up outside as she claimed, though not by the stile; indeed, she referred to the pump in her statement, and then sent Mary out to rouse the neighbours.

The rest we know for certain except that Mary, following upon some hasty attempt to tidy the bed which she had originally ignited, may well have became thoroughly frightened following the death of Sarah and decided to change her story, having no great love for her mother in the first instance. In part, supposition again, but perhaps nearer the truth than the girl's lurid conflicting tale and borne out by the mother's statement, though the youngster never did retract her own damning testimony. Insofar as medical opinion was concerned in respect of the burnt clothing and its alleged limited effect on the actual injuries, we can but observe that the face, upper breast and hands bore the most serious burns in any case. Shock probably did the rest.

What is much more definite is that Jane Crosby was quite unfit to have the sole care of two vulnerable children, probably suffering from some kind of personality disorder – witness her earlier abortive attempts to hang herself, as well as being a chronic drunkard. Her husband's extended absences probably didn't help but she still couldn't treat him rationally when he was at home. So should Mary have been allowed to go back to her mother immediately after the trial given all the background dynamics? In these times it is highly unlikely that such would have been the case, nor would the mother have been discharged, hopefully without some offer of psychiatric treatment. That is where the thinking of our predecessors differed from the current climate of social care.

Yet still there were undoubtedly many other grey areas in the case of Jane Crosby. Mightn't she have been lying asleep after all, as Mary Crosby was to claim, when the accident occurred? Could she have held Sarah over the flames if only to obtain a better look at the injuries in the gloom and finished the child off in the process? It is tempting to play devil's advocate but we don't really know, except that in more primitive times on the Cumbrian-Scottish border, Jane Crosby might jut have merited less consideration and been hanged for infanticide. But on balance, justice of a kind does appear to have been done in August, 1845.

3: PASSING THE POISON

The list of those for trial at Carlisle Assizes in August, 1847 was remarkably short, given the continuing number of wretches normally appearing in the Cumbrian courts. But from time to time there would be a genuine lull in criminal activity in one region or another, leaving aside routine offences of brawling or drunkenness dealt with along with other lesser matters in the lower courts. Or Peel's expanding police force might have been less successful than usual.

In this instance there were but fourteen for trial at Carlisle. An unremarkable calendar altogether in the opinion of Lord Chief Baron Pollock. Most were the usual insignificant offenders who could as easily have been dealt with at the Quarter Sessions; one forty-seven-year-old man had been charged with stealing a hen, a fourteen-year-old boy with stealing a silver fork. Further up the scale were a Penrith couple charged with keeping a house of ill repute, and a seventeen-year-old youth who had drunkenly stabbed a man in a fight. Bad enough, but nothing calling for the jury's grave consideration in the opinion of his Lordship – with the exception of one offence, a grave matter indeed, the case which had brought the crowds flocking to Number 1 Court on 6th August, 1847, John Thompson of Union Street, Carlisle having been charged with the wilful murder of his wife Mary by poison in May of that same year.

The prisoner, a presentable man of forty-two, a millwright to trade, pleaded not guilty in a firm voice with the hint of a Tyneside accent. There followed a flowing fruity delivery by the advocate for the prosecution, advising the jury, in effect, to give the case their very close attention and to bring in a verdict of guilty providing they were satisfied the prisoner merited such. But if they were not satisfied, then he would be most delighted to hear them find the prisoner not guilty.

A cordial beginning to a most serious affair destined to result in a unanimous verdict of guilty. But if John Thompson was in any way moved at all by his situation on 6th August he did not show it, presenting an indifferent countenance as though wondering at all the fuss. And indeed, in spite of the tremendous interest which the case had engendered already, through Cumberland and beyond. Thompson was not the first man to be charged in the county with poisoning his wife as we already know. Twenty years previously, twenty-four-year old Robert Fox, a farm servant from Gosforth, had stood trial in the same court on precisely the same count.

A few words now about Fox, who bore some quite disturbing similarities to John Thompson in personality and technique. He has been described as stout but good looking, but with traits which appear to have been bordering on the psychopathical. He had been married only a short time to his wife Sarah who was already heavily pregnant by him. Her ostensibly decent husband had gone to Whitehaven and openly purchased arsenic, seemingly to poison rats, but had used it to lace his wife's coffee.

Within a short time she had given birth to a dead child and died herself a few hours later in terrible agony.

Fox eventually made a full confession but motive was never properly established. What did emerge was that though born and bred in Cumberland, he had became a wanderer and had worked as far afield as Lancashire and elsewhere. Possibly he had became weary of Sarah and wanted to be on his way again, but had brought himself to wed her because she was expecting his child, or through sheer family pressure. Then perhaps it has became too much after all and he had decided to be rid of mother and child before the child itself was born. Or maybe there had been another woman somewhere in the wings.....

Be this as it may, though suave enough in manner; indeed, he reduced the judge to tears at the conclusion of his trial with ringing words of atonement, Fox hadn't been too clever. Because a second party was required to witness any purchase of poison, he had called upon a former acquaintance, John James, to fulfil this role. Speaking in innocent jest, James had put Fox on the spot: 'Surely, Bob, thou isn't intending to poison thy new wife already?' Fox stubbornly maintained that he wanted the poison to kill rats but ought to have had some premonition of danger in that the other man had unwittingly came so close to the truth in the hearing of the chemist. He might at least have postponed the operation or thought up a different tactic in the light of this. But he had gone straight home and administered the arsenic to his wife. Amidst all the subsequent gossip and suspicion, John James recalled his jesting exchange with Fox which was no longer a joke given unfolding events. He became a key prosecution witness at the trial along with the chemist.

Fox was hanged in the spring of 1827 alongside Philip Tinnaney, the frenzied killer who had battered out his girlfriend's brains with a hammer in the St. Nicholas area of Carlisle the previous September. Unquestionably two of the most sordid criminals to ever grace the Cumbrian gallows. But while Tinnaney had been a violently neurotic personality who had sank slobbering onto his knees to receive sentence of death, Fox had been cool and not entirely unintelligent. Nevertheless, he had been determined to have his way and dispose of his wife and child too. He had thrown caution totally aside, with no thought or concern for the suffering of anyone else so long as he could serve his own immediate ends. There were many echoes of John Thompson here.

Another trial for poisoning in Cumberland had been of much more recent vintage. In August, 1845, John Graham of Grinsdale had been tried for the wilful murder of his wife and father, again by means of arsenic. To the surprise of many, the failed farmer had been acquitted, due essentially to insufficient evidence though others had been found guilty and hanged on less. Graham went on to merit veiled hostile coverage in the local press afterwards, with reference being made to the fact that death by arsenic was up and up, implying that it could well be a popular means of illicit disposal too often undetected.

Whether or not Thompson had noted such journalistic considerations at the time is uncertain. But he could read and may have drawn the conclusion from this and other sources that it was possible to use arsenic to dispose of a burdensome partner with a good prospect of success and acted accordingly when he presently found himself having to choose between two ladies. This is mere conjecture but it would be interesting to have some indication as to just how many people did get away with the misuse of arsenic and other poisons in the last century, even with forensic detection of a sort slowly coming on stream. Though of course, poison as a whole had been misused from the time of the Romans and beyond, often with ruthless effectiveness.

Of John Thompson himself, not a great deal was known prior to his arrival in Carlisle with his wife at Whitsuntide the previous year. There was certainly no indication that he had ever been unfaithful to Mary Thompson until then and she was to speak well of him, even on her deathbed. What little was known by the time of the trial was that he had wed his late wife at All Saints' Church in Newcastle upon Tyne twenty years previously. Afterwards they had spent an extended period at nearby Camperdown. They then made their way westwards into Cumberland and lived in the Crosscanonby area for some years until moving to Carlisle in 1846. There Thompson found work as a millwright with a local firm and settled with his wife in a two-roomed dwelling in Union Street, off the main city thoroughfare of Botchergate.

A quite ordinary couple until then perhaps? And yet Thompson was quickly to begin practising duplicity to such a degree as to raise doubts as to whether he had ever really been the ideal husband, married as he was to a seemingly childless wife, who may long since have became tedious to him. Certainly they were no sooner settled in the old border city than he began doing the rounds independently of the local drinking establishments. It was at the house of one Edward McBride, a weaver, that he met a widow, Margaret Kane. McBride's residence was licensed as a beer house, an interesting example of the type of establishment favoured by many of the poorer classes in which to drink and carouse in the Victoria era. In this instance the living room was the tap room and McBride presumably made sufficient from the retailing of liquor over and above his regular income to compensate for any loss of privacy.

Indications are that Thompson was immediately smitten by Kane, who had been widowed some seven years. She had a boy of ten years and two girls but was still an attractive woman. Like McBride, her husband had been a weaver. His death had left her with little money so she returned to domestic service, placing the two children with her mother. But when the older woman died she immediately took the children back and exchanged the role of a house servant for work in the fields. She also made caps and took in lodgers. Clearly an independent industrious woman, but she may have been lonely too, welcoming the opportunity to get out occasionally and enjoy herself.

Thompson posed as a widower and called himself John Peel. The attraction was mutual and he was soon sharing Kane's bed, once she had been persuaded to get rid of her lodgers. He was to share it until his arrest some eight months later. Most nights he would remain with her until the early hours. Carlisle wasn't a very big place in those days. Kane lived only a brisk walk from Union Street. When she heard rumours that her lover had a wife, he denied it, and followed through with a letter purporting to be from one J. Brown, Parish Clerk, stating that Elizabeth Thompson, the wife of John Thompson, had died in 1841 and was buried in the parish of Crosscanonby. At least he now admitted that his name was Thompson, shedding the rather unimaginative choice of an alias. However, the envelope bearing the supposed confirmation of his wife's death and her burial miles away in West Cumberland bore a Carlisle postmark.....

In the light of this, Kane remained suspicious, but made no attempt to drive the amorous millwright from her bed which was in the same room as that of her son John. The youngster was eventually to testify that Thompson and his mother had slept together and yet he and his sisters appear to have had a good relationship with the affable adulterer. Their mother for her part was to present herself before the judge and jury as a decent woman who had been duped by a rogue. But her morals were to remain questionable.

Thompson talked often of marriage to Kane but of course he still had a wife very much alive and well in Union Street. She herself must have became increasingly aware of her husband's infidelity as he now crept home morning after morning around three a.m., knocking her up to let him in, but appears to have borne the betrayal stoically enough. Presently she simply left the door on the latch, even while hinting to neighbours that she knew of the other woman.

What finally decided Thompson to do away with his wife is uncertain. Perhaps the constant strain of two-timing had begun to tell though it seems more likely that continuing infatuation with Kane was the crucial factor, and possibly an ultimatum of sorts from the latter that he must make a decent woman of her or clear off. What is undisputed is that just as Robert Fox had done, he now went to a chemist's shop and purchased arsenic, ostensibly to kill rats in his Union Street tenement though there were no rats in the building. This was some three weeks before the death of Mary and almost immediately she began to feel ill, experiencing mild discomfort at first but eventually suffering violent stomach pains, prickling in the hands and raging thirst, accompanied by swollen eyes, flushed cheeks and vomiting.

Thompson continued to see his mistress and go to and from work as though nothing were amiss. When his ailing wife passed on a portion of veal pie to a neighbour and the latter and her daughter sampled it and became violently sick, he said blandly that he had eaten a piece of the same pie and felt ill himself. He went dutifully for the doctor when neighbours urged him to do so, and made the necessary sympathetic responses in the sick-room. But too many neighbours had became involved and when the end came on the Saturday morning of 29th May, the poor woman having died thrashing the bedclothes violently about her, they vociferously supported the doctor's recommendation that the coroner become involved, and talked darkly among themselves about the other woman.

As Fox had done and as Palmer the Rugeley poisoner was to do some nine years later, the bereaved husband accepted the recommendation with little demur, though he did question the need for it….? Afterwards, between further visits to Margaret Kane's cramped accommodation and an assurance to those there that the dead woman was only his lodging house mistress, he entered into negotiations to sell the Union Street furniture. He also paid to have the chaotic sick-room cleaned up. However, the neighbour involved refused to touch the numerous dishes bearing traces of boiled rice, gruel and vomit and the brimming chamber pot covered with a hat box lid. This because the doctor had instructed that all the latter vessels and their contents be left untouched. Nothing daunted, Thompson blatantly emptied and washed them himself, disposing of any evidence in the process. He may well have congratulated himself on this move because the place was sealed off and then searched shortly afterwards. But any smug satisfaction he may have experienced was in fact to be short lived. Ample evidence remained elsewhere.

The police were especially interested in a jar of oatmeal and marked the contents of this down for special analysis. They took dust samples from the pockets of Thompson's spare trousers and waistcoat. They also searched for the remains of the veal pie eaten by the neighbour and her daughter which had been thrown onto a nearby midden. They failed to find anything in this instance but as it transpired, already had enough to go on.

For the moment, Thompson remained at large, now totally debarred from his premises but still mouthing his innocence. Nevertheless, signs of agitation were observed when a neighbour advised him of rumours that Mary's body would probably be opened up. He had every cause to be agitated. The body was found to be riddled with arsenic. Arsenic was also found in the oatmeal and among the dust from his pockets; there had presumably also been arsenic in the veal pie. Almost certainly he had been feeding his wife small but deadly doses of the poison in her porridge and in other food. On 8th June he was arrested and charged with wilful murder.

Nonetheless, before and throughout his trial he maintained a veneer of confidence but forty witnesses were ranged against him including the pathetic Margaret Kane. The verdict of guilty was almost inevitable. Yet even as Baron Pollock put on the black cap, the guilty man was shouting his innocence. But then, like Robert Fox, though somewhat later in the tragic affair, he proceeded to make a full confession. The continuing parallels between the two poisoners are rather unique for both also made emotional speeches towards the end. Thompson was rather less profound in his delivery than Fox but did say that he forgave everyone including Widow Kane and that he hoped they forgave him. He did ask for Kane to visit him in the death cell but for some petty moralistic reason, the authorities refused his request. However, her children visited him and took an emotional farewell. Obviously he had been a better substitute father than he had been a husband.

Impressions if anything are of a chameleon, like Fox and Palmer and others of their ilk within the poisoning fraternity, cheery, plausible, but utterly remorseless when looking to their own needs. In these times of course, Thompson could simply have left his wife and moved in with his girlfriend and few would really have thought very ill of him or of her. The only anguished member of the troika would have been the betrayed wife, there being no known children of the marriage, but at least she would still have had her life. However, the whole social climate was different then and so an innocent woman died a slow agonising death for whatever precise reason we can only guess.

John Thompson was hanged on the east wall of Carlisle Gaol on market day, 21st August, 1847. Thousands came to witness the spectacle with many travelling in from the surrounding countryside. The bungling Calcraft officiated and for a time the prisoner struggled in the air after the trap was sprung. But death came soon enough and his body was cut down and buried within the gaol confines like others before him. The scene of the murder itself remained standing for almost a century more but the whole street was eventually demolished under a slum clearance scheme in the late 1930s. It was rebuilt and named Rydal Street and remains today, a quiet modest thoroughfare affording no hint whatsoever of what transpired there so many years ago. On the other hand, Thompson's was not the last case of poisoning to come to light in Cumberland as we shall see.

4: GENTLEMEN AND PLAYERS

Little more than two years after the dispatch of John Thompson, Cumberland was the scene of a macabre crime which might easily have resulted in another double hanging. John Hogg and Nichol Hogg of Bewcastle were accused of strangling Sir James Graham's gamekeeper with his own neckerchief at Bewcastle in November, 1849. However, in the event, the brothers were allowed to walk free. This decision by the court was based on the unsoundness of the depositions made by their alleged accomplice, Andrew Turnbull, who had made two contradictory statements prior to his suicide in Carlisle Gaol shortly afterwards. In sum, a doubtful witness, but his suicide may have came as an added Godsend to the Hoggs for evidence had originally appeared overwhelming against all three.

Whether the public as a whole agreed with the verdict was questionable but Victorian justice had again taken its careful course. The gallows on which the poisoner of Union Street had perished were not required again after all and would remain unused for some time. A further two years passed with little worthy of great attention on the Cumbrian crime scene at all. The majority of those appearing in the courts, be they burglars, thieves, poachers, shoplifters or wife beaters were generally mundane specimens and usually of the lower orders. All in all, a not unfamiliar state of affairs. But the Assizes of August, 1851 were rather different in that there were at least two white collar gentlemen for trial, one of them a clergyman on a charge of manslaughter, and two notorious 'highwaymen'.

George Ladyman, thirty years old, pleaded guilty to forgery and embezzlement. This was scarcely a crime unknown in Cumberland. But Ladyman had been employed as a servant of the County Court at Keswick, one of the bulwarks of the local establishment. He had not only forged a court receipt with intent to defraud but had also pocketed public money entrusted to him. The judge, Baron Platt, seemed intent upon making things hard for Ladyman. It may have been that the wretched man was self-made or had been helped into his post originally. At any rate, in a long monologue, he was reminded that he had betrayed the trust of others after having been fortunate to have been able to move among better people and be able to support himself in a respectable way by being thus placed. Unthinkable conduct in the eyes of his betters, more so in an age of continuing patronage and class distinction. His Lordship made it clear that an example must be made of him, so that others of lesser position in life would think twice before following in his footsteps. The fact that he had never been in court before was taken into consideration. But he was still sentenced to twelve months hard labour with all that entailed; his future prospects would henceforth be nil of course. No enquiry was made as to why the culprit had offended in the first instance? Intemperance or womanising or gambling perhaps…..

Ladyman appears to have taken his medicine calmly enough. He may well have expected much worse. In a way he was lucky. He could as easily have been transported. Thirty-two years earlier, in 1819, Gale and Townsend had been publicly hanged at Carlisle for similar offending. It could be said that British justice overall had came a long way in a short time insofar as many offences and individuals were concerned. But yawning gaps did remain. Only a short time previously, a seventy one-year-old woman had received an identical sentence to Ladyman's for stealing a handkerchief and a shawl at Whitehaven. But unfortunately for her, she had offended before. 'A very old woman, but a very old thief' intoned the judge, regretting that she was rather too old for transportation, but not too old to do hard labour. Needless to say, at seventy-one years old, she might surely have merited greater charity.

The Reverend Joseph Smith was far less phlegmatic than Ladyman. Irrespective of what his sentence might be, he probably knew he hadn't a great deal to look forward to, with his reputation already so diminished. What was he doing in court at all along with so many of life's misfits? Clergymen had been known to be hypocritical, self-seeking and intemperate in Cumberland as anywhere else but rarely if ever physically violent. This case involved a fatal shooting, the breaking of the sixth commandment, a total violation of the values the perpetrator was expected to uphold. Yet the truth of the matter was that the whole sorry affair need never have been. It occurred primarily because a man was in the wrong place at the wrong time.

Smith cut a sorry figure in court, slumped and despondent. His problems had begun the previous April. Prior to that he had been ministering to the needs of his flock in and around the village of Walton, near the town of Brampton. He had been in the living for some years and was held in sufficient regard. But Smith was of exceedingly nervous disposition and had became disturbed by the increasing number of burglaries and assaults in the countryside at large. When people fret about the crime wave today, they often tend to forget, or may not appreciate, that many of their law abiding predecessors were no strangers to such criminal activities either. These could be all the more terrifying in remote areas in an age without motorised transport or telephones, and when some rural areas were more thinly populated and less accessible.

Covertly, the timid clergyman had equipped himself with a revolver and put it carefully away, especially mindful that he was the only man in a household made up otherwise of three women and five children in a vicarage lying well off the beaten track. He was to claim that he only intended to use the revolver to raise the alarm should his home and its occupants ever be threatened and there the matter might well have rested.

However, on 16th April, 1851, a thirty-eight-year-old farmer named William Armstrong rode across the nearby Scottish border to transact some business in Brampton. Armstrong was a respectable family man by all accounts, the father of four children and well liked by all who knew him. A congenial individual, he also enjoyed a drink but hadn't appeared too inebriated when he set off homewards again at about nine p.m. He had been invited to stay overnight with friends in Brampton but had appeared intent upon getting home. At first he travelled in company, stopping off for a few more drinks some two miles along the Longtown road, Subsequently, now rather more intoxicated, he galloped away from his companions in the vicinity of Walton around eleven p.m., having some fifteen miles still to go to reach home. They never saw him again and assumed that he had simply outpaced them.

We now enter the realms of conjecture, not in fact the first or the last time we shall do so in this book. Armstrong had actually left the main road and turned off for Walton, despite his earlier intention to make for the border and home, and found his way to Smith's vicarage. This may have been due to drunken confusion on his part but we can't be certain. On the other hand, he did know of the place beforehand for a domestic servant, one Ann Glendinning, had recently left his service to go to work for the Reverend Smith. Thus it could have been that in his now mellow state, the farmer had decided to call and pay his respects to a woman who had been with he and his wife for several years previously. Or perhaps use such a visit as a pretext to obtain a bed for the night, given the late hour and the distance he still had to travel along lonely, inhospitable roads.

But we don't really know. What is more certain is that he must have ridden up the quiet lane to the vicarage, dismounted and walked up to the front of the dwelling. According to Smith, who was now making his final rounds inside after the family had retired to bed, he subsequently heard the sound of someone tapping on a window and completely panicked. It was close to eleven thirty p.m. and totally dark outside. He grabbed his revolver from a drawer, opened the front door and fired blindly before slamming the door shut again. Presently, he tentatively opened the door again once more, went outside and looked around but saw nothing. He returned indoors, secured the door and went upstairs to join his wife, feeling more relieved in himself. This at least was his account of the episode but in fact he was not destined to remain relieved for long. Early the following morning, Armstrong was found lying dead in front of the vicarage, shot three times; his steed had already been discovered grazing close by.

Smith had never attempted to deny his guilt and indeed, a servant testified that she had heard something heavy fall and the front door slam at the time the clergyman stated he had acted. The main question for the court to decide was whether or not he could have avoided killing Armstrong. Why hadn't he challenged the assumed intruder beforehand for instance, if only from behind the door? Had he really needed to fire so indiscriminately at all? And why hadn't he searched the grounds more thoroughly afterwards; the man might still have been alive then. On the other hand, just why had the farmer put himself on the spot that fatal night? That would never be completely certain. And as the judge emphasised in his summing up, a man had a right to defend his property, more so from a midnight aggressor, and there might not be a great deal of time for caution in some situations.

The trial lasted for some hours but finally a verdict was reached. The Reverend Smith was found not guilty and discharged, to the continuing anger of many who saw him as deserving of some punishment and who felt he had been leniently dealt with simply because he was a clergyman. Be this as it may, Smith remained a nervous wreck and as he had probably anticipated, was no longer wanted in his living at Walton, given the animosity he had already engendered. He was soon to leave the area for an unknown destination.

But all else aside, the highlight of the 1851 August Assizes had to be the trial of the two highwaymen, Tinning and Monteith. John 'Swift Nicks' Nevison, Dick Turpin and others of their ilk had long since became no more than overrated legends, wantonly embellished by writers such as Harrison Ainsworth. The actual offence of highway robbery was of itself still on the books and not uncommon, but now more likely to take the form of rolling a drunk in some quiet street or country lane, the Victorian equivalent of mugging. Thomas Tinning and Hughie Monteith were a twosome who did briefly reverse the state of play, literally causing a seven day sensation in the Carlisle area. Unlike George Ladyman and the Reverend Smith however, they were more akin to the general run of common criminals of the period. It was the sheer audacity of their crimes which set them apart, smacking more of the previous century and beyond, though neither was particularly bright.

They were an odd pair. Neither were Cumbrians, both originating from neighbouring Dumfriesshire, though they had been domiciled for some years in Carlisle. They had a mutual predilection for crime though there is no indication that they had known one another for any extended period. Indeed, Tinning was fifty years old, Monteith a mere eighteen years. Tinning was short, Monteith tall and presentable and something of a dandy. The former man was the more cunning and concerned to stay clear of the limelight though he owned the weapon involved in the short series of hold ups, whereas Monteith was brash and not at all averse to direct action and could have been dangerous, manipulated by his more seasoned companion. Both had girl friends in Dumfries. This may have brought them together in the first instance.

It was early on 5th July, 1851 that they made their first debut. A railway guard, Robert Carson, had been bathing in the River Eden, close to Carlisle's environs. He had only been in the water a short time. The water was cold. He jumped out onto a nearby path and began drying and dressing himself. Suddenly he was aware of a man with a covering over his face who made a number of trite remarks. Carson responded testily but became quickly aware that the stranger was intent upon more serious business. The semi-nude railway guard found himself looking into six barrels of a huge revolver. He was quickly relieved of his watch and loose change and humiliatingly searched before the stranger took off.

This episode quickly made headline news and the railway guard must have felt an utter fool but no arrest was made. The police were only looking for one man at this stage though as was later indicated, Tinning had set the crime up but stayed clear, albeit relieving Monteith of the watch afterwards.

A week passed. Then early on the Saturday morning of 12th July, 1851, two farmers, Robert Bowman and William Gibson, were making their way westwards towards Carlisle by horse and cart. A masked man in a bottle green jacket and moleskin trousers suddenly appeared and ordered them to halt. The same six-barrelled revolver was in evidence. The two rustics were completely intimidated, allowing their pockets to be hastily rifled and parting company with a watch and almost the equivalent of a week's wages in labouring terms. The robber was less careful in this instance however. He allowed his mask to slip and the farmers obtained a good look at his face before he made off. As quickly as possible they shakily reported the offence, having also observed a second man hovering in the background.

But already a further robbery was taking place in the same area. In this instance the victim was a chemist from Tyneside, one Backhouse Myers, riding in a gig. All appeared well with his world until a man in a green tailed jacket with a black handkerchief over his face emerged from a hayfield and grabbed the horse's bridle, shouting: 'Your money or your life!' Myers was relieved of his purse, his indignation giving way to fear when a revolver was trained upon him. He still had the presence of mind to keep quiet about an additional £500 stowed in the gig according to a subsequent press report. But this may have been no more than media hype.

Whatever he may have had or may not have had, Myers was certainly more prompt and vocal than the unfortunate farmers in reporting his ordeal. But the police had already swung into positive action. They had had their suspicions but insufficient proof. Now they had a description of two men and it was a fairly simple matter to check out the respective whereabouts of Tinning and Montieth who were well enough known to them in the city. The twosome were missing but had been seen at the railway station during the early evening of 12th July, headed for Dumfies and clearly in some kind of alliance.

Early the following Sunday, two policemen travelled by gig to Gretna where they knew Monteith's father lived. They quickly located Monteith Senior who passed on an address in Dumfries. The policemen's journey continued. They arrived late in the small Scottish town but by the early hours of Monday morning, had both rogues in custody, having found them in bed in two different houses attended by their women friends. There were quite sufficient grounds to warrant arrest. Monteith took one look at the policemen and lunged for the fearsome looking revolver in his green jacket hanging by the bed but was quickly restrained. Indications were that the brash eighteen-year-old would have used it. He also had a blue purse belonging to Robert Bowman. Tinning was found to be in possession of Carson's watch. Two additional weapons were also traced to him: a brace of pistols in good working order. By Monday evening the two criminals were locked up in Carlisle Gaol.

At the trial, Monteith totally implicated Tinning, who pleaded not guilty to everything. Alas for the rogue from over the border; it was true that he hadn't held anyone up but there was evidence enough to prove that the weapon used had been his. He had also lurked close by when Bowman and Gibson were threatened, presumably prepared to assist if necessary. And he had been a receiver and almost certainly the planner of the crimes in the first instance. Rather surprisingly, both prisoners went on to plead not guilty to robbing Carson, but Tinning had been found with his watch which was deemed evidence enough while the revolver trained upon the unfortunate guard had been his. To clinch the case, the two farmers were able to fully identify the teenager by his dress and features; and Myers recalled his voice which must have been conspicuous by its Scottish twang. And Tinning had been observed in the background of course, by Bowman and Gibson.

Both men had criminal records of a petty kind. Tinning was a weaver to trade but was better known as a poacher. Monteith had worked as a gardener but had been sacked for dishonesty. Neither had been very successful criminals. Both were now sentenced to fifteen years transportation apiece. Tinning looked startled but Monteith didn't appear to mind. Brazen to the last, he may have envisaged himself being given the chance to mine for gold down under, details of the Australian diggings being not uncommon. No convict under sentence had in fact ever been given the opportunity to take up such work. But they could always hope.

5: AN ELEMENT OF DOUBT

The Lancelow Bottom murder of November, 1854 is dealt with at some length by James Walter Brown in an informative article which was eventually reprinted in the first volume of Round Carlisle Cross. Brown has afforded us details of several nineteenth century Cumbrian crimes which all found their way into this nine volume series of pieces on local people and topics, by a man who was particularly interested in local crime. Brown is one of the few writers of his time to have left us with a tangible record of some of the more infamous Cumbrian cases. He died in 1930 at a fairly advanced age. It is to his books that many armchair criminologists still tend to turn when seeking a quick reference to various crimes in the county which made the headlines in their day, the writer having had personal recollections of several of them. Brown's style is clear and compelling but he does have a fault. He tends to see a number of the crimes and their outcome in black and white rather than in shades of grey whether he was around or not. This is especially true of his piece on Thomas Munroe and the crime perpetrated in Lancelow Bottom.

Munroe died on the same scaffold as John Thompson at Carlisle on Tuesday, 13th March, 1855, pleading his innocence to the end. Much of the evidence was purely circumstantial and many felt he would be reprieved. The anti-hanging lobby was itself in full cry. But Munroe was hanged regardless at the age of eighteen. Was he really guilty? There is a very strong possibility that he was and Brown leaves us with no doubt of his own views on the subject. He was quite convinced of the teenager's guilt. Yet to the more sceptical pundit of this modern age, there has to remain an element of doubt.

To better ponder the rights and wrongs of the case, it is essential to know something of the accused individual himself. Thomas Munroe was born in West Cumberland on 25th March, 1836. He was illegitimate but apparently brought up well enough during his early years by his mother and maternal grandmother. But both died and Thomas was left at a comparatively young age to fend for himself. A series of contradictions were to hang about him thereafter. Though described in court as imperfectly instructed, he was said to have been taken up and educated by a lady of means and to have been confirmed by no less a divine that the Bishop of Chester. It is recorded that he was sensitive and fond of books but came over in court at times as arrogantly indifferent with a monotonous tone of voice and we are never told what he read – the good book perhaps, for he was eventually to evoke the name of Jesus, but not until his final moments on earth. Described at the time of his remand as a 'simple, innocent-looking youth' he was also to be described as looking older than his eighteen years. Though said to be of good character by his aunt, the judge was to speak of his previous life as not free from crime.

But whatever advantages he may have had and whatever he may have been, he remained too poor to advance himself. By the age of seventeen years the only work he could find was that of a farm servant at Sellafield. But though liked by his employer, John Sharp, for his apparent propriety and mildness of temper, his health broke down and he couldn't go on in this employment. He also had money troubles and around Whitsuntide 1854, prevailed upon his half-brother, Amos Munroe, to take him in as a lodger. Amos, twenty-eight years old and married with two children, did more than that. He not only took the younger man into his home at Kirkland, a few miles from Cleator, he also found him work as an iron ore miner at nearby Kelton where he was already employed by Messrs. Lindow, a respectable well established company. The two half-brothers worked regular night shifts, mining for iron ore in a drift in the side of the Cumbrian mountains. It wasn't easy work but the former weakling appeared to cope with it. Two other men worked a day shift. There were no others employed at the Kelton drift except for the overlooker, Isaac Turner.

Turner was fifty-eight years old and had worked for Messrs. Lindow for more than twenty years. Impressions are of a sturdy resilient man and dependable to the extent that he was also entrusted with his men's wages. Every fortnight he would carry these from Cleator to Kirkland. He travelled through isolated countryside, the area in the mid-nineteenth century having yet to become as industrialised as it was to do a few years later. The drift at Kelton had itself been worked but a few months and Thomas Munroe had only been there some ten weeks when on the morning of Saturday, 4th November, 1854, Turner proceeded towards Kirkland as usual to pay out the four men. He had been given two £5 notes originally and changed these into gold and silver and smaller change at two public houses en route but partook of very little alcohol for he was normally of sober disposition.

Around 11.15 a.m. at what was subsequently to be defined as country time in court, he was seen by a farm worker, Joseph Kitchen, who was hedging fairly close to Kirkland. The two men weren't close enough to exchange greetings and Turner proceeded on and vanished into an area of low ground known as Lancelow Bottom. It was here that Joseph Kitchen came upon his body some fifteen minutes afterwards. A horrifying sight met the farm worker's eyes.

Isaac Turner lay face downwards in a pool of blood. His throat was cut from ear to ear. The man's hands were also cut, his clothing bloodied and his pockets turned inside out. There were signs of a terrific struggle and blood on a nearby incline. Turner's hat lay some yards away. The body was still warm. Obviously a savage murder had taken place and very recently. Kitchen at once went for assistance and returned with a farmer, Joseph Jackson. It was still but a short while past noon.

The two men turned the body over and discovered a half sovereign beneath it. Other small change was lying about. They placed the body on a cart for removal. Such a course of action would be unthinkable in these times of course. The police would be called and the entire area sealed off prior to a minute examination of both body and surroundings. As it was, another man lately arrived in Lancelow Bottom, John

Graham, now took it upon himself to pick up a broken razor from the scene and stow this away for future examination by those concerned.

Nonetheless, the police became involved soon enough. They were especially interested in a man both Jackson and Kitchen had seen loitering near the scene of the crime prior to the discovery of the body. Jackson had seen him as early as 9.00 a.m., wearing a dark blue shooting jacket and a blue cap. Kitchen had seen him some time later but described him as wearing a dark coat, waistcoat and cap. A much more damning witness was to be a twelve-year-old boy, Joseph Braithwaite, who had been cutting turnips in a field when he had seen a man in a dark square-tailed coat coming from Lancelow Bottom in haste around 12 a.m. But none of the trio had seemingly been able to get a proper look at the man's face.

The motive appeared to be robbery and as it transpired, the police weren't long in making an arrest at the instigation of none other than Amos Munroe, who led them to his half-brother Thomas. Nevertheless, the older brother and his wife Jane were both quickly destined to join the prisoner in the House of Correction at Whitehaven as possible accessories. The twosome accepted their incarceration quietly enough but the story Amos told at the ensuing inquest did seem feasible enough and he never faltered.

In short, he and Thomas had completed their night shift at nearby Kelton early on the morning of the murder and returned home. He went to bed and got up at 11.30 a.m. After eating his dinner he went to the local smithy where he met other men around noon, anticipating that Turner would arrive to pay them. The news instead was that the overlooker had had his throat cut. Still he never suspected his half-brother, Tom, until he returned home at 8.30 p.m. on the Sunday night, having joined a party searching for the murderer. Thereupon his wife had spoken of finding bloodstains on Thomas's coat. He hadn't hesitated, going straight to the police.

Jane Munroe testified in rather greater detail. She confirmed that her husband had returned home early on the Saturday morning. He had had his breakfast at half past six or seven o'clock, eating with Thomas. He had then had a wash before going to bed and had got up at 11.30 a.m. and eaten his dinner before going down to the smithy though she couldn't remember the exact time. Jane didn't appear to have her husband's memory for times though she was sure that he returned home early that evening at 6.00 p.m.

It transpired that Thomas had returned about the same time, remarking that 'it was a cruel thing about Isaac Turner'. His half-brother agreed. That morning, Thomas Munroe had not gone to bed as Amos had done. After breakfast he had washed and changed and gone straight back out. He had two jackets, one brown and one green. He was to claim to have donned the green jacket that morning though the blacksmith Joseph Thompson, who saw him at 8.00 a.m., claimed that the youth had been wearing a dark coat, with waistcoat and cap. Thomas later spoke of having gone out to see his auntie but that at 11.00 a.m. he had stopped off for a drink with one Bob Robinson in a public house at Wath Brow. By 1.20 p.m. however, he was at the home of his aunt, Bella Parker, who lived in Cleator Moor and paid her half a sovereign for a shirt which she was making for him. He went on to visit another near relative at Arkedon before returning home. A full day, all seemingly accounted for. There was only one problem. His alibi didn't hold water prior to the visit to Bella Parker. Bob Robinson remained untraced and the landlady of the pub at Wath Brow had no recollection of Tom having been there as he said, nor had her daughter.

Jane Munroe had further testified that when Thomas returned home early on the Saturday evening, he went to the room where he slept with his half-brother's two children and hung up his coat. He didn't leave the house again that evening, passing the time playing cards until retiring to bed some time after eleven o'clock. The following morning he went out again. His sister-in-law advised that she had afterwards taken down his coat to dry it, though the prisoner had spoken of having remained dry the previous day despite some rain, but he had had an umbrella. The coat appeared wet though none the worse but what she did discover were a number of bloodstains on the sleeves. Her brother, John Hellon, was visiting. In a state of some dismay she queried of him if he thought the culprit could be Tom, given her discovery? Hellon had no answer to this but the seeds appear to have been sown as from now, whether insidiously or not.

Amos having returned, events moved swiftly thereafter as we know and Thomas Munroe was soon in custody. Not however before his box had been searched, when other articles of his clothing were discovered, matching those he had allegedly been seen wearing the previous day, and also a clasp knife with dark traces upon it. But the police were still not fully satisfied as already noted, thus Amos and Jane Munroe joined the younger man in custody for a time. But not for long. The case quickly built up against Thomas who was shortly to be identified in Whitehaven House of Correction by several witnesses, despite the fact that they had appeared uncertain before about his actual features. With his alibi shattered prior to this and other evidence piled against him, he now appeared not only the prime instigator of the ghastly deed, but the only one. Nevertheless, he remained cool and indifferent and continued to maintain his innocence, even while his half-brother and sister-in-law were now walking free again.

His trial at Carlisle on Friday, 23rd February, 1855 was of itself a comparatively short affair. He was at an immediate disadvantage by the number of witnesses ranged against him who claimed to have seen him skulking about in the area on the morning of the killing; and of course he had no alibi to cover those early hours. There was also a footprint left by him close to the scene of the crime. He had obviously had money to spare too, immediately following the killing, and there was the additional evidence of the clasp knife discovered in his box, and the undeniable blood stains on his clothing.

The trial dragged on into the evening. It was eleven o'clock before the jury retired but by midnight they were back with a verdict of guilty, albeit with a recommendation to mercy given previous good character….. Thomas Munroe was unmoved. All along he had continued to maintain his innocence and proceeded to advise the court that he was as innocent as an unborn child. Sentence of death was then pronounced but he appeared to have little expectation that he would hang and was not without influential supporters.

Indeed, no sooner had he been sentenced to death than a meeting was convened in Carlisle by no less a personage than Robert Ferguson the mayor. It was uncommonly well attended. The focus of the meeting was Thomas Munroe's sentence. In this instance, while it was made clear that the issue was not any question as to the man's innocence or guilt, the recommendation to mercy clearly was. There was a call for the abolition of capital punishment altogether, Those present were reminded that no less than thirty innocent persons had been hanged in Britain since the beginning of the present century, which did perhaps indicate some questioning of the actual verdict after all in Munroe's case.

Others were more open in their support. A group of men, quite prominent in the affairs of the old city, sought a respite of the sentence on the grounds that the young fellow having been too poor to pay for a solicitor, had thus had no direct contact with the barrister defending him prior to the trial, thereby limiting his defence. Other points which it was felt merited a stay of execution included the fact that Munroe had been identified primarily in respect of his attire. There was also the question of the footprint actually pointing in the opposite direction to Kirkland. Nor had there been any marks of a struggle upon him and it seemed to have been taken for granted that the half sovereign paid to his aunt had belonged to Turner – but had it? And where was the real proof that he had even worn the bloodstained coat on the day of the killing? Would he have gone visiting in it afterwards if it had been the same garment stained with Turner's blood? Would he have hung it up at home, knowing it to be thus bloodstained? And why had none of the medical fraternity at the trial been prepared to swear that the blood found upon the sleeves and collar of the coat had in fact been human blood anyhow?

Valid points after a fashion. Nor had the razor found at the scene of the crime been traced to Thomas Munroe while the clasp knife found in his box had been rusty rather than bloodstained. But the condemned man knew nothing of all the attempts being made to help him and time was ebbing away. His execution was eventually fixed for Tuesday, 13th March, 1855. All along he had remained steadfast in his denial of any guilt. Now, on the Sunday preceding the planned hanging, he broke and asked to see the chaplain urgently. It is probably worth adding here that since the day of his arrest, some four months previously, not one relative or friend had ever visited him and this included the period of his trial, fairly short though the latter had been.

Closeted with the chaplain, what he now proceeded to do was dictate a statement. Brown makes full use of it and it can also be found elsewhere but since it is not without considerable relevance, is also produced here in its entirety, inspired in part it seemed by a visitation the prisoner claimed to have had from his mother and grandmother who invited him to tell all, knowing him to be innocent of the murder itself. It ran as follows:

> "I was never in the public house at Wath Brow Top with Bob Robinson on the day the murder was committed. I saw Bob Robinson at Egremont Fair, but was not in his company at that place. I was at the places where the witnesses on the trial swore they saw me on the day of the murder, but I neither committed the murder, nor did I see it committed. I was at the place where the murder was committed by appointment of Amos Munroe. I and Amos were working together at "night shifts", when Amos asked me if I could keep a secret if he were to tell me one. I said I could if he would tell me what it was about. Amos refused to tell me unless I would promise never to divulge it. I promised him I never would. Amos then told me he was going to murder Isaac Turner, and asked me to assist him. I said I would not do such a thing. Amos then promised to give me the whole of the money he got from Turner if I would go with him, as he was wanting to be foreman in Turner's place. I told Amos that I would not if he would give me £20. Amos then asked me if I could go across the fields; he wished me to go towards the spot where the murder was committed, and then run across the fields towards Cleator, so that people might think that some person from that neighbourhood had committed the murder. I suppose Amos must have worn my clothes, as I had not them on at the time. I said before that I had the waistcoat on, but that was not the truth. Amos told me he would give me money if I would run across the fields in the direction of Cleator. He said he would not give me the money until he got hired and settled in his place. I was on the side of the Gill towards Cleator, and saw my brother, Amos Munroe, on the opposite side of the Gill among the whins. Amos told me that Isaac Turner would pass the place about eleven o'clock. I was to look at my watch, and start to run about eleven o'clock in the direction of Cleator. I have no doubt the witnesses saw me when I was running. I made up the story about Bob Robinson in order that I might clear both Amos and myself. I would have confessed before, but I was expecting a reprieve, and I was anxious not to fetch my brother into the scrape. I did not think they would hang one so young as I am. If I had been reprieved I should never have mentioned what I have now communicated".

The chaplain wrote everything down then read the statement back to Munroe in the presence of the gaol governor. Munroe signed it and appeared much more relaxed. An interesting document indeed, but there is no mention of any visitation. If anything, the pathetic man seemed concerned only to get back at the man who had exposed and abandoned him, delay his execution in the process and possibly even eschew it. On the other hand, what he had done, however unwittingly, was admit to having been an accessory to the murder, still a hanging offence. Notwithstanding, the prisoner's supporters now attempted to obtain a stay of execution on the strength of the statement's revelations but as we know, to no avail. The Home Secretary was unmoved and the death sentence was carried out as planned with Amos Monroe remaining exonerated.

James Walter Brown was among those who implicitly believed that the original evidence totally disproved the condemned man's eleventh hour allegations and that Amos Munroe was quite innocent. Maybe, but anomalies did remain. It was actually not beyond the realms of possibility that Amos could have been in Lancelow Bottom as his half-brother stated. The place was only a short distance from Kirkland and there was only Amos and his wife to testify that he had risen at 11.30 on the morning of the murder. Jane Munroe wasn't too good at recalling precise times and may even have been an accomplice; in sum, Amos could feasibly have risen earlier and made his way across country to lie in wait for Turner.

No one had apparently observed any bloodstains on Thomas Munroe's coat either, until Jane had taken it down to dry it on the Sunday, though Thomas had visited other family members in it for most of the preceding afternoon. And he said that the coat had been dry afterwards, with no reason to dissemble then. Could another coat have been deftly substituted on the Sunday? The coat worn on the Saturday by Amos Munroe? Indeed, his half-brother had ultimately suggested, however vaguely, that Amos must have worn his clothes on the Saturday.....

Neither had the younger man a great deal to gain by killing Turner. He was single and earning 16s. a week, a princely sum in those days. He couldn't hope for promotion for a considerable time if at all, but was finally getting onto his feet with money in his pocket, a good wardrobe of clothes and a roof over his head. By comparison, Amos must have been less well situated, financially at least. He was married with a wife and two children to support and another on the way. He may well have coveted Turner's better paid responsible job. And the police had been sufficiently suspicious in the first instance to hold both he and his wife in custody, even after they had combined to expose Thomas as the villain.

Finally, the ambiguity surrounding a pair of cord trousers was never properly explained; the trousers, freshly washed, were presented to the police by Amos and

Jane shortly following the murder, ostensibly belonging to Thomas but without a great deal of rational explanation. Could they have belonged to Amos?

Consider too, all the other points put forward by the condemned man's supporters as grounds for a reprieve, with an additional mind to identification issues. While Thomas Munroe was undoubtedly a complex character in his own right and may well have been guilty of first degree murder, there have surely to remain some shades of uncertainty, even allowing for some persisting deviation on his own part.

His half-brother certainly presented in many respects as a better man originally, taking in his poorer relative, affording him a home and finding him a well paid job. After the ghastly crime in which he and his wife were for a time suspected of being involved, he distanced himself completely from Thomas and few could blame him for that in the normal order of things. He also remained clear in the face of the condemned man's final damning statement. And none of the missing money appears to have ever been traced to him, if it was ever traced at all.

But one tends to wonder too if a shadow did not continue to hang over Amos Munroe after all in the closely knit community of West Cumberland in which he lived and if this did not cause him to eventually move away altogether? What is certain is that within a few short years after the murder and its aftermath, there is no official record at all of he or his immediate family in the whole of the Cleator Moor area. Could this say something additional in itself.....?

6: THE LAST CUMBRIAN TO BE TRANSPORTED

Rather surprisingly, the Staffield killing of November, 1856 has never merited a great deal of mention in the annals of local crime. It drew ample press coverage and public attention in its day but may have quickly sank into obscurity because it wasn't premeditated, had its origins in poaching and drunkenness and ended with a verdict of manslaughter. Be this as it may, it was still infamous enough at the time and has surely to be of additional interest too in that its perpetrator, twenty-eight-year-old William Graham, was the last Cumbrian to be transported.

Transportation for its part had continued to be a popular means of disposal until the early 1850s by courts throughout Britain, as the law sought to maintain a policy of consistent social cleansing. However, New South Wales had already ceased to take convicts in 1840 from anywhere in the United Kingdom and Van Diemen's Land had closed its doors thirteen years later, being filled to saturation point with Britain's undesirables.

Then in 1853, the Penal Servitude Act had came into being, seeking finally to replace transportation altogether. Sentences under the new act could range from three years imprisonment to life in one or other of the new gaols now up and operational or in the case of Cumberland, perhaps in the existing institution in Carlisle. But the act allowed for some degree of remission too, and ultimately, a ticket of leave.

Henceforth, from Cumberland at any rate, transportation now more or less ceased. Nonetheless, there were those among the regional judiciary who still deeply regretted its passing and very occasionally resorted to transportation again as a means of disposal. They could do this for the reason that Western Australia was to continue to take convicts until 1868. William Graham, however, was the last prisoner to be sent from Cumberland, this probably because his crime fell just short of meriting execution and any other punishment would have seemed insufficient.

The scene of the crime was in an area of Cumberland still remote enough today in harsh weather, lying in the shadow of Carrock Fells, best known perhaps for the legend of the Croglin vampire, given over to fields, forests and narrow roads, with occasional villages, farms and disused quarries. There were larger communities in 1856 too, just as there are today, such as Armathwaite, Ainstable and Staffield but these of themselves not much bigger than they are in these times. Running through the area was the River Eden, just as mercurial then as now and following much the same course. By and large, a very rural community and ideal poaching country. It was near the banks of the Eden, in the vicinity of Staffield, that the crime took place on the night of 15th November, 1856.

William Graham was the second eldest in a family of six, and well known in the area as a 'wrong un'. His father is listed in the census returns for 1851 as a small farmer and quarryman and had for some years been settled on a place at Langdales, a hamlet off the Armathwaite-Staffield road. Their thatched dwelling gives the impression of overcrowding and low life and yet they were obviously a close family. Most of them were still at home. William had been married but had soon returned to the family home. Neither he nor his older brother, Henry, did much regular work but were well known poachers. Two other siblings, Anne and Joseph, were elsewhere in farm service but returned home regularly. The two younger children were in school. The mother, Nanny, was fiercely protective of them all and was to be active in attempting to destroy important evidence following the killing. The family don't appear to have been too popular, especially William, who drank to excess and had a penchant for violence away from his poaching activities. More disquieting, there were at least three guns in the Graham's farmhouse.

In such an isolated region of the county as Staffield and its environs then was, much went unchecked. Any man who took up as a gamekeeper thereabouts had an especially difficult job to do, the prime credentials being vigilance and stamina. But even those could sometimes be to little avail when dealing with a man like William Graham. Some four months prior to the killing, Graham had been involved in a vicious attack on a gamekeeper employed by Charles Fetherstonhaugh, a local landowner. The gamekeeper, Clement Richardson, was accustomed to keeping a close eye on all the Grahams but on the evening of the attack, forgot himself momentarily to his cost. Choosing to trade words with the black sheep of Langdales and neglecting to put himself physically on guard, he was knocked senseless with a heavy stick and lost his job as a result, a gamekeeper unable to defend himself being deemed of little use around Staffield.

William Graham had the gall to apply for the vacant post but Richardson having reported him for assault, the wastrel disappeared from the area for a time, his parents allegedly muttering darkly that 'Richardson should die with his shoes on'. The unfortunate Richardson presently obtained new employment with Sir Henry Vane of Hutton, near Penrith, but refused to let the charge drop. In the meantime, Fetherstonhaugh had taken on a new gamekeeper, not William Graham, but a formidable and determined young individual, Thomas Simpson, who took up residence with his pregnant wife in a cottage on his employer's estate. The Grahams of Langdales were his special care, William for his part having recently returned to the area as cocksure as ever.

About 10 p.m. on the night of Saturday, 15th November, Simpson was indoors with his wife when he heard the sound of a gun being discharged. He was sure it was poachers and went out into the darkness leaving his anxious partner behind. He never returned. Early the following Monday his body was found in the Eden. He had been beaten so severely about the head that his brains were protruding. He had about twenty-two skull fractures, had suffered great loss of blood and had been dead some twenty-four hours.

A search party had been combing the area for hours previously and helping in the search had been none other than William Graham. Now with the body discovered, the older Graham brothers all became prime suspects. As the law closed in on their dwelling, the police were alleged to have heard the mother ordering the burning of the apparent murder weapon: "Burn the remainder of that gun stock – here are the police coming". A young journalist with an overheated imagination perhaps…? But a gun was in the process of being burned.

The mother and her three eldest sons were all taken into custody and an inquest convened at the Crown Inn, Ainstable. Nanny Graham was soon released but Henry, William and Joseph appeared before the magistrates at Penrith the following day charged with the murder of the unfortunate gamekeeper. A charge of assault against Clement Richardson was also added in respect of William Graham. The latter remained nonchalant, the others stupidly indifferent. None were pleading guilty and £100 was offered in a bid to obtain additional information while the threesome were returned to the local gaol.

As was to be the case with several of those under scrutiny in this volume, a period of incarceration did exercise their minds considerably. And yet, nothing further might have been elicited from William Graham had he not fallen dangerously ill while remaining in custody with his two brothers at Penrith. All along, he had maintained his innocence, claiming to have been drunk and incapable on the night of the killing. But now the former swaggering misfit began to sink fast to the extent that his brother Henry was allowed to sit with him. It was to the latter that William confided his wish to make a statement on 21st December, 1856 and this wish was granted. The statement ran as follows:

> "Five weeks gone last night I went out to shoot in Eden Banks. I saw a man. He told me to stand. I ran away. After running about ten or a dozen yards I tumbled. He came up to me and got hold of me and we had a scuffle. He tried to get the gun from me. I cleared myself of him and then struck him with the small end of the gun. I think it was the third bat that felled him and the gun broke. It was broken off behind the lock. I then took the stock which was broken from the barrel, and brayed him till he was dead. I trailed him to the water and put him in. My brothers Henry and Joseph are both clear; they had nothing to do with it. I was dead drunk when I went out. When the man came up to me I thought it was the gamekeeper at Staffield. When I was running away he fired a pistol at me. It did not hit me." Signed William Graham.

The statement was read over to Graham and he agreed it was correct. Clearly he had thought he was going to die and had sought at least to absolve his brothers before expiring. But nothing is ever so clear cut in law. Joseph Graham was now released but any part he might have played in the crime was doubtful anyhow. Henry was not released. Nor did William die. He began to improve and was deemed fit to stand his trial on 26th February, 1857 before Mr. Baron Martin, though played the part of the fragile patient. He also pleaded not guilty. Plainly he sought to escape a verdict of murder and the penalty it carried.

The trial drew crowds akin to those patronising a popular music hall matinee. According to the press reports of the time, there was a rush for admission, clothing was torn, women fainted; there was scratching and bruising. Altogether a most distasteful scene, with his Lordship pushed and jostled as he attempted his grand entry. Yet those who were able to obtain seats in the crowded Carlisle courtroom may well have felt that the struggle outside had been well worthwhile as a tale of wanton behaviour in the more isolated reaches of Cumberland gradually unfolded, away and beyond the content of the prisoner's short statement.

The unfortunate Simpson, whose pregnant widow had only recently been confined, would appear to have been at definite risk hours before his fateful encounter with Graham, as the wastrel prepared for mischief throughout the foregoing day. Freshly back from his enforced exile following the assault upon Clement Richardson, he had lost none of his dislike for gamekeepers or anyone else who attempted to thwart him. He had begun that fateful Saturday by getting drunk, though not drunk enough to be totally inhibited. With the intention of taking in some illicit shooting he had gone to a shop in Ainstable and purchased a pound of shot, some powder and caps. Some time in the late afternoon he arrived home and quarrelled with his father over the care of a horse. In a drunken rage he grabbed one of the guns kept in the farmhouse and despite the protestations of his mother, made off into the encroaching darkness and back to the public house.

Around 7.00 p.m. he arrived at the home of some friends, the Hogarths. He threw himself into a chair, the long-barrelled percussion gun beside him, and fell into a drunken sleep, lying sprawled out in his dark velveteen coat and ribbed trousers until 10.00 p.m. Upon waking up, he was entreated by the woman of the house, Susan Hogarth, to go home. Aware of his intention to shoot game she warned him that the new gamekeeper would be a different proposition to Clement Richardson. This may have served to inflame Graham further rather than deter him though he did make off initially back in the direction of Langdales. At one stage he banged on the door of an elderly neighbour, Ned Stuart, the latter giving him much the same advice as Susan Hogarth but to no avail.

Graham was bent upon mischief and went off to shoot. Simpson confronted him. At first he turned tail but then in a drunken frenzy, after being seized, he went on to take the man's life, his statement saying all this. In court, greater detail was afforded as to how he had then dragged the body through brushwood and long grass to the river, leaving him exhausted. This was scarcely surprising, given the amount of alcohol he had earlier consumed. Thereupon he stumbled home as though nothing had happened. Later he made a point of joining the search for the missing gamekeeper but this ploy proved abortive. As the police net closed in on him after the discovery of the body, it was left to his mother to attempt to dispose of the offending weapon while his brothers covered up for him, apparently remaining ignorant at the onset of the full magnitude of the crime.

There was one witness at the trial who could have brought William Graham closer to the scaffold had his testimony been accepted. This was Francis Bousted, a farm labourer well known to the Grahams, who had gone to the police some time after the arrest. He claimed to have been engaged on behalf of Graham's uncle for a few hours prior to the crime, when the accused man had fallen into conversation with him: "Now, Frank, art thou at work?" To which Bousted had assented, noting that his employer's nephew was the worse for drink, the latter then proceeding to speak violently: "I'm going out to shoot tonight. If the bloody keeper comes to me this night out goes the bastard's brains, but I will speak once to him. I will tell him to stand back and if he stirs an inch towards me after I speak, out goes the bastard's brains. I will never die with my shoes on." And on he had apparently ranted in similar vein.

But there was something in Bousted's testimony which didn't quite ring true and he received a humiliating drubbing from the defence counsel. Why hadn't he spoken up and warned the gamekeeper beforehand? Why his delay in coming forward at all? Bousted's response was that he had been frightened of Graham and concerned also to keep his job with the latter's uncle, John Goulding. This wasn't good enough. The defence counsel, Monk, virtually accused the miserable Bousted of malice aforethought with the intention of getting his hands on the £100 previously offered for further information. The judge also had some hard things to say and Bousted departed ignominiously.

There remained the matter of the pistol Graham alleged had been fired at him by Simpson. If this was the case, then the prisoner had had a right to act in self defence. Ever in such situations, most Victorian courts were prepared to afford the accused some benefit of the doubt, more so when there was a possibility of the drop. In the event, after some deliberation, a verdict of manslaughter was finally reached, though indeed there was no indication that the crime was ever premeditated, with Bousted already humiliated and dismissed.

There were loud cheers and clapping of hands. William Graham had his fans after all. The unfortunate Simpson was already assuming a secondary role. But the judge still had the measure of the man in the dock. All along, Mr. Baron Martin had sought to have the trial conducted as fairly as possible and had extended every courtesy to the emaciated wretch before him. But now he emphasised the magnitude of Graham's offence, almost akin to actual murder, given the barbarity of the attack and committed very much as a result of excessive drinking – the assault against Richardson having for its part became a mere appendage. Sentencing William Graham to transportation for the remainder of his natural life, he appeared to engender some surprise among those in the crowded court, even while the older brother, Henry, was discharged as anticipated.

William Graham himself was nonchalant as ever. It was doubtful if he had ever spared much thought for the honest man he had cut off in the prime of his life, or for his widow and her child, recently born posthumously. He may even have welcomed the opportunity for a free passage to Australia as others had done over more recent decades, given the discovery of gold in the land down under. But we don't really know. Like many another before him he was taken below and along the connecting underground passage to the gaol to await transport to the hulks and there is no further word of him.

Whether he died on the voyage out, given his continuing fragile state, or whether he did go on to make a new life for himself in Western Australia remains unknown. But the Cumbrian courts had definitely sent their last felon overseas.

7: EARLY ONE MORNING

People are contrary and those in 19th century Cumberland no exception. Thus, when William Graham was cleared of murder, the locals in the public gallery clapped their hands and cheered. This may have had its origins in the fact that his unfortunate victim was a representative of authority, gamekeepers, water watchers and their likes having never been very popular with the majority of Cumbrians. This dislike was ingrained in their psyche, a not uncommon condition anywhere perhaps, along with not unnatural sympathy for the underdog as the unsavoury Graham had gradually became to some extent. But other defendants, and plaintiffs, could as easily become the subject of ribald laughter in any Cumbrian court.

Paradoxically however, when thirty-one-year-old Jacob Skelton was cleared of murdering his aged father-in-law in February, 1858 at the Cumberland Spring Assizes, the audience hissed repeatedly, demonstrating their rabid dislike of the man in the dock and their disagreement with the verdict, as surely as their kind had angrily made their feelings felt following the carefully considered Jane Crosby verdict, and the acquittal of the Reverend Smith. Skelton was disliked from the very onset and while he probably was innocent, his case is of particular interest given that many had deemed him guilty before he was even tried.

The scene of the death was Fenton, a small hamlet some seven miles to the east of Carlisle and linked by a network of roads to the nearby communities of Faugh, Warwick Bridge and Howmill. The pleasant hamlet has probably not changed a great deal since Skelton's time, consisting of just a few houses and farms, some of the properties dating back to the eighteenth century. Here, eighty-five-year-old Robert Irwin, a retired farmer, had lived for some months with his only daughter, Mary Ann, her husband, Jacob, and the couple's three young sons. The old man was known to have savings amounting to some £260; local gossip had it that the amount could be even greater. Irwin was also a devout Methodist and a former preacher. On Christmas Eve, 1857, a close neighbour, William Parkin, invited him to a prayer meeting at six o'clock the following morning at the home of an elderly farmer, Thomas Taylor, who also lived nearby, who may incidentally have been the same individual who had attempted to make a decent man of John Pearson of Randylands some twenty-three years earlier. Skelton was said to have grumbled about his father-in-law going to such a meeting so early in the morning but Robert Irwin was in favour of it and refused to be deterred. It was to be his undoing.

He rose early the following morning with Skelton and apparently set off alone at 5.55 a.m. towards Taylor's house carrying only a small lantern. He was never seen again until about 8.00 a.m. when a farm worker, John Bell, discovered him lying bleeding and unconscious by the roadside about fifty yards from his starting point. Given Robert Irwin's age and frailty, it was not beyond the realms of possibility that he had been taken suddenly ill and fallen down, hitting his head in the process. This was to be the immediate assumption. He was taken back to his lodgings and Mary Ann Skelton had some hard words to say about Christmas morning prayer meetings.

Had the old man lived he might have been able to eventually shed rather more light on the affair. A doctor was called and everything done to assist and revive him. However, at one a.m. the following morning, he died without having ever regained consciousness. It was a post mortem following hard upon the death which first led to suggestions of foul play, the victim having sustained two distinct wounds. The first was above the left ear with some evidence of fracturing about it but was innocuous enough. The second wound, on the crown of the head, was much more serious, the skull being smashed straight in; it gave the impression of having been caused by a heavy instrument, leaving an indent the size of a hammer head. Tongues quickly began to wag, the finger of suspicion pointing unswervingly in the direction of Jacob Skelton.

Skelton was a garrulous uncultivated man with the knack of upsetting those about him. The police investigated the burgeoning rumours. It emerged only too clearly that the big noisy man had never got on with his father-in-law who had been given to upbraiding him for his unprincipled way of life. Skelton had openly called the old man 'a methody bugger' and wished him dead. The family had only been a short time at Fenton, Skelton normally making his living as a farm labourer. But it subsequently emerged that he had had ambitions to be on a farm of his own and had been especially resentful because Robert Irwin wouldn't put up the money to assist him. And now, not only had he seemingly been the last person to speak with the old man but possessed a hammer of a size which it was felt could have killed him.

Skelton's conduct immediately following the discovery of the body had further told against him. He had quickly taken possession of Robert Irwin's watch and then flown into a rage when it was taken from him after the old man's death by his wife, who wished to retain it for their eldest son: "Thou'll only lose it or break it, Jacob." And when Mrs. Skelton had called upon him to assist in shopping for provisions for the funeral tea, he had cursed his father-in-law and refused out of pique. Such conduct as this was scarcely sufficient to condemn him irrevocably. But it served to underpin other details which the police were rapidly uncovering about Jacob Skelton and which had begun to convince them that he was their man.

There was another suspect nevertheless: William Parkin, the neighbour who had invited the old man to the prayer meeting in the first instance. He hadn't been around to collect Irwin that fatal morning as he had half-promised to do. He claimed to have overslept until 7 a.m. while it was estimated that the old man had been struck down around 6 a.m. Still he had no witness to his movements and Irwin had been discovered lying close to his gate. And he had a similar hammer to Skelton's. His home had been searched at the same time as the latter's who had been quick to advise him that he could be arrested as surely as he himself could be. But Parkin had no cause to harm old Robert. If anything, he had appeared fond of him. It was Jacob Skelton who was eventually arrested on 27th December, 1857 while having his evening meal. Coarse and loud as ever, he jeered and suggested that he have another cup of tea before he went.

To be charitable to Skelton, unlikeable though he was, he went on to receive abysmal press coverage which could have prejudiced the outcome of any kind of trial before it well commenced. Under the constantly recurring headline: THE FENTON MURDER, he was variously described as one who had been to prison for stealing, and someone who had left various places 'under discreditable circumstances'. Possibly, but not only was there insufficient evidence at the onset to establish that there had definitely been foul play but there was little to suggest either that the prisoner was much more than a poorly-educated oaf of a man whose main fault was his loud uneasy temperament. Nevertheless, the eventual outcome of the protracted inquest was a charge of murder and Jacob Skelton was listed to appear at the 1858 February Assizes. Such a form of preliminary press coverage one would add, was not uncommon in those days, any more than it has been in our own times on occasions.

At the commencement of his trial however, there was no indication that the prisoner was any less confident. He pleaded not guilty in clear tones and appeared quite indifferent to those packing the public benches. He was off to a good start. He had an excellent defence counsel, the young pushy Campbell Foster, beginning to make his name on the Cumbrian circuit. On the other hand, the case against him looked grim enough.

Steadily, the police had continued to amass evidence. At first Robert Irwin's body had been quickly interred. But then it had been exhumed for further detailed examination. The conviction had grown that the old man's skull had been smashed in with a hammer of the kind owned by Skelton. It was further believed that he had accompanied his father-in-law outside on that fatal morning. Equally as damning, they had witnesses prepared to testify in detail to the appalling relationship between Skelton and the old man, following on from evidence already given at the inquest.

The first of these, a labourer named Joseph Armstrong, spoke of the twosome agreeing badly to the extent that Robert Irwin had received a black eye from Skelton the previous summer, after which he had cursed the old man and his religion and offered Armstrong £10 to shoot him. This too was when Skelton had spoken of his wish to be on a farm on his own, blaming Irwin for thwarting him in this.

A washerwoman, Ann Burrough, testified against both the Skeltons, speaking of their harsh treatment of the deceased and of Jacob Skelton's threat to knock the old fellow's brains out when he had questioned his son-in-law's wisdom in buying some geese shortly before Christmas. Old Robert had asked if he could come and live with her. She had always found him quiet and civil and had felt sorry for him.

Otherwise, it seemed that the couple hadn't been doing too badly out of their elderly lodger at all. He had been paying 5s. a week towards their rent and an additional 2s. when they couldn't make up the weekly amount. And they had been able to afford to pay Ann Burrough to do all their washing following his arrival. And Mrs. Skelton had had access to a dressmaker.....

Skelton himself had spoken of his father-in-law having up to £1,000 in savings. He had appeared quite obsessed about this. And on Christmas Eve 1857 he had seemingly given the impression of not wanting William Parkin to go to the prayer meeting either. The insinuation was that there might have been some darker reason for this.....

And yet, as the trial progressed, the scene began to change somewhat. Skelton was not denying that he had risen with his father-in-law early on Christmas morning – perhaps making him all the more suspect. But it was noted too that he had apparently taken it upon himself to light the fire and offer the old man some food. This had seemingly been refused, but Irwin had accepted a drink of water. Thereupon Skelton claimed to have seen his father-in-law to the door but no further, bolted it behind the old man and returned to bed. His wife confirmed this in part for the entire family slept in a room off the main passage and she had heard the door close and spoken with her husband when he came back to bed. However, the precise timing of this appeared somewhat ambiguous. And it had already been claimed by another witness at the inquest that Mrs. Skelton had spoken of her husband as having seen the old man as far as the sheep fold. Mary Ann had subsequently denied this.

Likewise, Skelton hadn't appeared too concerned when the body had been brought into the house and made no attempt to deny his aggressive attitude afterwards with regard to the watch and the funeral provisions. But Skelton was never to claim that he had had any great affection for his father-in-law. Whatever he might have been it was clear he was no hypocrite and this might even have impressed the judge and jury to some extent. And clearly he had been against both Parkin and his father-in-law attending the prayer meeting, albeit for purely practical reasons perhaps.

Another major point which may have caused both judge and jury to ponder was the account of what had been found in the old man's pockets after he had been brought in from the roadside. He had been carrying a hymn book, his watch, and £5.15s., a considerable amount of money in those days, yet none of this had been taken. Thus robbery presumably hadn't been the motive of any would-be attacker.

As for Joseph Armstrong, he had sounded concerned at the inquest about Skelton's attitude towards Robert Irwin. But at the trial he didn't speak of Skelton with any great virulence. He confirmed the origin of Robert Irwin's black eye and the bad relationship between the two men but had gone on to treat the big noisy farm worker and his offer of £10 to have the old man shot as no more than a crude joke it seemed, having jestingly implied too that Skelton probably wouldn't have been much use as a farmer and had said this to his face. It seemed in fact that the old man had received the black eye while the family were living just outside Carlisle, at Kingstown, where Skelton had been briefly endeavouring to run a beer house. This would obviously have been against all Robert Irwin's religious values. He may have been lecturing his son-in-law yet again in the light of this, on his way of life and the state of his soul, something he often did, and thus provoked the assault from an irate and harassed Skelton, though this was never made clear. Needless to say, it was still a despicable action on the part of the younger man. On the other hand, Mary Ann Skelton had recently claimed that the twosome had begun to get on rather better of late.

Ann Burrough's evidence for its part had been damaging enough but her character had gone against her. She had had four illegitimate children and was well known locally as a drunkard. She had no cause to like the Skeltons having recently lost some of their washing whilst inebriated, causing Jacob Skelton to threaten legal action against her which she had deeply resented.

More complex was the medical evidence. Robert Irwin had evidently been struck by something and the paramount damage appeared to have been done by a hammer. But a sharp stone had also been discovered with hair and blood upon it near the scene of the old man's demise. Nor had there been any footprints at the scene of the alleged murder or any sign of a struggle.

A deal of time was spent considering the geography of the area. The road through Fenton led to Howmill which then had a thriving railway station: horses and ponies were regularly upon it at all hours taking riders and passengers to and fro. There was also a nearby pond where animals went independently at times to drink. Mightn't Robert Irwin have been struck by one of the foregoing, bewildered by the light from his lantern? The only problem about this was that no one locally had heard any horses or ponies abroad on Christmas morning. Neither was there anyone available to confirm that they had been using the road then. Parkin himself had stated that he had heard nothing on the road, though apparently he had been asleep until 7 a.m. anyhow. Skelton hadn't committed himself.

Altogether it was a confusing picture. Campbell Foster capitalised on this. In his speech for the defence he reminded the court that despite any past animosity, his client had got up on the fatal morning to attend to the old man's immediate needs and see him off, the prayer meeting itself having been expected to last about two hours. And what had the accused man to gain from his father-in-law's death anyhow? The wily lawyer reminded the court that Robert Irwin had been paying the Skeltons 5s. a week and sometimes more. The couple would have lost out immediately if he died for then such payment would obviously cease as indeed it now had done. There was also a will. Jacob Skelton had known of its contents: he was to receive nothing.

Mrs. Skelton was to receive the interest on the old man's capital of £260 during her lifetime, with the money to go to the couple's children following her own death. His client could have destroyed the will perhaps; he knew where it was kept, but he hadn't done so. He had spoken of his father-in-law possessing other money but this had to be fantasy. There was no other money.

Foster continued, now in full flow. The body had been found close to Parkin's gate. Parkin obviously had no reason to kill the old man, but likewise he had spoken of the love and reverence Mrs. Skelton had invariably demonstrated in respect of her father, discounting Burrough's allegations further. And would Jacob Skelton himself have gone so close to Parkin's door to strike down his father-in-law when the other man might just have been there to meet him. Neither had Jacob Skelton's footprints been discovered near the scene of the crime. And he had willingly surrendered his hammer to the police when requested to do so. Of greater importance still, the prosecution had failed to show that the wound to the crown of the head could not have been caused as surely by the hoof of a horse or pony, with the old man possibly tottering and falling onto the stone beforehand, and then receiving the accompanying wound as suggested. Thus in sum went the case for the defence, with the emphasis that robbery was clearly not the motive.

The judge himself was obviously reluctant to bear down too heavily on Skelton. There were too many contradictions. His summing up was balanced and fair and far from detrimental to the prisoner. The jury were undoubtedly swayed by his thinking and what they had heard beforehand. Skelton was not a likeable individual but they obviously felt he merited the benefit of fair play. They were only out ten minutes before returning with a verdict of not guilty.

Almost immediately, hissing began. The verdict was an unwelcome one to many of the onlookers. They might cheer for someone like William Graham but Robert Irwin was a more pathetic victim than Thomas Simpson, a defenceless old man who had deserved better in their estimation than a black eye and a blow to the head on a dark morning; Skelton had to be guilty. But while applause or laughing might at times be acceptable in most Cumbrian courts, hissing was not. Angrily, Baron Martin threatened the culprits with two years imprisonment if they persisted. Silence fell and his Lordship thanked the jury and was at pains to emphasise for the benefit of all the sceptics that the case had been 'one of mere suspicion with insufficient evidence to convict anyone of the crime'.

Thereupon the prisoner left the dock to rejoin his wife who had stood by him throughout the whole affair. He appeared to take his acquittal very much for granted and justice did appear to have been done despite some remaining ambiguities. Yet the unpleasant fact remained that had many had their way, Jacob Skelton would surely have been hanged.

8: 'A QUITE RESERVED SORT OF MAN'

It is a depressing fact that several of the more serious episodes already covered in some detail here happened directly or indirectly as a result of heavy drinking. But for excessive imbibing on the part of such reprobates as John Pearson and William Graham, their unfortunate victims might well have remained unscathed and the culprits spared the subsequent courtroom drama and its attendant punishment. Many lesser criminals of the period had doubtless been drinking too before plunging into wrong-doing. Nineteenth century judges, and magistrates, were often wont to deliver a lecture on the evils of drinking and its consequences in the fair county of the Celts, even while ignoring other reasons for offending.

We shall encounter more drunken crimes as we proceed for those domiciled in Cumberland could drink as hard as any outside the county and drink was never far away. In and around the small town of Brampton alone, there are said to have been at one period in the nineteenth century, around thirty licenced hostelries, even while the population thereabouts had not grown much beyond 2500 by the 1880's. Yet in an age which still tended to view drinking as a means of blotting out the tedium and drudgery of everyday living, and with so much social and business activity continuing to be centred around pubs, it is perhaps little wonder that so many drank to the extent they did, these including perpetrators of crimes, and victims themselves, such as the farmer William Armstrong, already known to us of course, who died by the hand of the Reverend Smith.

But not everyone drank either, in Cumberland or anywhere else. As the nineteenth century progressed trends did begin to change, with such alternatives as tea and coffee becoming more popular. Nevertheless, the temperance movement still gained ground pitifully slowly. Even while paradoxically, in the following case of violent death, it was not a drunkard who was the perpetrator of the crime, but one who simply abhorred drink and its effects.

The scene of the tragedy in this instance was Whitehaven, grown from a small fishing settlement in the mid-seventeenth century to one of the most important seaports in Britain in just a few decades, noteworthy for shipbuilding, a thriving coal trade with Ireland and the import of tobacco, spirits and sugar from the Americas. Many thousands of people were employed in its shipyards, mines and docks. The town itself had largely been the creation of the Lowther family, its fine Georgian architecture and symmetrical layout of streets remaining impressive to the present day.

Yet beneath the veneer of bustle and prosperity and architectural gentility there was another Whitehaven. The place would not begin to slide back commercially until well into the nineteenth century following the American Civil War and with the advent of the railways and competitive deep water ports elsewhere. And local coal and iron ore would long continue in demand requiring a huge labour force along with accompanying industries. But this had had a detrimental social effect in its turn. Given the overwhelming need for housing for the workers and the families, cheap residential property without adequate sanitation had eventually been erected in the very heart of the town itself and beyond, degenerating into overcrowded slums which would not disappear for many years and with ale houses in most streets. This was the state of play on 15th November, 1859 when residents in the neighbourhood known as the Ginns, close to the town centre, learnt of a violent crime in their midst.

Earlier that day, neighbours had observed the victim, thirty-four-year-old Jane Usher, out on the street. She was friendly and cheerful as usual and well known, having lived in the area most of her life, before and after her marriage. As was often the norm in those days her own parents, the Shepherds, lived only a few doors away. She had other relatives in the vicinity and three healthy boys of her own aged six, four, and sixteen weeks. But Jane Usher was possessed of one great handicap; she had a drink problem. This had already blighted her marriage to a man twelve years older than herself, William Usher, the father of her children, who was as serious as she was outgoing.

Jane was well liked, Will Usher was an unknown quantity, described as 'a quite reserved sort of man' who didn't mix with his neighbours and who worked solidly day after day as a coal bagger. Born in 1813 at a time when few working class youngsters received schooling at all, he had striven to achieve a measure of literacy and might have gone further in a different age. Respected if not particularly well liked, he was of religious inclination and had seen to it that both his older children attended Sunday School. Dedicated to his home and family, he nevertheless had a low tolerance level and detested drink for no given reason unless he had seen it blight his own childhood. When his wife began imbibing to excess he left her, though the origins of her drinking may have grown out of his own stifling piety and rigidity in part. But we don't really know.

Neither do we know who had the care of the two young boys during this period of separation; possibly the wife's family with some oversight from Usher. What is known is that Jane Usher continued to drink for some time during the separation but that family and others remained supportive and prevailed upon the aggrieved husband to take her back. He agreed to do this after she had signed the pledge and for almost a year afterwards the couple enjoyed a satisfactory relationship. In the words of one family member: 'she could have anything she wanted except drink'. Presently there was an addition to the family, another boy, who might have served to bring some kind of lasting stability to the marriage. On the other hand, the child may have been the means of placing additional strain on a still vulnerable woman.

At the onset, when the family began living together again as a complete unit, the husband remained cautious. He felt he knew his wife well enough not to trust her totally and may well have felt he was assisting her towards a complete cure by denying her the means to buy drink. Thus he kept the purse for a time but gradually began to allow her housekeeping money again and within a few months she was in full charge of household expenses as she had been before.

Yet who can really claim to be irrevocably cured of any addiction? Stronger beings than Jane Usher have foundered. It can take very little to upset the fine balance between enforced self-control and cloying inner weakness. The birth of her youngest child came and went and still she resisted the curse of drink. But came the day when it was all too much. Though not too well-endowed with money she felt the burning need for a drink and it wasn't difficult to find a second-hand shop prepared to buy a bag of the children's clothes. The money received for these was exchanged for a bottle of rum, the contents of which were covertly sampled and the bottle hidden away.

Two days passed and she continued to secretly imbibe. Usher suspected something but said nothing; perhaps his wife was able to conceal her condition to some degree. Then it all became too much. The brooding husband who had had such high hopes returned for his dinner at 3.00 p.m. on 15th November after a pre-dawn start on the early shift. The meal had been purchased for him at the communal oven and he ate this while noting that his wife's condition had worsened. He rounded on the pathetic woman angrily and left her in tears. Returning around six o'clock he found her lying down and ordered her to get up but received a torrent of verbal abuse from one who was normally so compliant.

Something snapped in Usher. He laid savagely about his wife until she fell and struck her head on the chimney corner. The angry trembling husband picked up his youngest child and sought to pacify it. What could he do now? The scene is not difficult to imagine with the two older boys eyeing their mother anxiously as she lay on the floor moaning. Usher, the anger ebbing out of him, asked the eldest to go and fetch his granny as he had requested often enough in the past.

The little fellow ran to Mrs. Shepherd and asked if she would come and make them their coffee?

Where was mammy then? Why couldn't she make the coffee herself?

"She's lying on the floor," retorted the youngster.

Liz Shepherd hastily put on her bonnet and shawl and hurried to the Ushers' home with her grandson. Her son-in-law stood over the sprawled body of his wife, still rocking their youngest child in his arms.

In great consternation, the grandmother enquired what had gone on? The husband indicated his wife. "She's drunk, that's what's wrong. It's been on her a few days." He sounded terse and distressed.

"But couldn't you have just put her out into the street, Will, and sent for me?"

"I'm sick of sending; I think I'm to be tormented by a drunken wife all my life!" A pathetic likeness here to Stephen Blackpool from Dickens' Hard Times.

The mother attempted to lift her daughter onto a chair and give her a drink of milk but without success. Minutes later, Jane Usher was dead. By this time the small house had begun to fill up with family and neighbours, anathema to a man who preferred privacy. Then the police arrived and he was taken into custody. He made no attempt to conceal the facts surrounding his wife's death but voiced his regret at his hasty temperament. And when charged with her murder he said that he wished he had never heard such a charge. It was a subdued unhappy man who was remanded to Carlisle Gaol.

The trial took place the following March. Usher had had time to think and had been prepared to accept legal guidance. He proceeded to plead not guilty though indications were that the odds remained against him. Neighbours had heard him assaulting his wife behind the thin walls. And though she was known to have had a drink problem, so had many another and they weren't prepared to swear that they had ever seen her greatly the worse for drink. A post mortem had revealed external and internal bruising. But it wasn't felt that the victim had died from falling against the chimney corner, but from a blow, or from a man falling upon her.

However, the defence had been ready for all this. The emotive picture of a hard-working man at the end of his tether with a drunken wife and three dependent children was presented to a not unsympathetic judge. Relatives were already known to have spoken of Usher's better qualities and two important outside witnesses were now called upon to testify in his favour. The first was his overseer at the colliery who had been in charge of him for fifteen years, speaking of a quiet industrious man and an agreeable workman. The overseer was followed by the prisoner's local clergyman who considered him sober and industrious and a good provider for his family. By this time Usher had been advised to change his plea to guilty of manslaughter. The judge was clearly moved by all he had heard and said that he would consider the whole painful matter carefully before reaching a decision. Usher was taken below again to await sentence.

His was not the only serious case to be heard at the 1860 Cumbrian March Assizes. Another individual, Barnaby Baines, was on trial for the manslaughter of a man on the railway. And a sixty-one-year-old midwife, Mary McVitie, was accused of causing the death of a young woman in labour through gross ignorance and incompetence, the girl's child having also died. Given that in those days, midwives were often illiterate and known to double up as washerwomen on occasions, this tragedy was perhaps scarcely surprising. McVitie herself was illiterate and quite untrained. A tragic state of affairs nonetheless, the fact that the dead girl had been a policeman's wife being quite irrelevant to the court.

McVitie aroused particular ire but in the event she was found not guilty amidst a confusing whelter of medical testimony. Baines too was acquitted. Others received a variety of custodial sentences as was almost inevitable with property involved. This left Usher and his Lordship took some time and care in addressing the subdued collier from Whitehaven. He felt that if Usher had used a deadly weapon with malicious intent, then he would have been given up for execution. But this was merely window dressing. Clearly the prisoner had hit out in momentary passion. He had not intended to murder his wife and had evoked considerable sympathy eventually and generally made a good impression in court. He was sentenced to fifteen months at hard labour.

Punishment enough perhaps. The reserved insular man would have the death of his wife on his conscience all his remaining days and would have his children to face again soon enough, and other members of his extended family. It is difficult not to sympathise with the man to some extent. He was a hard worker with good standards. He probably loved his wife in his own fashion as surely as he loved his children. In an era when heavy drinking remained the norm among many, he had turned his back firmly upon it. But he was all the more intolerant of his wife's penchant for alcohol as a result; when pushed to the extreme he reverted to the behaviour not uncommon among many of his peers in those days, setting about his partner because he couldn't take her change of personality and 'bad mouthing' and possibly feeling justified in doing so at the time, in his passion.

It might have helped if he could have sought some kind of professional advice but there was little help available for drunkards and their families in those days beyond the intervention of the fledgling temperance bodies or the platitudes of the church. And then, as now, the patient had to genuinely want help. The victim's mother thought she had an answer, to put the culprit out into the street to sober her up. But Jane Usher needed more than that. Perhaps unfortunately, no one ever sought to discover just what did trigger off her binges or why she was an alcoholic to begin with. And ironically enough, the sentence on her husband was probably little different then as to what it might be today under the same circumstances. Both alcoholism and resulting marital stress still remain grey areas.

9: THE KILLING OF ANN SEWELL

Cumberland could rightly claim to have moved ahead both economically and socially as the nineteenth century advanced, keeping in step with many other regions. Even by 1820, thousands of acres of hitherto neglected land had been enclosed and cultivated or converted into meadows. From 1835 the railway network began taking definite shape in the county. The Carlisle Canal had opened in 1823. The roads too had greatly improved, facilitating much speedier communication. There was a continuing upsurge of multifarious industry, particularly in Carlisle and West Cumberland.

Yet for many, life remained hard in Cumberland as elsewhere in the country. Nowhere was this more true than on the farms and the region had an abundance of the foregoing. Any improvements brought about by enclosure or otherwise had not been passed on to the farm servants. They still rose around 5.00 a.m. like their counterparts elsewhere, working until well into the evening most days for as little as £8 per half year. The women continued to have it almost as bad as the men for they often had to combine their household duties with labour in the byres and fields.

The general emphasis was on drudgery and boredom and Cumberland was no exception. The majority of the farms lay well away from any town. Away from work there were few recreations. Many agricultural labourers still couldn't read properly if at all and if they were able to read, they weren't encouraged to. Most hadn't travelled far in spite of improved communications so there wasn't a great deal to talk about. The major recreation of the unattached males might be drinking, providing there was any money to spare, or sweethearting the maidservants. Such was the background to the killing of Ann Sewell at Beckhouse Farm, several miles east of Cockermouth, in March 1860.

On Monday, 26th March of that year, Thomas Fearon of Beckhouse, a secluded hamlet in the Vale of Embleton, went off to Cockermouth market in the early forenoon with his widowed mother, Isabella. Thomas Fearon was one of the better-off Cumbrian farmers for it has to be said that some were almost as poor as those they employed. But thirty-six-year-old bachelor Fearon owned his 290 acre farm at Beckhouse, employing a hired man full-time, two day labourers and a female house servant. The stone-built farmhouse and its adjacent buildings are still there today, reached via a narrow lane running up from Embleton church. On this occasion the house had been left in charge of the female servant, an attractive girl of twenty-six named Ann Sewell, while the men went about their everyday tasks.

By 5.00 p.m. Mrs. Fearon was back home again, only to find the house locked up and the whole place deserted. She went to a neighbour's house and requested the assistance of the servant there, Sarah Earle. The servant got into the house through a window and saw Ann Sewell lying on her side in the kitchen passage. At first sight and given the position of the body, it seemed the girl might have fainted, as she had been prone to do in the past. She was still in her clogs and working dress and the house seemed undisturbed. But a closer examination revealed the true horror of the situation. The girl's throat had been violently cut and she was lying in a pool of blood. In her hand was a long-bladed kitchen knife.

The alarm was raised and the hired man brought from a nearby field where he had been harrowing. Twenty-four-year-old George Cass, big and burly, galloped swiftly into the farmyard on the horse he had unyoked. He declined to enter the house via the window, opening the door instead with a piece of iron hidden in the eaves which he utilised apparently whenever he was out late. A neighbour who went in with him presumed that the girl had cut her throat. An uneasy Cass agreed.

But a more detailed examination revealed a different state of affairs. The unfortunate girl's throat was so violently cut that the spinal cord had been entirely severed. She couldn't have held on to the knife afterwards in this event. And the knife had been found in her left hand; Sewell was right handed, further discounting any theory of suicide. There were also signs of a struggle with bruising on the girl's right hip and forearm and blood elsewhere in the passage. She had no money about her though she was known to be thrifty. She had almost undoubtedly been murdered, perhaps robbed, but by whom?

The blood had been beginning to dry upon discovery of the corpse but the girl had been last seen alive as recently as noon and beyond when she had served dinner to six men: the three farm servants and three Keswick men who had called to collect a consignment of grain. There had been some good-natured banter then but by 2.00 p.m. all the men had returned to their work. The farm dog had been heard barking later around 3.00 p.m. The Embleton parish clerk, John Robinson, had crossed the field from the church at 3.30 p.m. to return a mop and pail he had borrowed that same morning to assist in cleaning his hearse which was kept in a building beside the church. The house had been silent and locked then. This put the time of the crime at perhaps half an hour earlier.

No strangers had been observed in the area that day. Suspicion thereupon fell fairly quickly upon one of the day labourers, James Eland, who had already been in prison for poaching. But it transpired that he had been observed at work most of the afternoon by an independent witness as had his fellow labourer, James Boak. The parish clerk said that he had noted Cass's horse in the stable at the time he had returned with the mop and pail. But Cass claimed to have merely unyoked and stabled the animal while he had been repairing his harrow in the field and that he too had found the house locked up at the time, even while admitting that he could get into it independently, but claimed also to have seen Robinson trying the doors from his vantage point in the field.

Suspicion of a kind subsequently lay upon the unfortunate Robinson for a time. But further enquiries revealed that Cass was something of an unsavoury character. He drank heavily whenever he had money and was currently in debt to his employer. A Whitehaven girl, Jane Atkinson, had had a child by him fifteen weeks previously. He was also known to have a violent temper. He and Ann Sewell had both commenced working for Thomas Fearon the previous November. At the onset, the coarse-looking, imperfectly-educated hired man had attempted to sweetheart Sewell but she had put him off by saying she was already engaged; this was indeed true, though she had seen little of her boyfriend for some time.

Emnity had reigned between Cass and Sewell thereafter in their rather isolated environment. They quarrelled over the tasks they were required to share and he referred to her as a damned lazy bitch because she wouldn't always fodder the cattle. He had spoken of cutting her throat before the term was out. She had threatened to get the law onto him. But she had never apparently spoken ill of Cass to others and at times they still seemed to relate well enough. If anything, she had appeared to be unhappy at Beckhouse mainly because of the lack of social amenities.

Notwithstanding, the hired man was placed under close surveillance at the personal instigation of the Chief Constable himself, John Dunne. The latter, a remarkable individual in his own right, had only been three years in post. But he had already succeeded in melding the previously uncoordinated local police forces into the Cumberland and Westmorland Constabulary following the County and Borough Police Act of 1856. The Sewell episode was the fledgling force's first great murder mystery and a test of its reputation. Dunne therefore took an especial interest with good result for though Cass had been a prime suspect almost from the start, there had still been little to make a charge stick initially: the corpse had been discovered within a house locked from the inside and the suspect had neither key, nor blood upon his clothing; fingerprinting still remained an unknown phenomena, neither was he saying anything to give himself away.

Almost a fortnight passed and still no arrest was in fact made. But surveillance had fairly soon established that the farmhouse door could be locked from the outside as well as opened, by means of the piece of iron plyed by Cass whenever he was late back. It was also established that he had been in possession of additional money of late from an uncertain source.

George Cass was finally arrested on 6th April, 1860, charged with Ann Sewell's murder and placed in a police cell at Cockermouth. His clothes were sent away for analysis and minute traces of blood were to be discovered soon enough on his waistcoat. Yet the evidence against him would have doubtless remained flimsy had he not now gone ahead and quickly made a statement, ostensibly at least of his own free will. This not only served to afford some insight into the killer's twisted psyche but also became the means of incurring a verdict of wilful murder when the suspect might still have saved his neck. The statement, as strange and intriguing as any ever made, read as follows:

> "How was it done, you know, she made me mad, you know, and I was coming from righting a ewe. She was in the passage or lobby as some folk call it, coming out of the front door, leading into the yard opposite the stable. I had been in the orchard before the house righting the ewe. She wanted me to do something with her caulkers; and then, you know, as I would not bother with her caulkers, and then she began to bother me and to call me. She had a knife in her hand and I was standing between the stable door and the house door and then she threw the knife at me and the half just catched me on the cheek bone. Well then, I clicked it up in my madness and I just took it up and threw it at the deceased Ann Sewell. She was then standing just within a yard from the door in the passage and it struck just about there (prisoner pointing to the apple of his throat) somewhere about the part of the throat which projects out. Well then, you know, she ran from there down to the bottom of the passage. She did not scream out "Oh dear", she says; "come here and put me away altogether". She said she could not find it in her heart to go out again. Well then, I said I did not like. She begged and prayed of me either twice or three times to do it, and then I just took up t'knife which I had in my hand and just came a stroke across the left side of her neck. When I was coming a second time she put her hand up to the left side of her face and she said it did not seem to go far enough in. "Give us another". I gave her a second one, when she asked me; and then she stood a little bit and then she dropped and she laid there. Then I came up into the kitchen and I took the knife up with me and I thought I would wash it and then I rued – I would not; and I just went and put it into her hand and then there was just a drop of blood about the size of a halfpenny on here (pointing to his waistcoat) and then just with that John Robinson came up to the door. I was in the back kitchen at that time washing my waistcoat breast with my hand. I just stepped aside till he went away and he went into the stable and then he came out again and went away home. When I saw him off I washed my hands and waistcoat out and then I went like down into the kitchen and out of the front window into the orchard and then I got my mare out of the stable and then when I got her into the field she would not stand still till I got the gear on. She went galloping back into the fold. Then I went and brought her back and yoked her. About quarter of an hour after that I saw Mr. Boyes going down. A little bit after that there was a young lad went down on a cuddy and then I saw nothing more till Mr. Boyes' girl came to take me home at night. Then when I got home Mrs. Fearon told me to go in at the front window and I said: No, I could get in at the back door. I had got in many a time at it and then I opened the door for the mistress. I opened the door with that piece of iron that Mr. Brown had there (there

came a second caution, but Cass said he only wanted to tell the truth). Then at night after we had all gone to bed I went upstairs into Ann Sewell's room. Her and me was down at Cockermouth one night before that a bit and she wanted to get some things and she had forgotten her purse and she asked me if I had any money in my pocket and I said I had half a crown if that would do aught for her, and so I lent her it. So as I thought I had lent her the half crown I thought I would have it back again. Then I just looked into her box and there was a little bag, you know, that they hang over their arms, and I opened this and found a purse in it, and I just opened it and there was just eighteen pence in it, and then I just put the eighteen pence in the purse in my pocket, and then I grouped her frock-pocket as I thought there might be something more in it and there was half a crown in it. I put that in my pocket. In the morning I was putting the half crown into the purse with the eighteen pence and at one side of the purse there was a little hole in it and a sovereign in it. I did not know what to make of the sovereign and I owed our folk a sovereign and so I was over home on Wednesday night after I got the sovereign and I just left the purse and sovereign with my mother. Then I spent the half crown and got some drink on the road. And then I had eighteen pence left and then I ran out of bacca and sent for another ounce. Then I had like fifteen pence left. But Sarah Dixon the person I sent for the bacca only gave me three halfpence instead of threepence. I had given her sixpence out of the eighteen pence. That is all I think. I do not wish to add anything more to this statement. I have made it voluntarily and of my own free will. It would be as near half past three as near as I can tell when this happened. There was no one with me. I have done it all myself and I was very sorry after I had done it." Signed George Cass.

This was a dictated statement and must have been edited to some degree for Cass was only semi-literate and spoke very broad Cumbrian. However, it is still possible to get the flavour of the man's manner of speaking from it, affording the whole thing a measure of authenticity. Yet so much of the content of the statement was clearly fabricated too on the part of the accused. Just what had gone on in this brutish creature's mind while dictating his confession? Would such a presentable thrifty girl, well thought of by her employer, with a sweetheart and a modest amount of money in a savings account have really invited someone to kill her? And how could she have ever done so in any case with a knife stuck in her throat. Where the caulkers came into the matter must remain a mystery of itself for her only pair of clogs were found to be in no need of repair. And it appears extremely doubtful if her murderer could have gone to her room on the night following the killing in search of money. Those left in the house that first traumatic night including Sarah Earle, borrowed by Mrs. Fearon for company, slept very little and never heard anyone pass along the upstairs corridor of the comparatively small Cumbrian farmhouse.

Did Ann Sewell's killer simply feel too ashamed to admit that he had stooped to robbery immediately following his beastly crime? Or did he wish to emphasise that robbery was not part of his original conduct with a view to lessening his chance of hanging? In the event, it didn't really matter. What did matter was Cass's confession to the killing. As it transpired, he had now literally signed his death warrant irrespective of his reasons for the crime. Though indeed it was queried in some quarters too as to what tactics had been applied in order to obtain such a confession in a custodial setting so quickly, when the suspect had been so reluctant to confess until then.....

But then in Carlisle Gaol awaiting trial, Cass changed tack anyhow, speaking of having been asleep in the barn in the afternoon of the murder when the dog awoke him and he sighted a man coming from the house with a billhook who spoke of having taken a life and who gave him twenty-four shillings to keep quiet. He appeared to be implying that the man was James Eland though the disclosure availed him nothing. No one took it seriously. Yet still he seemed to think that he wouldn't hang, remarking to another prisoner that his case wasn't as serious as William Usher's whom he may have met in gaol and who was in the process of beginning his fifteen month sentence for manslaughter. But William Usher had to be a rather different individual to George Cass with much more to mitigate in his favour and with various people having been prepared to speak up for him. There was no one prepared to speak up for Cass, and nothing remotely tangible to excuse his crime.

The trial itself on 2nd August, 1860 was of fairly short duration, being almost a replay of the inquest in many respects. Cass pleaded not guilty, hopeful that he might be found guilty at least on the lesser charge of manslaughter but to no avail. The case had already engendered so much horrific publicity that it seemed doubtful if a single juror could have been found throughout the length and breadth of Cumberland who was without some kind of prejudice. And yet, as Baron Martin emphasised in his summing up, without the damning statement of the accused 'there would have been no evidence to go to trial at all – on the other hand, if they the jury believed the statement, then the accused was guilty of murder'. There was little doubt in the jury's mind. They were out but half an hour before returning with a unanimous verdict of wilful murder, but with a rather surprising recommendation to mercy.

A hush fell over the courtroom, crowded to capacity with women and members of the farming fraternity as the judge pronounced sentence of death, only punctuated by loud sobbing from one of Cass's sisters. The burly man in the dock, hair cropped short, eyes staring before him and looking older than his twenty-four years heard the sentence without any show of emotion. He is said to have smiled as he was taken below though this might have been no more than a journalistic flight of fancy.

George Cass really had little to smile about. Yet he now proceeded to damn himself even further by making a final statement: in short, he had been smoking his pipe after dinner when Ann Sewell had begun calling him names and taunted him about his bastard child and thrown cinders at him. He had jumped up and cut her throat, then changed his clothing and rifled her box for money. This may have been nearer the truth. With his master and mistress away for the day he might well have taken the opportunity to spend additional time lounging in the parlour. But it seems doubtful if the maid would have showered him with cinders, given that an integral part of her duties was to keep the house spick and span and with her mistress due back before nightfall. What may actually have happened is that Cass had gone back into the house prior to repairing his harrow and became over-familiar in the knowledge that no one else was present. Sewell would scarcely have welcomed the hired man's latest overtures; she had endured them before if some were to be believed, but made it clear then that she was already engaged. Or paradoxically, he may have been bullying her again over some task he wanted her to perform.

Either way, she had possibly retaliated by pouring scorn upon him. Only that morning the mother of his child had been to the farm seeking maintenance. Cass had had to send her away empty-handed. Sewell had witnessed this. She also knew of the fool he tended to make of himself while in drink and that he commanded little respect. She would have plenty of verbal ammunition and may well have made the fatal mistake of getting behind the defences of a man on a short fuse at the best of times and with a low level of intellect and self-esteem. Consequently he could easily have snapped there and then with fatal result but also taken his victim's money afterwards, being insolvent as usual and feeling she owed him something. Needless to say, we can never be truly certain as to just what did happen in the farmhouse that Monday afternoon, though Cass seemingly did change out of his bloodstained clothing all right, allegedly hiding it in an outhouse where it was never discovered. Then later he claimed his friends took it away and destroyed it. Yet for some reason they were never charged as accessories. And who were those friends anyway? Nor was it ever established why a hammer and pincers were lying on the kitchen table of Beckhouse Farm at the time of the murder. Some anomalies certainly did remain…..

On the other hand, George Cass had long been known as a misfit and even as something of an eccentric. His family were actually hard-working and respectable people who had lived in the neighbouring community of Eaglesfield for many years, variously employed as farm servants and coal merchants. Cass was one of seven children and apparently well loved but grew up a difficult youth taking quickly to drink and womanising, with an added reputation for unpredictability. He had been fired by at least one employer and was on his second time round with Thomas Fearon who was however only paying him £7.10s a half year and could probably humour him and was prepared to put up with him.

Ann Sewell was a native of Lamplugh. Not for her the ongoing love of decent parents and extended family; she had became an orphan at an early age with only one sister. She must nevertheless have benefitted from the basic educational amenities gradually coming into vogue for the offspring of poorer people from around 1833 onwards for she was fully literate – a freshly written letter to her sweetheart, a miner named John Farrish, was found in her box after her death. All in all, a bright and articulate young woman, which may have led to her final undoing. Ironically enough, she hadn't intended to remain more than six months at Beckhouse. But though all the other players involved eventually went from there, she remained, buried in St. Cuthbert's Churchyard five minutes walk from the place where she died, her resting place marked by a stone generously paid for by public subscription. Unfortunately, the grave is now sadly neglected and the stone itself is becoming weather-worn and has long since begun to lean, the inscription only just discernible now after so many years and reproduced as follows, less only the now rather anachronistic biblical quotation which accompanies it.

SACRED
To THE MEMORY OF
ANN SEWELL
WHOSE LIFE WAS TERMINATED
BY THE HAND OF AN ASSASSIN
While in the discharge of her humble duties
On the 26th day of March
AD 1860. Aged 26 Years

Insofar as her assassin was concerned, following his arrest, trial and sentence, various unfounded rumours began to circulate about him; that he had threatened to kill anyone in the gaol who came near him in the event of a guilty verdict, that the Governor had contemplated putting him in chains, that his mother had died of a broken heart. In fact, perhaps surprisingly, Cass was a model prisoner. Leaving aside his final wild statement he listened sensibly and carefully to the Chaplain and took a final respectful farewell of his immediate family and the mother of his illegitimate child though could not face his mother for fear of upsetting her any further. This aside however, there is no evidence that he expressed personal sympathy for his victim then or ever.

On 21st August, 1860, the date set for his execution, he walked with a firm step to the scaffold on the front wall of Carlisle Gaol and is reported to have kept his eye steadily on the cross beam above him before being hooded and haltered and launched into eternity. Several thousand saw him go. Being stout and strongly-built he dropped heavily and expired fairly quickly, the first man to be hanged in Cumberland for five years. Unfortunately, his crime was to the be the forerunner of several more quite horrendous episodes to now hit the county as the decade got under way. It would not be too long before the scaffold was again in use.

10: THE BODY IN THE FIELD

The Embleton murder resulted in an almost obsessional interest in the crime throughout Cumberland and beyond. More than a thousand people awaited the train bringing Cass from Cockermouth to Carlisle even prior to his trial; they watched in hushed silence as the manacled prisoner was escorted from the railway station under close guard and taken into the nearby gaol. The short trial itself resulted in a full house and more and as we also know, thousands attended the execution.

But there was considerable shame and revulsion too among Cumbrians at the time. There was already a strident abolution movement there as elsewhere. It is probably true to say that it lost considerable support following Ann Sewell's demise.

1860 saw several particularly horrible murders in Britain, most notably the Youngman killing in Walworth, in which the twisted killer took the lives of his mother, girlfriend and two brothers over a paltry £100 in insurance money. But to the consternation of thinking Cumbrians, they very quickly had another violent slaying on their own doorstep a mere fifteen days after the killing of Ann Sewell.

On Tuesday, 10th April, 1860 a man named George Pattinson was making his way across the fields lying just beyond the Townhead district of Penrith. It was six a.m. on a cold frosty morning. Pattinson had risen early as usual to feed a horse and some sheep belonging to his employer. He had almost reached the animals when he saw an ornate walking stick lying on the ground, an unusual object for such a place. He picked it up and as the warmth of his hand thawed the hoary covering, discovered his hand to be sticky with blood and noted gore and hair clinging to the stick's head. Seconds later he came across the body of a man lying within the angle of a stone wall, a few yards from a small stream.

As the shocked Pattinson endeavoured to make sense of it all, he observed a young raffish character known locally as Tommy Grey coming from the direction of a pig shed in the immediate vicinity. Pattinson called out to the latter for assistance but received a lukewarm response. The man spoke of having no time as he had horses to meet at Penrith station. But he did finally consent to come closer. Pattinson called out to the man lying on the ground; he moved his head slightly but made no sound. The man known as Grey volunteered the information that he had observed the body lying there earlier but that nothing had passed between them. Pattinson requested that the younger man inform a policeman given every indication that foul play had taken place; there was evidence of a struggle with foot marks everywhere. The man on the ground had received a violent blow to the head – the back of his skull was smashed right in and a broken ash sapling lay nearby coated with blood. There was blood in the nearby stagnant stream, a hat floating on the surface of the water and blood on the stone wall close to the body. The young man made off. Pattinson, a conscientious and sensible individual decided to notify the police himself, not being too sure of the other man's reliability. He acted wisely for 'Grey' never did report the episode to the police.

The latter were quickly on the scene and to their credit, conducted a thorough on-the-spot investigation under Superintendent Carson with some result, even though the man in the angle of the stone wall was now dead. The investigation was all the more impressive considering that Cumberland was not normally a place with a very high homicide rate and that the officers involved were more accustomed to dealing with brawlers, drunkards and thieves. But the calibre of the new Cumberland and Westmorland Constabulary had already became evident in the current case of George Cass and was not destined to be found wanting throughout this latest tragedy and its finale.

Following minute examination of the entire site and the corpse itself, the body of the unfortunate victim was removed to the Penrith Union Workhouse. Penrith wasn't a large place then with many locals knowing one another. A number of people were questioned to good effect leading to 'Grey's' arrest at Patterdale later that same day. The latter proved perfectly able to speak up for himself. Appearing presently in court he demonstrated little concern for legal etiquette, promptly informing all those present that his proper name was Sowerby and contradicting the police evidence persistently, a young man of twenty-seven years, garbed in menial attire, with an unwashed countenance and dark matted hair.

Things looked bad for Thomas Sowerby. He had blood on his clothes and gaiters and had been seen drinking in a Townhead pub with the dead man on the evening of 9th April. He had also been observed in his company after closing time. But Sowerby dismissed the stains on his clothing and gaiters as sheep's blood. He maintained that he had remained in the pub, the Grey Bull, just short of an hour after the dead man had left it and would not admit to being with him afterwards. All in all, he gave as good as he got: 'I can tell t'truth as any man that steps'. When remanded in custody for a week and advised that his clothes would be taken off him for testing, he enquired impudently if he would be stripped altogether? Confirming that he could read, he had accepted a bible but without any indication that he would attempt to seek solace from it: 'they can nobbit hang me and I have no one to fret after me'.

The suspect was in custody. But who exactly was the victim? No one ever really established who he was. It was quickly supposed that he was a German because he had said he was and because he seemingly spoke German fluently. But how many of those he had earlier spoken with in Penrith knew the language sufficiently well to authenticate this? A man of around fifty years of age with dark hair and a moustache and quite well-built, he was further assumed to be a Jew given his looks, but this too was supposition. He had only arrived in Penrith the previous Saturday, variously advising those he encountered that his name was Simon Manassa or alternatively Davidson, that he had a wife and three children in Newcastle upon Tyne, but giving

Shap as his normal place of domicile to someone else. He had worn a white apron and was said to have been travelling about dressing hats, but had also described himself as a jobbing gardener. A peculiar character altogether, not unintelligent, but probably just another of the deviants who travelled the roads of Britain in those days, tolerated by the majority but standing out from the mainstream and inviting insult and abuse on occasions. Indeed, we still have their likes about today but to a lesser degree in our technically-orientated age, allowing for fewer opportunities to earn a casual living.

Meanwhile, it was already believed that the dead man could have been decoyed down to one of the pig sheds in the field under the pretext of finding him somewhere to sleep for the night and perhaps robbed. But his pockets had appeared undisturbed even while his clothing had been saturated with frozen dew and his head was a bloody mess. A little over two shillings had been found upon him and various personal items: a knife, a snuff box, soap and comb, needle and thread, a box of pens, all intact. So what had really led to his death?

An inquest quickly followed at the local workhouse and a number of witnesses were called headed by George Pattinson, who repeated his account of events that cold April morning with emphasis on his encounter with Thomas Sowerby. The latter, it transpired, worked as a kind of general labourer at Hetheringtons Stables in Penrith and had had every reason to be in the field that morning for his employer had livestock in the immediate area as had Pattinson's employer. But his volatile behaviour at the time was particularly noted. On the other hand, it seemed that the prisoner's clothes had not yet gone off to London for a full examination. It was proposed sending them to a Dr. Taylor but a juror remarked that Taylor had made mistakes in the past.

"Who hasn't?" retorted the Coroner.

Laughter ensued, while it was remarked that the only difference between human and animal blood was the difference in the diameter of the globules. Despite considerable advances in police methods, such were the limits to forensic knowledge still prevailing at the time. Obviously any evidence which might be gleaned from the prisoner's clothing was going to be ambiguous at best.

The inquest was adjourned shortly afterwards, having concluded with a statement by a Penrith watchmaker, who spoke of having given the deceased man sixpence doss money on the day of his arrival in the town. When asked by the latter if he couldn't give more, he had handed over a box of pens which explained why Manassa had been in possession of the foregoing at the time of his death. One other piece of information which had emerged on this occasion was that the wanderer had been prone to fits and hadn't been well on the day prior to his demise, or so he had said. This information would be utilised later to good effect at the subsequent trial.

When the inquest resumed on 21st April there was more information available. The police had remained zealous. Their efforts to establish the victim's true identity had proved abortive. But they now had no fewer than twelve local witnesses available to testify. The medical evidence was of additional relevance. The dead man had been less healthy than he had looked. It was remarked that his body beneath a generous layer of clothing had been positively emaciated and there was evidence of heart disease, this over and above the possible propensity to fits. And though his skull had been fractured, it was inferred that the blows he had received were not the direct cause of death. Yet evidently the shock to his already weakened system by such repeated blows and loss of blood and exposure to the cold air over a period of hours had to have been the indirect cause of his demise at least, with the dead man's stick being confirmed as the assailant's instrument along with the ash sapling.

Yet still there remained the motive. Manassa, as he now irrevocably became known, hadn't been an easy man. This was evidenced by witnesses who had encountered him on his last fateful weekend and afterwards. Impressions were of a man with the unfortunate habit of upsetting others and drawing unwelcome attention upon himself. Arriving first in Penrith, he had booked into a common lodging house where he had stayed two nights. The lodging house keeper spoke of his quarrel with a fellow lodger on the last day of his life when he had brandished a pocket knife menacingly. That same evening he had been drinking in the Grey Bull, downing rum and ale and boasting tactlessing of having five pound notes and sovereigns about him, though he had never shown these. Later, the landlord had offered to 'escort him home' given that he was the worse for drink and a stranger to the locality, a rather touching demonstration of Cumbrian courtesy. But Manassa had refused the offer and gone stamping off alone, clutching his stick. Sowerby had been talking to him earlier in the bar but hadn't left the place until later – in fact he had been put out around 11.30 p.m., a good half hour after the deceased man, but was identified as one who had been with him again afterwards. Had the motive been robbery? This still wasn't clear. But it was confirmed that Manassa had not been allowed back into his lodgings that night where several men and women remained in residence owing to his earlier trenchant manner. Thus by around 11.45 p.m. he was definitely homeless, and within hours he would be dead and discovered to be almost penniless.

All the while Sowerby was present, brought once more from custody to attend, as was the norm in those days. He remained nonchalant enough by and large. However, he kept twisting his cap too and interrupting the proceedings. Finally, with still no verdict in sight and another remand proposed, he blurted out excitedly: 'Put it off t'th Sessions or 'Sizes and hang me. What's t'use of keeping a fellow here?' There followed further complaints from him about 'lack of t'truth' before a further adjournment was announced and he was locked up again.

Indications were that the prisoner was beginning to break though indeed, in the minds of many, it was not really a question of who had committed the crime, but still a question of why? Finally, the following Saturday, Thomas Sowerby went some way towards answering that question. Suddenly, but perhaps not totally unexpectedly, he expressed his wish to make a confession. Since the confession of George Cass had been the prime means of hanging him but Sowerby's the additional means of assisting him to escape the noose, it is reproduced her virtually in total for the reader's additional edification. Impressions are of a man, locked up alone in a Penrith police cell, who was in fact almost relieved to confess in the end, in spite of his earlier familiar, unhelpful manner. He spoke as follows:-

> 'When I went out of the public house he went out afore me and there were two little lads Pelter and Hilton who lived down Crudmire. First when I went out of the pub I went out by the back gate; then I went down Crudmire to see if the two little lads had gone home. I did not see nowt of them. I went down that back street as far as the lodging house is beside the old House of Correction and I met him beside John Varty's gate. He asked me if I knew any place where he could lay down and sleep a bit. I said I could not tell I was sure. Then he said he would go home with me. I tell't him she had nea room where I stopped at and I was not gen haeme just then. Then he asked me if I could find him a place to lay down a bit and I said we would go into the back building of Willy Hetherington and I would see if there was any hay or straw or owt. I could not find owt. The back door and stable door were both locked. There was not any other place that had owt in it. I tell't him I knew of a building where we had put a cartful of straw that day. He said that would do then. I tell't him that it was about three fields length off. With that he got hold of my arm and said let's be away. We went down Thackerbeck. We did not go down the field; we went through Willy Hetherington's back meadow. When we got there I let him see the way up and he could not get up inside because there was not any ladder. Then he began a swearing at me; then I ran away. I ran down the wall to the bottom gate. When I got over the gate he threw his stick after me; then he came up to me. I got his head under my arm and threw him over my buttock. He began cursing and swearing and I got hold of his stick and I was frightened what he was going to do with me, he was threatening. I struck at him several times with the stick; then I threw the stick over the dike across the back into another field. Then he got up again. There was an ash stick ligging. I got hold of it. I broke it and then I ran up the wall beside the hog house again. I came up the fields to the Townhead by the Willow Grove and left him. I did not think I'd hurt him half as sare as I did.
>
> All I have to add is that if it had not been so frosty I don't think he would have died.'
>
> Thomas Sowerby
> (Signed by himself)

Much more was therefore revealed and the confession had some ring of truth about it. Yet given the extent of the victim's injuries and the amount of blood splattered about, the question had to remain as to just how defensive Sowerby's action had actually been, even allowing for his excitable temperament and inebriated condition. The walking stick had been thoroughly coated with blood and he had gone on to break the ash sapling in two. The impression was of someone rapidly transformed into a state of frenzy rather than continuing in a state of fear. And Manassa scarcely appeared to have been a very formidable opponent, antagonistic though he may well have became. However, the confession-cum-statement was undoubtedly much more authentic than the one provided by George Cass, intellectually limited though both prisoners appear to have been. It was sufficient at any rate to assist those conducting the extended inquest on Simon Manassa to now record a verdict of manslaughter against Thomas Sowerby though he wasn't out of the wood yet.

At his trial the following August the prosecution were still eager to find him guilty of wilful murder. However, weather conditions at the time had almost certainly played a part in the victim's death, perhaps abetted by his already run-down physical condition. Nor was there tangible evidence to prove the accused guilty of robbery which was of crucial importance in the determining of his fate. He had had very little money when arrested at Patterdale and it was eventually assumed that he had probably never heard Manassa mention money in the Grey Bull, if the wanderer had ever been possessed of additional means to begin with. Certainly the latter's pockets had appeared undisturbed after the killing and what money he had had then had been minimal. Much play too was made on the victim's hasty temperament and his apparent medical problems and many points in the statement rang true, even to the extent of straw having indeed been placed in the pig shed on the day Sowerby mentioned. Neither had any previous dispute been evident between the victim and his slayer, while Sowerby wasn't denying having been in drink either, at the actual time of the crime. In the event, the jury returned a verdict of manslaughter without even retiring but the judge had been toying with the idea of an extended period of penal servitude and only a recommendation to mercy spared Hetherington's odd job man a longer sentence. As it was, he was probably fortunate to receive no more than eighteen months hard labour which he appeared to accept unconcernedly.

Throughout his trial he hadn't appeared greatly concerned and this was a rather intriguing feature of several major Cumbrian defendants of the period, notably John Graham of Grinsdale, William Graham and Jacob Skelton. All appeared to feel that justice was on their side and that they didn't have much to worry about. In a majority of instances such proved to be the case, Sowerby for his part receiving a lesser sentence than that normally meted out to a common thief.

Chief Constable Dunne was one who may have had other ideas about Thomas Sowerby and the true magnitude of his crime. Extensive press clippings on the Townhead killing appear on a day to day basis in a scrap book kept by Dunne which survives today in the police's Black Museum at Penrith. He had obviously followed the case closely and may well have been disappointed at the eventual paltry sentence.

Meanwhile, the unfortunate Manassa had disappeared into an unmarked Cumbrian grave. It only remains to remark upon the odd likeness between victim and assailant. Both were deviant characters living from day to day, accustomed to dossing where they could, possessing little more than the clothes they stood up in, though Sowerby did apparently have one change of shirt. Both were of excitable temperament and drank more than was good for them. Their coming together was transitory but the result was tragic.

11: FATAL LIAISON

There's no fool like an old fool, they say, with a mind perhaps to some elderly man who ought to know better, enamoured of a beguiling younger woman. But the reverse can apply too of course and there have been some famous affairs both true and legendary: Elizabeth and Essex, Phaedra and Hippolytus, springing expressly to mind, though unfortunately ending badly.

At a rather lesser level but with similar tragic result was the case of Jane Davidson and William Horsley, whose affair and its outcome made headlines in Cumberland during the spring of 1861.

It is doubtful if William Horsley envisaged any kind of trouble when he married Jane Davidson's daughter, Mary Ann, in 1858. At that time he was a presentable young man, a nineteen-year-old apprentice draper from Penrith and the son of solid respectable people. Despite all this he was said to be weak and indecisive. Yet he might still have made a reasonable husband had he not quickly fallen under the sway of his mother-in-law. She appears to have became besotted with him from the onset and to have quickly shown her hand.

A native of Scaleby village, Mrs. Davidson was then into her forties but still attractive with a seeming penchant for younger men. She had married her husband, George Davidson, years before and borne twelve children. But the marriage appeared to have gradually fallen into decay, with the wife going much her own way.

At the time Horsley came into the family, his in-laws were managing a Penrith hostelry, the King of Prussia, but Jane Davidson was the controlling force there, probably as in much else relating to the marriage now. William and Mary Ann moved into their own house in Penrith but Mary Ann was very soon complaining that her mother was keeping William from her for extended periods. She eventually appealed to her mother-in-law who confronted her son but he appeared unable or unwilling to break free from Mrs. Davidson's charms.

Matters seemed to be improving when Mary Ann gave birth to a baby girl. But the child soon died and was followed a few months later by its mother. By this time Horsley's relationship with Mrs. Davidson was being much talked about in the area and the younger woman's death gave rise to some ugly rumours. These were without foundation; Mary Ann had died of consumption. But as it was, Jane Davidson did take the opportunity to use the event to her further advantage. Ostensibly she assumed the role of comforter to the young widower. Nevertheless, this must have went well beyond the normal bounds of itself for Horsley's mother surprised the couple in a compromising position. Thereafter she could scarcely bring herself to speak to Jane Davidson, who was almost as old as she was.

Things could not continue like this. The gossip intensified and Horsley's friends finally prevailed upon him to move to Carlisle away from Jane Davidson. By this time he seems to have genuinely wanted to break off the relationship. Having completed his apprenticeship some time previously he succeeded in finding a position with a Mr. Hyslop in Carlisle in whose home he also arranged to lodge and was quickly installed there.

Nothing daunted, Mrs. Davidson proceeded to bombard her son-in-law with letters. On one occasion she enclosed a poem, which if her own composition, was no mean effort for one who was little more than imperfectly instructed:

> I felt it was like a dream too beautiful to last.
> Would that I could, but never shall forget the past.
> When he told me that he loved me how little did I know,
> That he was then deceiving me I could not think it so.
> Oh believe me it is better when you find you've been deceived,
> By one whose love you felt assured could ever be believed.
> The burden of that sorrow causes bitter tears to flow.
> Though there is a bright tomorrow, the present's nought but woe.

Her own verse or not, this and the thirty-eight letters she wrote to the young draper from Penrith appear to have had some effect. Horsley continued to travel to Penrith to see Mrs. Davidson, even while his father was to testify that the young man, still only twenty-two, had been attempting to shake her off.

Be this as it may she was a persistent woman and early in 1861, moved with her remaining children to Carlisle where she took up as landlady of the Pack Horse Inn in Water Street behind the railway station. Meanwhile, her husband was no obstacle at all; he was generally working long hours for a farmer some miles out in the country. When he came back on occasional visits he now slept with his two young daughters while Mrs. Davidson had a bedroom to herself, surely an unpleasant and unhealthy state of affairs insofar as the children were concerned, even in those less sophisticated days.

Horsley became a regular visitor to the Pack Horse and slept there on a number of occasions. There is no evidence that he was actually sleeping with the older woman at that time. But tongues were beginning to wag afresh and the young man's employer banned Mrs. Davidson from calling into his shop. He also threatened to sack Horsley for staying away at nights as though he were some kind of juvenile delinquent. Such however was the power of the master in those times.

This may have brought matters to a head. Horsley had now begun seeing a younger woman in any case. Whether this affair was serious or not is debatable but Mrs. Davidson learnt of it. She had already spoken with another young man of her acquaintance and said she would be Horsley's end some way or other after she had quarrelled fiercely with the latter on a previous occasion at Penrith. In her present state of desperation she consulted a fortune teller who prescribed a number of worthless charms. On a more insidious note, she set someone to watch the subject of her infatuation closely and attempted to instigate a breakdown in the new relationship.

Harassed and frustrated, Horsley expressed his intention of going to the Pack Horse and ending the affair once and for all. He went there on the evening of 11th April, 1861 and sat closeted with his mother-in-law in the front kitchen where they had spent time together in the past. But once more he seemed to have found difficulty in breaking with the woman he had spoken of as 'very dangerous if one got the wrong way with her'. The hours passed and he drank steadily, yet no voices were heard raised in anger while the couple tarried alone.

Mrs. Davidson had an older daughter, Margaret, and the latter's husband William Robinson temporarily living with her as well as her two younger dependent children. Around midnight she came upstairs leaving Horsley in the kitchen and spent some time rummaging through a drawer in the Robinsons room. She did not appear too agitated but was heard being sick through the night.

The following morning Robinson rose early and observed Horsley lying on the kitchen floor, head resting on a pillow and covered by an eiderdown. He thought nothing of it and departed outdoors leaving his brother-in-law lying there, Horsley having slept in the kitchen before. Some time later Robinson returned and his wife instructed him to wake Horsley up and get him out. But when he drew the eiderdown back and attempted to rouse the figure on the floor, he quickly observed that Horsley was lying in a pool of blood. His neck tie was drawn very tightly about this throat, tied in a single knot; he was obviously dead.

The police were called. No sooner had an enquiry been initiated than there was a commotion elsewhere in the house. Mrs. Davidson was found gasping agonisingly for breath. Within hours she too was dead.

Gradually, all the ignoble background details were pieced together. It was surmised that Horsley had finally plucked up the courage to tell his mother-in-law that he was ending the affair, but that she had continued to ply him with drink and then found it comparatively easy to strangle him with his own necktie, his blood bursting from nose and mouth in the process. What was beyond question was that she had then sought out a packet of arsenic which she had earlier purchased and secreted in the Robinsons room, having possibly intended to use it on Horsley as a last resort. As it was, not wishing to live without her young man, she had taken a massive dose of this herself after presumably choosing to strangle him, a post mortem affording evidence of a large quantity of the poison in her stomach.

Following the evidence of all those involved including the elusive fortune teller, the required inquest resulted in a verdict handed down in ten minutes: 'Wilful murder of William Horsley against Jane Davidson and self-murder against the same Jane Davidson'. No one disputed this verdict and the couple had already been laid to rest at Penrith. Had Mrs. Davidson lived to stand trial the whole thing would have became a cause celebre and she would probably have been the first woman to have been hanged in Cumberland that century. But she had died along with her unfortunate victim and the whole sad affair soon became yesterdays' news and only those immediately concerned were left to continue mourning the passing of this ill-starred pair.

12: INSUFFICIENT EVIDENCE

In these more enlightened times, we tend to forget that suicide was a criminal offence in England and Wales until 1961. Indeed, many went to prison for attempting to take their own lives as late as the 1950s. However, in Cumberland during the period under scrutiny here and even beyond it, local courts generally appeared to favour a more sensitive means of disposal. This was perhaps as well for Cumberland had more than its share of suicides and attempted suicides over the years. Most did succeed in killing themselves. But those who survived and came before the courts might only go to prison for a short token period and were more likely still to be free on recognizance of a small payment, or bound over, providing they weren't deemed too unstable, after being subjected to a moralistic lecture.

Yet some local verdicts still bordered on the ludicrous in respect of those who had succeeded in their aim. For instance: 'deceased committed suicide during a temporary fit of insanity induced by drinking through the week'. No mention of possible causes closer to home such as the sheer misery of everyday living experienced by the lesser fortunate leading to abuse of alcohol prior to ending it all, or chronic alcoholism and damaged brain cells as a result of the rampant liquor trade which had continued unchecked for many years in Cumberland and throughout the country. And was there anything at all to match the archaic verdict handed down in respect of Jane Davidson? She was rightly held responsible for the wilful murder of her toy boy, Horsley. But then she was also labelled a 'self-murderess' albeit with the insanity rider being conveniently omitted in her case. Obviously it was a matter of horses for courses insofar as Mrs. Davidson was concerned.

Whether acceptable or not, the fact remained that suicide and attempted suicide had long been yet another grey area and was as poorly understood in previous centuries as it can often be today. An especially complex case in Victorian Cumberland was that of Sarah Carrick, a fourteen-year-old servant girl who died on 19th September, 1861 in the Dalston area from rat poison. Had she sought to take her own life while her mind was unbalanced? Or had she been driven to suicide due to the harsh treatment allegedly meted out to her by her employers? These were the two paramount queries. On the other hand, had she even intended to commit suicide at all and had there simply been a case for involving an accredited child psychologist all things being equal? The reality was of course that no such creature existed in 1861 while Durkheim's pioneer monograph on suicide was thirty-six years off and not even destined to be translated into English until 1951. There was little to guide any jury in such cases beyond basic facts in those far-flung days.

As for Sarah Carrick, she had worked for Mr. and Mrs. Hornsby of Dockray Hall near Dalston as a house servant from Whitsuntide, 1861. She doesn't seem to have been entirely untypical of many another young working girl in those days. At least not until early one morning when another servant, eighteen-year-old Isabella Irving, reported to the mistress, Elizabeth Hornsby, that Sarah wasn't well. To the apparent credit of Mrs. Hornsby, who was later to be so maligned, she called the fourteen-year- old to her and enquired as to what was amiss? Sarah complained of pains in her stomach. She was immediately offered tea and advised to return to bed. She declined and ate her breakfast with Isabella and worked until lunch time when she ate with the other servants. She then asked permission to go out and gather potatoes in the field but fell sick and was put to bed. Late in the day she was invited to take supper. She did this but continued in bed.

The following morning, Sunday, she was no better but after breakfast in bed, claimed to feel improved and got up to go into the fields. Before long however, she was retreating through the rain and had to return to bed. Mrs. Hornsby examined her all over but the only problem appeared to be a stomach disorder. Again she rose but merely sat about, though was fit enough to take her tea with the other servants. However, she again took to her bed at the time she would normally have been going with the others to church. The situation worsened and at two a.m. the mistress discovered that the girl had vomited. Her hands too were stiff and she spoke of going deranged. Something was clearly wrong.

Shortly afterwards, one of the male servants reported that Isabella and Sarah had taken poison though both girls claimed that this was untrue. But then Irving changed tack and admitted that they had taken some after Sarah had discovered a pot of rat poison and had apparently disclosed all the details to the manservant afterwards. An alarmed Mrs. Hornsby called the doctor but he merely prescribed caster oil and Sarah seemed improved again. By now the manservant was also complaining of sickness though whether or not he had also been a victim of poison was never confirmed. Certainly he quickly recovered as did Isabella Irving. Sarah Carrick was less fortunate; she continued to hover between slight improvement only to lapse again. The following Tuesday her mother arrived following an urgent summons and the girl was taken home in a cart.

This was the story told by Mrs. Hornsby at the subsequent inquest for on the following Saturday, Sarah Carrick died. Most of the foregoing was confirmed by the other servants with the mistress denying any acrimony between the girl and herself. What Sarah had told the doctor was that she had taken the poison because Mr. Hornsby had ticked her off for impertinence the previous Friday. She had discovered a pot of phosphoric paste for use in poisoning rats and had determined to take some, though without any mention to the doctor of ending her ife.

Enter Isabella Irving, who testified that Sarah had came to her on the Friday forenoon saying that she was ill with sickness and a headache. Later that same day she had said she was going to take some poison and that she knew where she could find the same. Had she already indulged? What seemed certain was that she was already indisposed and had been complaining bitterly of her master's earlier reprimand. At any rate, Irving claimed to have remonstrated with the fourteen-year-old, stressing the religious implications. Sarah retorted that she would take the poison regardless. The two girls were then interrupted by Mrs. Hornsby but after dinner, Sarah took up the theme again and invited Isabella to take poison too. Perhaps to humour the youngster though this was uncertain, the older girl had agreed to take some but had only tasted her portion lightly from the pot produced before throwing the residue into the nearby river while going to bring in the cows for milking. She couldn't say how much Sarah had taken but was adamant that the girl had said that if the poison didn't kill her, then she would put matches into boiling water and that would do it, saying too that she was going wrong in her mind.

The Coroner then enquired off the eighteen-year-old if Sarah Carrick had any reason to be dissatisfied with her situation?

Irving had no answer to this.

The Coroner sharply reminded the witness that she had sworn by the name of Gold Almighty to tell all she knew.

But the unhappy girl was unable to say any more.

William Thompson, the head husbandsman, was called. He was of necessity perhaps, careful in what he said, but claimed emphatically to have heard nothing of the difference between the dead girl and her master. He understood only that Sarah had been impudent and had laughed at Robert Hornsby but had, he noted, been lively enough again afterwards. He had heard of the poison taken, but felt that there was nothing wrong with the workplace. Isabella Irving had told him that Sarah had had sweetheart trouble. He felt that this might have been the cause of the trouble. All in all, a discreet witness.

Whatever the truth of the matter, by the following Friday, the girl was unconscious with a yellow pallor; she had been cold and delirious and by the evening was in a coma and dead shortly afterwards.

The deceased's mother, Mary Wilson, spoke caustically to the jury, saying that Sarah had claimed to her to have taken the poison because of her master being hard on her. She spoke of her daughter having ran way from Dockray Hall about a month previously because of alleged ill-usage. She had taken her back and Mrs. Hornsby had been so charming that she had persuaded her daughter to stay. But Sarah had cried and shook and hadn't really wished to remain.

Thereupon the Coroner summed up, advising the jury that given the evidence, it was their duty to determine cause of death. If they were certain that she had died from taking phosphoric paste, then they must ascertain the possible reason for her taking it.

And if they believed she had wished to end her life by the taking of the poison, had she been sane or insane at the time?

The jury fairly soon returned with a verdict to the effect that the girl had definitely died from taking phosphoric paste but that there was insufficient evidence to show what state of mind she was in at the time, or why she had taken the poison.

In the meantime, the Coroner had not been idle. He had been quizzing Mrs. Hornsby relentlessly in another room as to the authenticity of what the girl's mother had said. But the mistress was adamant that she had always treated Sarah with the greatest kindness with her servants vouching for this.

What was the real truth of the matter? What did emerge, aside, was that Sarah Carrick was a not untypical adolescent girl who had told Isabella Irving on the crucial weekend simply to let her sweetheart know that she couldn't see him and that he would have to come back another night. But also it appeared that if she had a wrong word with anyone, then she was liable to fly into a passion and was very difficult to keep in at night. But there was clearly no tangible evidence at all that she was in any way of unsound mind.

So allowing Mrs. Hornsby the benefit of the doubt, was the victim in fact no more than a rather capricious young woman of vindictive disposition, prone to blaming others, who wished to attract attention to herself and punish others by the abuse of rat poison, the taking of which had got tragically out of hand, the manservant's food having been wantonly doctored in the process? Or was she merely an immature, homesick little girl crying for help who ought not to have been parted from her mother at all at such an early age and who might well have survived otherwise?

Given that it is still the prescribed norm to part some children from their parents at an early age, whether by accident or design, can we perhaps learn something even after the passage of more than one hundred and thirty years from the fate of Sarah Carrick in these more psychologically-orientated times? That has to remain debatable.

13: THE CLUE OF THE SPARABLES

Methods of police detection have became increasingly sophisticated over the years but simple coppering is still an integral part of police work and always was. We have already seen some local evidence of this in the cases of such reprobates as George Cass and Thomas Sowerby. But nowhere was it more apparent than in the case of the Durranhill killer, who was arrested and convicted at Carlisle well in excess of a century ago, due almost totally to sound fundamental work on the part of the police officers concerned.

The original scene of the crime itself on the east side of Carlisle has long since became lost amidst a sprawling industrial estate, linked by a convolution of roads. But at the time, it consisted merely of a small isolated cottage and garden at Durranhill, close by the North Eastern railway line which alone survives, and a level crossing linking Botcherby and Harraby. The seventy-two-year-old victim, Jane Emmerson, was the crossing gatekeeper who lived in the cottage. Her hours of work were arduous by present day standards but she didn't appear to mind, remaining a well made robust individual. Each night, after the last train had gone by at ten thirty p.m. she would pull the crossing gates across the line and they would remain in this position until four a.m. She would also bring in two lamps which hung close by on either side of the track. Presumably she was actively employed during certain daylight hours too and was well enough thought of by her employers to have been kept on following the death of her husband some years previously.

It was during the early morning of 22nd November, 1861 that the old woman's body was discovered lying close by the track, just a short distance from her front door, the lamps beneath her. She had been beaten about the head with ferocious force and one of her eyes had been forced well back into her skull. She had been dead only a few hours.

A hedge slasher which she had been accustomed to carrying for protection was discovered close by, covered with blood and hair. The front door of the cottage had been kicked in, with some prior attempt having been made to gain entry by a window. The place had been ransacked. Linen and silver teaspoons were said to be missing and a reasonable amount of money which the victim had had put by. Under her bed was found a pickaxe, also covered with blood. Everything seemed to point to robbery as the motive, by someone who knew the victim and her environs quite well. Mrs. Emmerson would normally have had her daughter and two grandchildren with her but they were away visiting relatives at the time in Liverpool, further indicating that the killer had known when best to strike for it was estimated that death had probably taken place late the previous evening, her assailant leaping out of the darkness, after the elderly widow had closed the gates across the line. Though indeed, the gates were now pulled back. But by whom?

In those days, fingerprinting as a means of identification remained an unknown phenomena and there were no other obvious clues, except for a number of footprints. In this respect the killer had been decidedly careless, even to leaving the mark of his shoe sole on the cottage door. The prints themselves were particularly conspicuous in that the design on the sole was of an unusual kind, comprised of numerous nails or sparables forming a pattern at variance with most normal designs.

Yet time passed and the local police appeared no nearer to catching the killer. Almost a month elapsed and it seemed to the public at large that the trail must have gone entirely cold. They were not to know that behind the scenes, the police had been carefully building up a picture of the person they were seeking and were now sure as to who he was, but still required sound evidence to secure a conviction. From the onset, they had appreciated that the footprints would be a vital part of such evidence and had taken plaster casts of the latter. They had still however to lay hands on the shoes themselves and were conscious of the need to maintain a total veil of secrecy lest the suspect be panicked into doing something rash which might in effect destroy the case being built up against him. They therefore maintained a very low profile, while linking up with the local press and worked with them in turn to give the impression that progress remained minimal.

Then finally, shortly before Christmas 1861, they felt confident enough to act. On Sunday, 22nd December, they arrested a man at his home in Harraby Street, off Carlisle's London Road and close to the local engine sheds, a comparatively short distance away from the scene of the crime. The suspect was a thirty-two-year-old engine driver named William Charlton with a wife and three young children who passed the Durranhill crossing regularly on his run to and from Newcastle. The incriminating shoes were found in his house but with a number of the sparables missing. However, the tools presumably utilised in the removal of these, a chisel and a pair of pincers, the property of the Newcastle and Carlisle Railway, were also found in Charlton's house and the missing sparables themselves discovered hidden on the premises, with another in the arrested man's pocket. The shoe soles clearly matched the plaster casts of the footprints made shortly following the discovery of the crime, even with the studs missing, for a vigilant policeman had originally shielded the footprints from the elements with buckets so that a perfect match had been obtained.

Charlton, of average height, slimly built and of presentable appearance though afflicted by a deafness, appeared calm and unconcerned and stoutly maintained his innocence. Appearing in court on 28th December, the incriminating shoes with him, he was remanded back into custody but now proceeded to commit a crucial error which was to prove his final undoing. Obviously possessed of an element of low cunning but not an especially clear thinker, he must have already realised that whoever was proved to have worn the shoes at Durranhill would be deemed the murderer. But without a great deal of further thought, it seems, he now proceeded to name his wife's brother, Thomas Robinson, as one who had borrowed the shoes from him on the eve of the crime and the latter quickly joined him in custody. Readers will note a similarity here to the allegation made by Thomas Munroe six years earlier though in this case, there was to be no element of doubt. Robinson gives the impression of having been something of a rake; he also had a previous conviction for dishonesty – ever an onerous liability in a Cumbrian court. But in this instance he was able to provide a complete alibi, proving that he had been elsewhere on 21st November and during the days immediately following and was soon released.

Thereafter, the finale was almost a foregone conclusion. Charlton was brought to trial early in 1862. Even while his plea remained one of not guilty, the case put by the prosecution was almost faultless, allowing for only minimal assumption. Charlton had indeed known the elderly victim and her movements and way of life very well. He had had a garden close to her cottage. He had been a visitor there and had actually borrowed the pickaxe used to bludgeon her for use in his garden some time previously. He had then returned it and knew where it was kept. He had possibly became aware of the money kept in the cottage during his visits or from gossip elsewhere and had sought to enrich himself.

What followed is not unakin to the plot of a second-rate detective novel. On the night of the crime, presumably aware that Mrs. Emmerson's daughter and grandchildren were away, he was believed to have made his way furtively to the cottage, quite close to his home and place of work, and yet remote too in its rural setting. Either he had hidden himself and then leapt on Mrs. Emmerson in the darkness as she brought in the lamps after closing the crossing gates, or she had surprised him as he sought illegal entry to the cottage, locked up while she performed her duties. Be this as it may, it was a stormy night and any cries she may have made had gone unheeded by anyone who might have been close enough to hear them. What does appear beyond doubt is that it was he who had brutally murdered her, then taken her savings and other items of value. Returning home and aware that his footprints might well give him away but still reluctant to part with a good pair of shoes, given that he was fairly confident that he might well never be caught anyhow, he had simply removed most of the sparables as a precautionary measure and concealed them for who else would have done so? Though later of course, once in the hands of the police, he had stupidly sought to incriminate Thomas Robinson to his final detriment.

But meanwhile, before commencing his journey to Newcastle early the following morning, he had returned to the scene of the crime and opened the gates across the line. He denied this though had subsequently been sighted, returning to the engine shed from the direction of Durranhill. He claimed to have been performing an act of nature then though in fact there was a toilet in the depot. During the actual train journey itself, before the discovery of the body around six thirty a.m., he had claimed to see Mrs. Emmerson standing in her doorway, while he engaged his fireman in distracting conversation. This was another ridiculous lie. The old woman had already been dead for hours. But it was the clue of the sparables which really did for him and his attempt to blame Thomas Robinson once he was caught.

He was hanged on the south wall of Carlisle Gaol before a crowd of several thousand the following March, stubbornly maintaining his innocence to the end but claiming paradoxically to have had a fair trial and finally exonerating the unfortunate Robinson completely. Few doubted his guilt or his motive but the question remained as to why he had ever felt the need to embark upon such a crime in the first instance?

It was a valid question for given the age of glaring inequality in which he had grown up, William Charlton hadn't done too badly for a young man of working class origins. Born in Longbenton, Northumberland, one of a large family, he had gone on to obtain employment with the Newcastle-Carlisle Railway Company and had fairly soon risen to become an engine driver with all the responsibility such a situation entailed. For at least twelve years he had lived in Carlisle, probably settling there due to his courtship of a local girl, Margaret Robinson. They married and she bore him two boys and a girl and was pregnant again at the time of his execution. The marriage appears to have been happy enough with Margaret staying loyal to her husband until the end.

When arrested, he had been living for some time with his family in a terraced house which was a cut above many of the overcrowded, sub-standard properties to be found in the lanes and streets of such areas of the city as Wapping and Rickergate. The Charltons' neighbours included a master carpenter and a police detective and by 1891 William Charlton was earning six shillings and six pence a day for a six-day week, a very good wage in those days – Jane Emmerson by comparison was paid only ten shillings a week.

It remains to be said that Charlton was popular with his workmates and of harmless interests without a criminal conviction to his name. Yet there was a darker side to him too. Though recommended to mercy at his trial on the grounds of previous good character, it did emerge that he had been suspected of thieving from his employers some eight years previously. Seventy pounds had gone missing from a guards van and he had been charged but then acquitted for want of sufficient proof. And just prior to the murder, he had been hard up to the extent that he had been obtaining beer on credit in a local bar. Consider too, his callous attempt to implicate his own brother-in-law in the crime at Durranhill and the very ferocity of the attack on Jane Emmerson, almost old enough to be his grandmother, and there are indications of a different type of individual altogether beneath the veneer of mundane respectability.

Attempts at mitigation by Charlton's defence counsel were of themselves tenuous to the effect that no blood had been discovered upon his shoes or clothing and no stolen coins found upon him. But of course several weeks had elapsed before the police felt ready to arrest him and he had had some time to cover his tracks, including removal of the sparables. Some mystery remains as to what happened to the stolen linen and the silver teaspoons? One rumour had it that at least some of these items had been discovered in a local pawnshop but this tale was unsubstantiated. And then there was the question as to how much his wife really knew or suspected? She had fainted at the time of his arrest and had later been caught attempting to slip a note to him in the condemned cell advising him to remain silent given attempts being made to help him on the outside. Maybe she knew more than she was prepared to admit. But here we are once again in the realms of assumption.

What is beyond dispute is that Charlton's crime was one of the most heinous ever committed locally. He never achieved the lasting notoriety of many of his peers on the national scene, remaining a small fish in a larger pond. Still the murder of the aged crossing gatekeeper continued to be talked about for years afterwards in the county itself. Her killer also had the dubious distinction of being the last criminal to be publicly hanged in Cumberland and public executions had ceased by 1868 throughout the country. But above all else, his arrest and conviction has to remain a lasting tribute to good fundamental police work.

14: CARLISLE'S FAGIN

In the lengthy annals of crime, the receiver has remained a shadowy but dominant figure, taking and disposing of stolen property but playing at times too, the dual role of informer. Never was this more true than in recent centuries. Who for instance has not heard of the notorious eighteenth century villain, Jonathan Wild, who dealt with thieves, while covertly reporting them to the authorities for a generous fee. Others, like the infamous Ikey Solomon of the following century, on whom Dickens based the character of Fagin, were rather more subtle, training boys to pick pockets and making good profits from the subsequent loot, only disowning the juvenile thieves when they themselves were in any danger of exposure.

The picture varied as it always has, but the receivers or fences of old might be bent pawnbrokers, innkeepers, or even domestic tradesmen who were in a good position to select lucrative targets from the inside, set up a robbery and receive a generous share of the spoils afterwards, many living in comfortable circumstances from the proceeds of their illicit gains, working at times through middle-men. Or at the other end of the scale they might be no more than shady second-hand dealers like Fagin, often encouraging youngsters to go out and steal for them but no less averse to grassing than their loftier counterparts to save their skins as needs be. In the last century, Cumberland had a fair share of the latter around the more heavily populated areas such as Carlisle and Whitehaven as records indicate.

Such was William Young, who appeared at the Carlisle Assizes in February, 1862 and who was to become known as Carlisle's Fagin, though in reality, he was scarcely in the same league as Dickens' original creation; twenty-eight-year-old Young, semi-literate and describing himself as a tailor, was charged with receiving a waistcoat from a fourteen-year-old youngster, John McNealey, the previous month, well knowing the article to have been stolen.

Mr. Campbell Foster, pressing hard on behalf of the prosecution in this instance – how deftly his likes could change sides – was adamant that he would prove that the youngster had been sent out with a bag by Young to steal some cloth but having been unable to obtain the required merchandise, had stolen the waistcoat instead and sold it to the tailor; McNealey had already confessed so he had nothing to lose it seemed, having admitted that the waistcoat had been stolen and that Young knew it to have been stolen. The owner of the stolen article having now identified it as his, Mr. Foster called another boy named Johnstone to testify that he had been given a shilling to change by Young, so that McNealey could be paid sixpence for the waistcoat.

The indefatigable Foster next called a local pawnbroker who testified that Young's wife had pawned the waistcoat at his shop, requesting two shillings which she received the same day it had been stolen. The pawnbroker, Blakey Marshall, was followed into the witness box by Master McNealey who reiterated his earlier confession and said he had taken the tailor other stolen articles.

Young declined to examine McNealey himself, perhaps feeling it to be pointless, but the youngster did confess that he had a previous conviction for felony.....

Police Constable Bond was next sworn. He said he had received certain information and interviewed the prisoner who said he had bought the waistcoat from an old man dressed like a navvy and given him one and sixpence. This hadn't satisfied the policeman. He had taken Young to the lock-up and sufficient grounds had been found to hold him. After a few days in custody, the tailor was heard to say that he had bought the waistcoat from McNealey.....

There were no further witnesses and the Judge invited the tailor to address the jury as he was not defended. Thereupon, Young launched into a long plausible speech, advising the gentlemen of the jury that he made his living buying and selling articles and had just happened to buy the waistcoat from McNealey, not being aware of his bad character at the time but adding that he wanted them to know that the boy's mother was a very bad character who had been apprehended for stealing and that her son had been in court eight or nine times. The court must also understand that young McNealey had been one of three confederates offered half a crown to swear against him by Mr. McNealey Senior and then a pair of shoes had came to light and for this he had been locked up for nine days. He admitted to buying cheap and selling as dear as he could but it was difficult for him to tell what was stolen and what was not in his line of work: "That is all I have to say, gentlemen."

His Lordship proceeded to sum up briefly, advising the jury that their main task must be to ascertain whether or not young McNealey was telling the truth. If they felt he was, then they would have to bring in a verdict of guilty.

Without even retiring, the jury found against Young. Thereupon the judge gave it as his opinion that the boy and others had been made a tool of the tailor's for the purpose of robbery. The prisoner already had a previous conviction of a similar kind and recidivism was almost inevitably the metaphorical kiss of death in any Cumbrian court. His Lordship decreed that Young be kept in penal servitude for seven years! McNealey himself profited little from his confession of guilt and exposure of Dickens' namesake for he received a sentence of twelve months hard labour, no doubt on the strength of his criminal record.

Some years previously, in a not dissimilar case, a shady Whitehaven storekeeper had got off after a protracted legal argument. And he had already won back most of the money paid out to one of the two teenagers concerned in a game of cards. The first youngster got off after turning Queen's Evidence. His partner was sentenced to custody and a whipping. To some extent it appeared something of a travesty of justice at the time. But receivers were often more fortunate than the thieves themselves for they were more devious and might it not be the same today?

In this instance however, despite their attempts to smear one another, both culprits went the journey and in a region where breaking into a hen house could of itself still merit six months hard labour, they could scarcely have expected less than they received given all the dynamics involved.

15: DEATH ON THE RIVER

It is doubtful if reference to the Brocklewath murder would strike a chord with many Cumbrians today, or anyone else, unless they were devotees of James Walter Brown and even his reasoned account of the crime has been out of print for almost fifty years. Yet at the time of the violent deed and its aftermath in early 1862, it was headline news and remained a favourite topic of conversation in the immediate locality for some years afterwards. Even though the charge of murder was finally reduced to one of manslaughter, this did not detract from its interest value.

There are probably a number of reasons for this, foremost of these being that it coincided with the Durranhill murder by just a few weeks, the two trials running more or less in harness, the prisoners all being tried at the same court and by the same judge. It and the Charlton trial also proceeded the trial and execution of George Cass and the trial of Thomas Sowerby by little more than a year, the latter of course also beginning with a charge of murder. The result of all this was considerable morbid excitement in Cumberland, but some continuing soul-searching too, given that there had now been four big murder trials in the county in less than two years, when capital crime had previously appeared distinctly on the decrease there.

Yet there were some wide differences between the various players involved. George Cass had evidenced a definite strain of instability. Sowerby had been a drunken nondescript, quite different to the odious Charlton, who had been quietly set upon a premeditated mission of gain, irrespective of past goodwill on the part of his victim and prepared to lie to the end. The three men involved in the death of Edward Atkinson on 15th January, 1862 were different personalities again. They were uncomplicated countrymen, a trifle rough-hewn and macho perhaps, but people who in the normal course of events, would probably never have gone out of their way to seriously harm anyone, harbouring some resentment of authority figures but a far cry again from the likes of William Graham of Staffield notoriety. Entering the dock at Carlisle Spring Assizes the following March, they might all have been wondering why they had ever landed themselves in such a mess at all, which could rob at least two of them of their lives in the event of being found guilty.

The trio facing charges of wilful murder were Robert Robinson aged fifty, a blacksmith from the village of Cumwhitton lying some miles east of Carlisle, his son William Robinson aged twenty-two, and his brother-in-law Hugh Earle aged forty. The crime had been committed in the vicinity of a place known as Brocklewath on a small island in the River Eden, a reasonable distance across the fields from Cumwhitton and just two and a half miles up the river from Wetheral, noted for its links with the ancient King Constantin. The crime stemmed from salmon poaching, such an activity having been a local way of life for centuries and continuing along with other kinds of poaching, despite fixed penalties, well into the twentieth century. Indeed, just short of a century after the occurrence at Brocklewath, three men were in court at Carlisle charged with going to the extreme and literally blowing up fish with dynamite in the neighbouring River Esk and being heavily fined like others of their kind along the way. A fine, or a short prison sentence might have been all that Earle and the Robinsons faced had their own situation not got completely out of hand. But as it was, they were now all in very deep trouble.

There were four other players in the drama aside from the unfortunate Atkinson, who was river watcher for many of the local gentry and as popular with the local poaching fraternity of the period as traffic wardens are with the average motorist today. Nonetheless, as already noted elsewhere, like others of his kind, gamekeepers, excisemen and their ilk, he was only doing the job he was paid to do. On the other hand, the prisoners themselves were held in some regard within their own community and continued to remain so. The threesome had an accessory in James Milburn, a forty-year-old tenant farmer who lived close to the island. Milburn may have been partly responsible at least in eventually sparing them from the extreme penalty though earlier he had made a statement implicating all three under the eye of the ever-vigilant Chief Constable Dunne. Ranged against them on the fateful morning along with Atkinson had been the latter's fellow watcher, Robert Bowman, and two others enlisted to afford them assistance as needs be: Jeremiah Cowman, a policeman, and John Irwin, a labourer.

On the previous evening, Milburn and the three prisoners had fished off the island with nets kept at Milburn's farm. The water around the island was fairly high at the time and their catch was small. They gave up around nine thirty p.m. and returned home, the Cumwhitton men intending to return early the following morning. At the same time, Atkinson had observed the water in the river dropping elsewhere. Knowing that this would render the salmon more accessible and make for more lucrative poaching, he promptly gathered his band about him in anticipation of a possible coup.

In the small hours, the four watchers secreted themselves on the island not necessarily with a view to apprehending Robert Robinson and his group but ready for action in the event of any poacher who was likely to come by. Shortly after six a.m. their patience was rewarded. Robert Robinson appeared and began plying his net in the subsiding water between the island and the meadowland below Milburn's farm. They watched him for some time and then he whistled as though to enlist help. At this Atkinson and Bowman moved in on the blacksmith and Atkinson ordered Bowman to tie his wrists, having taken firm hold of him. The man from Cumwhitton said there was no need for that and promised to go quietly, loathsome though he probably found Atkinson, whom he knew of old and who was no more than a few years older than himself and still in the peak of physical condition.

What followed is rather imprecise. Cowman had made off along the shore of the island with Irwin where they quickly encountered the younger Robinson, and Earle.

Both were carrying heavy sticks and hurrying towards the scene of Robert Robinson's capture. Whether it was a reflex action fuelled by anger and indignation at the older man's situation, or sheer personal frustration given the watchers' intrusion into activities which they didn't really consider criminal, or merely a wild impulsive desire to escape is uncertain. However, they set about Cowman and rendered him insensible. They also made to afford Irwin similar treatment but he escaped and hid nearby. He was to claim that he saw the twosome making towards Atkinson and Bowman and heard the sound of further blows though wasn't certain who was the recipient of these. But Bowman too was certainly rendered insensible for a time. Upon recovering his senses the latter found himself alone but recalled Atkinson being confronted by the two men and manhandled by one of them. He met up with Cowman shortly afterwards, likewise bruised but again fully conscious. They could see no sign of anyone else and left the immediate vicinity.

It was Irwin who discovered Atkinson lying unconscious and saturated with water by the side of the river though he appeared to have been dragged some way along the shore before being abandoned. Meanwhile, the three salmon poachers had retreated to Milburn's farm and the older Robinson had blurted out that they had killed Atkinson. Milburn remained cool and told them to make off homewards. He did nothing until Irwin attracted his attention shortly afterwards, probably not wishing to become immediately implicated in what seemed to auger very serious trouble. Subsequently, he and Irwin put the huge insensible Atkinson into a cart and took him to the farmhouse but he was dead within hours, never recovering consciousness.

It was footprints which again assisted the police but they also had the benefit of several vocal witnesses on this occasion. The Robinsons and Earle were in custody much sooner than the wretched Charlton, having scarcely had time to dry their clothes, Milburn soon joining them, though only for a short time prior to making his statement. This cleared him though he had to run the gauntlet of threats and jeers from a hostile crowd afterwards.

At the subsequent trial of the three, it was held that William Robinson had struck the fatal blow with a large hedge-stake, assisted by Hugh Earle, the stake being produced in court. Some play too was made on the whistle that Robert Robinson had allegedly given just prior to his apprehension by Atkinson and Bowman. But it was explained that this was a common practice used simply to indicate that a fish had been netted and not to summon help; thus the older man was exonerated from any deliberate call to provoke deliberate violence.

By way of further mitigation in respect of all three accused, much play was made on the fact that the watchers had not been formally appointed under the recent Fisheries Act. And Milburn claimed the legal right to fish at Brocklewath on behalf of the man from whom he rented his property as his predecessor had also done for many years. Could this right have included those he chose to fish with him, who used nets stored in his farm buildings? This was not made clear. Nor was the fact there may have been an element of provocation on the part of the victim, over-zealous to prove himself in the service of his betters.... The immediate foregoing may just have carried some additional weight with the jury but in any case, the judge himself directed in his summing up that should they decide upon a verdict of guilty, that this should appertain to manslaughter rather than murder, presumably with especial mind to the non-appointment of the watchers and the spontaneous nature of the assault itself.

Thereafter it was soon over. The jury, drawn in this instance from beyond the immediate Cumwhitton area, given the ties and popularity enjoyed by the three accused men in their community, brought in verdicts of guilty in respect of all three but in each instance they were found guilty of manslaughter rather than murder, Robert Robinson being strongly recommended to mercy. Robert Robinson thereupon received a sentence of twelve months imprisonment with hard labour. William Robinson and Hugh Earl each received ten years penal servitude.

The two younger men were probably luckier than they may have thought. Some years previously they might still have been transported or even hanged, just as surely as William Charlton was already preparing to meet his maker. But they were of previous good character; this and the points of law raised by their defence counsel along with other background details probably spared them a harsher sentence, though ten years penal servitude was still severe enough of course. And the older Robinson had not been totally spared either.

All in all however, it was perhaps surprising that there were not more episodes of the Brocklewath kind in nineteenth century Cumberland, given the amount of illicit whisky distilling still going on in the remoter regions of the county and the constant poaching on land and water, by those who at times actually relished outwitting the despised authority figures appointed to catch them out, but who could be desperate too when cornered. Indeed, it would only be a few years before another water watcher died violently in the call of duty near Cockermouth. We shall come to him presently.

16: GUILTY BUT INSANE?

On 9th February, 1862, the naked body of a three-month-old baby boy was discovered washed up on an island in the River Eamont some three miles south of Eamont Bridge. The discovery followed the finding of a pile of child's clothing in a field near Penrith a few days previously.

Following the finding of the clothing and receipt of a letter written apparently by the child's mother, the police had already gone to a lodging house in Penrith. There they found a twenty-four-year-old servant girl, Catherine Simpson, in bed with her pregnant sister Margaret whose husband was away tramping in search of work. Catherine accompanied the police back readily enough to the station. Following a tearful disclosure she was charged with murdering her son John with rather undue promptitude by those concerned, while appearing to be under the influence of some kind of narcotic. She had it transpired attempted to take her life with laudanum hours previously but without success, the eventual recovery of the baby's body appearing to justify the earlier charge of wilful murder to some extent.

The case of Catherine Simpson was not one to evoke a great deal of countrywide interest, being deemed comparatively mundane. In those early weeks of 1862, her crime was also overshadowed locally by those of William Charlton and the Broklewath Three who made for much wider coverage. Infanticide of a sort was all too commonplace in Cumberland and beyond anyhow during the nineteenth century and before, whether or not the authorities wanted to admit it, now rarely resulting in a full-blown conviction.

Yet the Eamont case is interesting nonetheless both from a social and historical perspective, for the distinct light it throws on poverty-stricken young single women as a whole who had illegitimate children in Victorian Britain and what could happen when they simply couldn't afford to keep them, with the additional question of insanity in this particular case. But come to that, just how insane was Catherine Simpson at the time of her crime? Just how far did the jury simply wish to keep its head buried in the sand for a variety of reasons?

The accused girl had given birth to her child in Penrith Workhouse; the father was nowhere to be found. She had loved the child well enough to suckle it and have it baptised and had named it after its father. But she was quickly out on the road and destitute. Her father was receiving relief from the Penrith Union and her mother was in the Dunston Lunatic Asylum so there could be no parental assistance. She came to the lodgings of her pregnant sister Margaret and took up temporary residence there with the child but left on 29th January, 1862, ostensibly to take the infant to a nurse at Hutton End. She returned that same evening without the child. The next day she wrote a letter for an illiterate neighbour, Hannah Armstrong, then wrote a letter of her own to one John Irving which was left with the Armstrong woman. This was the epistle recovered shortly afterwards by the police at Armstrong's instigation. It read as follows, a pathetic testimony to the girl's state of hopelessness:

> 'Oh John. Should these lines ever reach you it will make you think of the sad bend you have rought us both to by your bad baver. I put my child out to nurse but I cud not rest so I brote it back to meet a watery grave, now as this is the last you hevr here of me the child is yours shud you see these few lines I hope it will be a warn to you never to deceave a young girl again. I had no home but the Workhouse and all thure your bad baver.'

It transpired from her account to the Penrith police that she had smothered the child in Longwathby Woods. She had then wandered about for some hours before going down to Eamont Bridge where she took the child's clothes off and put it into the water. She had then hidden the clothes closer to Penrith where they were later discovered. That same day she had written the letter and had intended to drown herself but then felt there were too many people around to drag her out of the water. The attempt to end her life with laudanum followed but there was insufficient to complete the deed. She returned to her sister's lodgings where she was arrested on 1st February, 1862.

Under caution, she said she had not taken her child's life because she disliked it but through distress. Seemingly since she had given birth, she had received nothing but harshness and unkindness and she could not obtain work to provide sufficient money for food and clothing.

At the succeeding enquiry at Penrith Police Station, the body having by this time been recovered, the Coroner was not unsympathetic and felt that a more lenient view might be taken elsewhere but that for the moment, a verdict of wilful murder must stand. The distressed young woman was therefore committed to stand trial for murdering her defenceless child.

She appeared at the same Assizes as William Charlton and the three Brocklewath men, sobbing bitterly. The prosecution opened the proceedings with a statement to the effect that this had to be more than an ordinary child murder as the child had been three months old; an incongruous utterance to the uninitiated of today perhaps, but with a mind no doubt to the many unwanted children who were simply disposed of at birth by their desperate parents in those times. They were acknowledging nevertheless that Catherine was rather different to the single mothers who normally appeared before the courts charged with such a crime. But they were also keen to prove that she had still known what she was doing when she suffocated her child. They produced back-up evidence from her sister Margaret who was guarded but refused to brand Catherine mad, and from the Penrith Medical Officer who had felt the prisoner to be of sound mind when he had seen her following the offence.

Here the judge chose to intervene, sagely noting examples of individuals recalling while sane, acts committed under sudden impulse while in the grip of homicidal mania. There had also been some who had confessed to a knowledge of what they were doing at the time while thus afflicted…..

The defence made no great play on words. With an obvious mind to the stark reality of their client's situation, their simple plea was for pity and charity followed by an immediate attempt to prove that Catherine was definitely of unsound mind. There was pointed reference to the girl's mad mother. Then her father was called and he confirmed that he was epileptic, as though that of itself must indicate further seeds of instability. Scarcely very complimentary to victims of such an unfortunate affliction. Sadly however, such misconceptions still remained in those days in the minds of many in respect of epilepsy; it would be early in the next century in fact before there was any real medical breakthrough and even then, some prejudice continued.

More telling in this instance however, was the older man's reference to his daughter going off to service eighteen months previously. She had been fine then as he recalled but some six weeks later she was returned, quite out of her mind. She had recovered and returned to work but relapsed again in a month. Again she returned to service but was soon deranged. No detailed description was given of her deranged condition which needn't of course have been linked to any homicidal tendencies. It was all rather ambiguous but suited the defence perfectly. The latter continued to firm up their case, rounding off with the calling of the two farmers who had previously employed the unfortunate girl; they unhesitatingly gave weight to allegations of her former dubious state of mind, as did her brother-in-law, but without going into specific details.

Still the prosecution wasn't satisfied, asserting that the prisoner had known perfectly well what she had been doing when she smothered her child. However, they had made little tangible attempt to reinforce their case along the way.

All too soon it was time for the judge to sum up. Given the social and medical implications especially inherent in the case of Catherine Simpson, his observations are noted here much as they appeared in the report of the trial at the time. He observed as follows: 'the prisoner was charged with the crime of murder and however painful the case might be it was the duty of the jury to calmly weigh up the evidence and return a true verdict. The law of England assumed every man to be sane until proved to the contrary'. Stopping off to read the pathetic woman's letter to the child's father and sparing the latter no praise but calling him to no grave account either, he went on to intone 'that if all the prisoner had said and done since the commission of the act led them to think that she was in a sound state of mind to know what she was doing when she committed the murder, if she did commit it, it was his duty to tell them that they must find her guilty. If they thought she was not at the time in a state of mind to know what she was doing was wrong, and if they were satisfied with regard to the identity of the child, then they would acquit her on the grounds of insanity and she could be placed in the care of the Secretary of State. If they came to the conclusion that the prisoner did not kill the child, or that the child found was not the child John Simpson, then they would acquit her entirely.'

A basic, albeit not unsympathetic summing up but with no great depth to it and no reference to the stifling misery and poverty of the times, obviously experienced by the deserted single parent. It was easier to move on to the insanity factor, to afford some veiled support to the defence, even while no specific diagnosis had ever been made, with at least one medical professional feeling that the prisoner had actually been of sound mind when he had seen her. For if the unfortunate woman was deemed guilty of coldly and rationally murdering her son, poverty-stricken or not, she could face execution and who wanted that? She had taken her son's life, of that there could be no doubt, so of course there could really be no question of acquittal either.

Therefore his Lordship endeavoured at least to take an objective stance and afforded the jury three choices with some convenient emphasis on insanity. But the jury had all but made up their minds already it seemed. They retired for only half an hour before returning with a verdict of not guilty on the grounds of insanity.

Was Catherine Simpson really insane? She may have been the victim of some kind of hereditary psychosis on occasions, and may even have been suffering from a degree of post-natal depression around the time preceding the murder. But given the state she had been left in and the treatment she had received in an unfair society, sheer hopelessness and want appear above all else to have driven her to do what she did to her child in Langwathby Woods on 29th January, 1862. The jury must surely have appreciated this however reluctant they may have been to speak out. Notwithstanding, they didn't really want her to hang so they took the easiest option, made rather more easy for them by the judge. We are not told what became of Catherine Simpson afterwards, or if her worthless lover ever did put in an appearance, but she has to be one of the saddest figures to come to our attention to date.

17: CONCEALMENT – OR MURDER?

It appears almost incredible now but in 1856 no less a personage than the Bishop of Oxford publicly complained at the decrease in the number of hangings in Britain, with some emphasis on women who were escaping the scaffold. Such a statement from a man of the cloth or anyone else in a public position here would be all but unthinkable now, whatever his or her true feelings.

Even in those rather less genteel times the divine's remarks were still deemed reactionary enough. While attempted murder, burglary, arson, robbery, forgery and a host of other lesser crimes no longer brought their perpetrators to the drop, this state of play generally continued to be acceptable to most thinking Victorians. True, there was a continuing crime wave but alternative sentences were generally harsh enough. Indeed, thirteen still died on the scaffold in 1857 following hard upon the bishop's postulating.

What in fact the latter appears to have been particularly driving at in his passion was the situation relating to the type of woman touched upon in recent pages. Not necessarily creatures quite as pitiful as Catherine Simpson but still single parents, who though frequently accused of killing off their unwanted offspring at the very onset, were often getting away with it in court on the lesser charge of concealment of birth or getting off altogether.

This state of affairs was noticeably prevalent in Cumberland and perhaps scarcely surprising given the number of illegitimate births there. As the 1850s drew to a close, single parenthood in Victorian Cumberland was running at over 10 per cent as opposed to a possible rate of 4.2 per cent in London, equalled only in Westmorland and Norfolk. Why there should have been quite so much illegitimacy in Cumberland is uncertain. The living conditions of farm servants have since been held up as a possible cause. Consideration too has been given to cultural norms with prospective brides supposedly permitting their boyfriends free licence on the strength of a promise of marriage only at times to be betrayed. But the major cause may simply have been the abundance of girls employed as farm labourers or domestic servants or both, often in quite isolated areas, bored and uneducated to begin with. Yet the whole business has still to remain something of a riddle for not all the girls who fell prey to unwanted pregnancies were necessarily living in cramped isolated circumstances either, on farms or in towns, and many were far from gullible, or quite as poorly educated as Catherine Simpson had been, and even she was semi-literate. Education was beginning to make some mark in Cumberland, however tentatively. But fall they did and then the outcome was still almost inevitable if the father refused to accept responsibility and there was no family support. Poverty, unemployment and despair would prevail, at times leading to tragedy akin to that surrounding little John Simpson, But many single parents never allowed things to go that far. Into this category fell the subject of our next case study: Jane Byers.

Byers, a neat respectable looking young woman appeared at the Carlisle Assizes in August, 1863 charged with the wilful murder of her female child in the Brampton area the previous February. She appeared composed enough, pleading not guilty. But what was she really thinking? The case against her was more telling than most. Lots of victims were simply found buried in middens or washed up on the shores of lakes with scarcely a mark upon them. But Jane's daughter had borne distinct evidence of violence. She could be in deep trouble and was without the defence of insanity. No woman had been hanged in Cumberland that century to date but there had to be a first time.....

In point of fact, two women with links unpleasantly close to home had been hanged only the previous year. Mary Reid had been turned off struggling at Dumfries for the killing of a neighbour at Carpshad, Kircudbright. And Constance Wilson had been hanged before Newgate for poisoning Maria Soames, albeit with another presumed victim, a Mrs. Atkinson, having lived as close as Kirkby Lonsdale.

Thus women were still being hanged all right, regardless of the Bishop of Oxford's earlier pontificating. But Reid and Wilson had been much more dangerous than a young Cumbrian woman who had found herself with an unwanted child. Reid had manifested all the traits of a psychopath, doing her weaker victim to death with a mallet and a butcher's knife following a simple domestic squabble. And Wilson, a self-styled nurse, had been described by the judge who sentenced her to death as 'the greatest criminal that ever lived'.

Jane Byers was never in that league, bad though her case appeared. What she was was a girl of poor family akin to those who only recently had been afforded aid via the local Carlisle Relief Committee, many of whom were having an especially bad time right then following unemployment in the textile trade due to the American Civil War. On the other hand she had been shady enough and had almost got away with her crime until 26th February, 1863. Then a slater, Robert Eilsdone, had begun taking slates from the roof of an old outhouse at Beckriggs, near Brampton. He looked through a hole in the roof and saw what he assumed to be a bundle of rags. Having then dropped his hammer he went into the building to retrieve it and saw a child's foot protruding from the bundle. The local police were called and investigated. A child's body was revealed which had been wrapped in a variety of clothing with a piece of cloth knotted around the neck so tightly as to have almost severed the head from the body. The doctor who subsequently undertook the post mortem found the body badly decomposed but he had floated the lungs in water and was of the opinion that the child had breathed.

By this time Jane Byers had been traced, presumably through the clothing in which the child had been wrapped though no doubt local gossip had also been of some assistance. She had been taken into custody and questioned but denied having ever had a child. She even offered herself for physical examination and was promptly taken up on this. The results of this rather embarrassing procedure were inconclusive but it transpired that a local doctor had felt she could have been pregnant as recently as November, 1862 when she had consulted him.

In the end however, none of this really mattered for after only a short time in custody, the prisoner had taken the course of Cass, Sowerby and their ilk and decided to make a statement, a solitary period in a Cumbrian lock-up seeming to exercise the mind quite considerably in those times, allied perhaps to some subtle persuasion from elsewhere.... She was duly cautioned but said she wished to tell the truth, admitting that she was the mother of the child and that she had put the cloth around its neck and put it down the hole. She also named the father but adamantly refused to admit having killed the infant.

In court she stuck by her story; neither were her mother or brother too helpful when called upon to give evidence. They had nothing definite to add and were if anything, protective of the accused girl which wasn't unnatural. Thereafter it was soon left to Thomas Campbell Foster to address the jury on behalf of the defence and he was his usual loquacious self. He did not dispute that the prisoner had had a child – she had admitted that. But had the child been born alive? If it had not been alive, he submitted, then murder could not have been committed. The surgeon had concluded that because the lungs floated the child had been born alive but by the time of his examination decomposition had set in and thus he suggested that the lungs had been exposed to the air during that time and thus inflated. He then made a deal of play on the short length of the sleeve around the child's neck, barely long enough to go around it, omitting to mention that the sleeve had in fact been so tightly tied, deftly contending that the prisoner had other means at her disposal if she had really meant to strangle the infant; for instance, the weft from a loom with which she had tied up the body. He submitted that there was no evidence to show that the child had had a life of its own and that there could therefore be no evidence that the prisoner had intended to commit murder. With regard to the other minor charge of concealment which it then resolved itself into, he shrewdly left that in the hands of the jury.

The judge was less airy in his summing up, contending that there was a preponderance of evidence to show that the child had breathed but insufficient for a verdict of wilful murder though he felt there were strong grounds for suspicion. With regard to the charge of concealment there was the evidence of the prisoner's statement and he left it to the jury to decide on that.

The jury thereupon consulted briefly and then retired. Within about ten minutes they were back with a verdict of guilty of concealment of birth.

His Lordship then proceeded to sentence the prisoner. He obviously still had his own doubts about Ms. Byers and was harder than some of his kind, commenting that no one but her would perhaps ever know the truth. He also noted that the offence of concealment seemed to be on the increase following former lenient sentences passed. He therefore sentenced the defendant to twelve months imprisonment with hard labour. Indications were that he would have liked to pass a longer sentence.

Jane Byers was luckier than she might have been all considered. Nevertheless, young women like her were to continue to come before the Cumbrian courts for years to come, as elsewhere in the country. Many continued to get off altogether, the majority were pitiful creatures though others were calculating too. The fact remained that it would take long-overdue changes in the laws of social welfare and bastardy to finally right the situation but that would be well into the future. In the meantime, their trials almost invariably rated secondary status evoking in the main, a combination of pity and embarrassment and even applause on occasions, following a verdict of acquittal.

CARLISLE IN OLDEN TIMES. THE ENGLISH GATE AND OLD GAOL

CARLISLE COURT HOUSES IN 1829 WITH THE NEW GAOL IN THE BACKGROUND

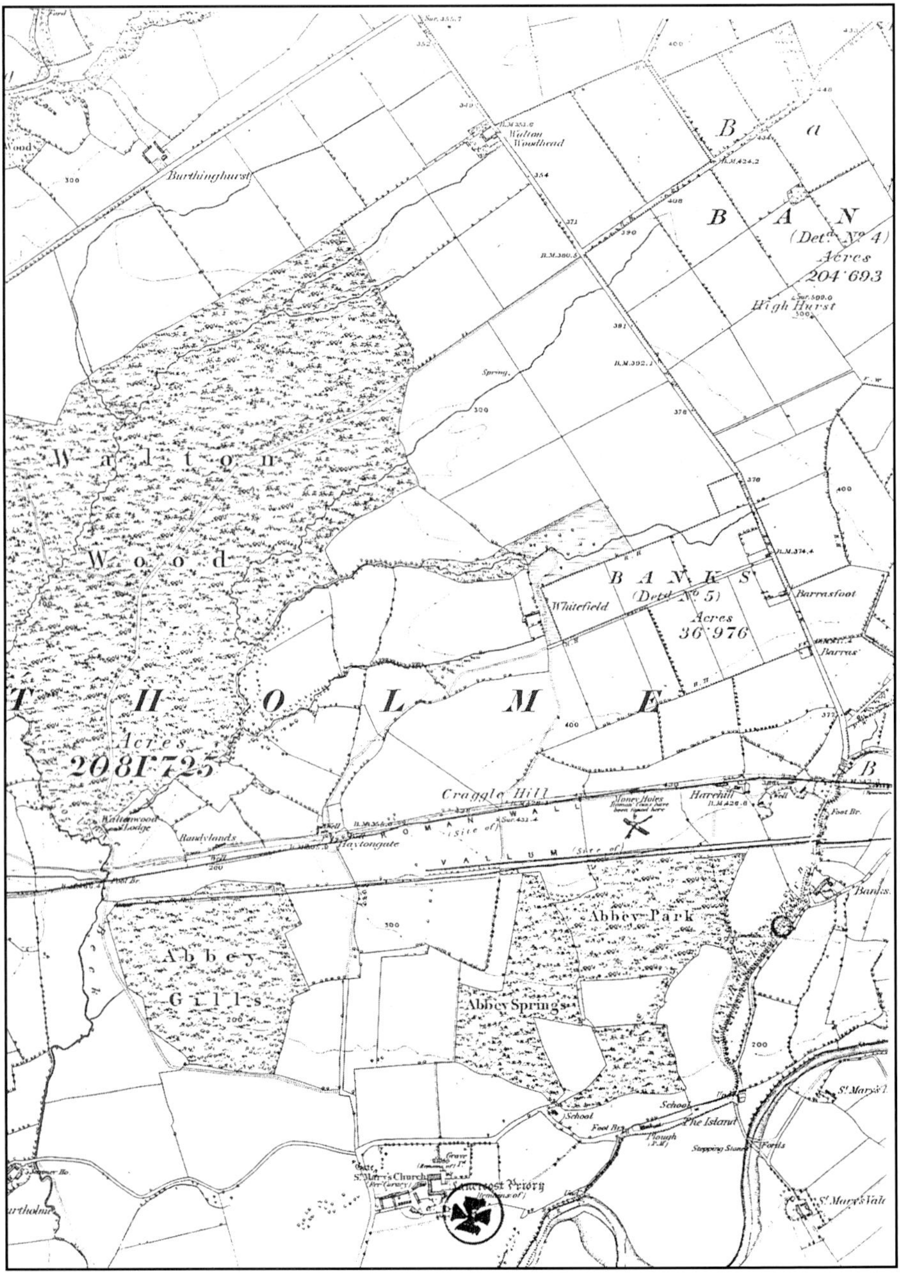

PART OF A NINETEENTH CENTURY MAP OF THE LANERCOST AREA, SHOWING RANDYLANDS IN ITS RURAL ISOLATION. (Carlisle Library).

ABOVE: THE BRIDGE JANE PEARSON CROSSED ON HER LAST NIGHT ALIVE.

ALL THAT IS NOW LEFT OF THE HOVEL WHERE JANE PEARSON WAS MURDERED.

UNION STREET, CARLISLE, SCENE OF THE THOMPSON POISONING: ONE OF THE MOST SOCIALLY DEPRIVED THOROUGHFARES IN THE CITY. (Carlisle Library).

BECKHOUSE FARM TODAY, STILL IN ITS PEACEFUL SETTING, WHERE ANN SEWELL DIDN'T INTEND TO REMAIN TOO LONG.

ANN SEWELL'S TOMBSTONE, PAID FOR BY PUBLIC SUBSCRIPTION.

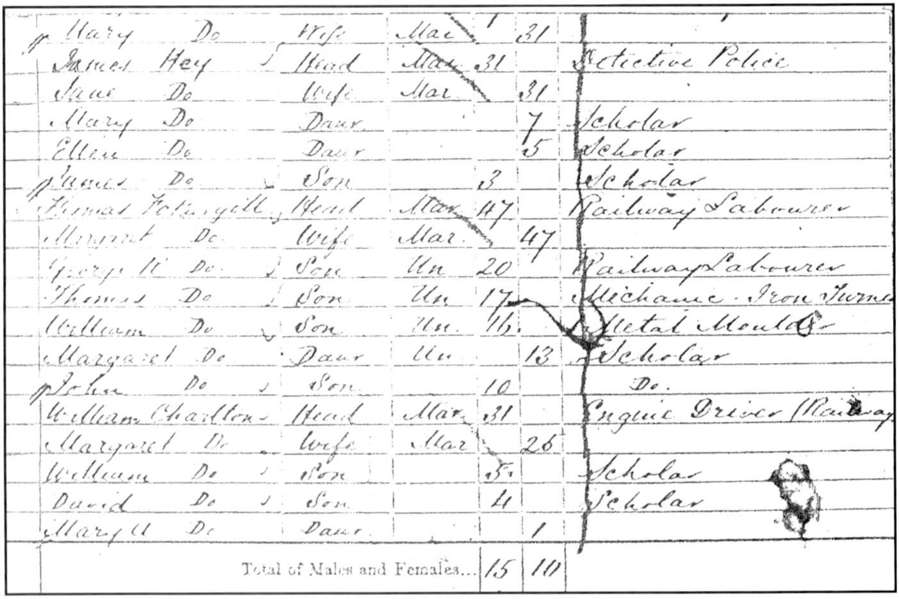

Name	Surname	Relation	Condition	Age (Males)	Age (Females)	Occupation
Mary	Do	Wife	Mar		31	
James	Hey	Head	Mar	31		Detective Police
Jane	Do	Wife	Mar		31	
Mary	Do	Daur			7	Scholar
Ellen	Do	Daur			5	Scholar
James	Do	Son		3		Scholar
Thomas	Fothergill	Head	Mar	47		Railway Labourer
Margaret	Do	Wife	Mar		47	
George R	Do	Son	Un	20		Railway Labourer
Thomas	Do	Son	Un	17		Mechanic - Iron Turner
William	Do	Son	Un	16		Metal Moulder
Margaret	Do	Daur	Un		13	Scholar
John	Do	Son		10		Do.
William	Charlton	Head	Mar	31		Engine Driver (Railway
Margaret	Do	Wife	Mar		26	
William	Do	Son		5		Scholar
David	Do	Son		4		Scholar
Mary A	Do	Daur			1	
			Total of Males and Females...	15	10	

IN THE 1861 CENSUS RETURNS, WILLIAM CHARLTON IS RECORDED AS JUST ANOTHER LAW-ABIDING HOUSEHOLDER. (Extract from 1861 census returns © Crown copyright)

ALBERT STREET, PENRITH, LITTLE CHANGED SINCE DALGLEISH'S TIME, WHITE LINES AND TRAFFIC SIGNS ASIDE.

ANTHONY BENJAMIN RUDGE

JOHN MARTIN

JAMES BAKER

P.C JOSEPH BYRNES

THE THREE NETHERBY BURGLARS AND THEIR UNFORTUNATE VICTIM. (Cumbrian Newspapers Ltd.)

ABOVE: NETHERBY HALL IN 1993, EMPTY AND RUN-DOWN. (Cumbrian Newspapers Ltd.)

prisoners for being a tool of the Chief's and Mr Collins. The young fellow the night previous to his hanging himself in a cell in B. hall at Portsmouth had an interview With the chief warder, the only noticable thing that leaked out after the (I was about to write murder) suicide Was that the poor tool asked for protection and the performance of certain promises. Should you, sir, wish to know more of this matter, as the unfortunate was a jew, the best and I think perhaps straightest plan would be to write to the Rabbi of the prison. The baneful influence of such rascality in ~~such~~ office Who can language. I will give the general opinion of convicts concerning appointed commissioners Who's office it is to visit convicts establishments. Tis this. that it's a respectable farce By some or other it is known all over prison, like a flash When they come, everything wears it's best face by the time they see it. What really would do good would be for them to ascertain meal times and drop into the Kitchen just previous. and dont taste what is offered them but pick for themselves ~~from~~ from some of the tins ready to be sent to prisoners, and not from any readied for visitors I dont mean to infer that they will discover anything shocking but it might somewhat alter their opinions especially if they compared with the dietary list what realy was sent to prisoners. I will now conclude this scrap, for tis but a scrap, of my experience. by repeating What I said to judge When sentence to death tis this If there were more govners like the governor of Carlise gaol, Mr Leavers, that there would be less desperadoes willing to pull the trigger. And Why this? Because he has shown, and it has come with with full convic[tion] on my mind, that a fatherly endeavour for a prisoners goo[d] is compatable with a perfect discipline.

A. B. Rudge

A PAGE FROM RUDGE'S DEATH CELL MEMOIR. (Cumbria Police Museum).

JOSEPH WILSON, THE LAST KILLER TO BE EXECUTED IN CUMBERLAND. STILL A PUZZLING FIGURE.
(Cumbrian Newspapers Limited).

SIR JOHN DUNNE, DEPUTY LIEUTENANT FOR CUMBERLAND, AND CHIEF CONSTABLE OF CUMBERLAND AND WESTMORLAND.
(Cumbria Police Museum).

CARLISLE GAOL SOME SEVEN YEARS AFTER JOSEPH WILSON'S EXECUTION THERE, HEMMED IN BY THE GAS WORKS, RAILWAY STATION AND VICTORIA VIADUCT AND NOW UNDOUBTEDLY OUT OF PLACE. BUT NOTE TOO HOW QUIET THE VIADUCT IS COMPARED TO TODAY. (Carlisle Library).

18: A GARROTING OFF TANGIER STREET

On 9th April, 1863, Andrew Brotherton left the tranquility of Lochmaben in Dumfriesshire to travel down to Whitehaven on business. The West Cumbrian seaport hadn't really changed a great deal since the Usher killing several years previously. There was rather less work owing to the American Civil War but it was still a thriving port with continuing emphasis on coal and iron ore.

On the other hand, Whitehaven continued to have its seamier side too. It was a place which had had links with both smuggling and the slave trade in its day and had maintained a hard-worked police force long before other areas of the county had came fully into line following the County and Borough Police Act of 1856. In 1863 it still had more than its share of crime and criminals.

Brotherton's visit for its part was not destined to end happily. He concluded his business fairly quickly and that same evening went drinking with two acquaintances named Gibbon and Wales. Indications were that a considerable amount of pub crawling had ensued by the time the trio encountered two local misfits, Sam Mooney and Jim Doran, Brotherton buying the twosome a drink apiece in passing and appearing to find their company congenial enough.

Some time later, the Scotsman apparently went off alone and failed to get into the Golden Lion where he had anticipated spending the night. There are already some echoes of Simon Manassa's situation though no evidence that Brotherton was in any way obnoxious, merely a comparative stranger stranded out on the streets of a strange town and a little the fresh for drink. Beginning to feel fed up and far from home, it was then that he encountered Mooney and Doran again and asked them if they could show him a suitable place where he might spend the night. This at any rate was his story.

The two wasters seemed happy to oblige but then led the hapless Scot off Tangier Street, the main thoroughfare, and through an archway. He was to claim that Mooney then put his arm around his neck and under his chin and effectively choked him. He was bent rudely back and felt hands going into his pockets but such was the tightness of the grip that he could neither speak nor shout. He came to himself lying on the ground with a sovereign, half a crown and his keys gone. He was not too drunk to call upon the police for help and Mooney and Doran were quickly arrested.

By the time the trial commenced before judge and jury almost a year later, Doran had already been sentenced and imprisoned for another offence and twenty-three-year-old Mooney stood in the dock alone charged with violently and feloniously assaulting Andrew Brotherton and stealing from his person, one sovereign and half a crown. For some obscure reason he had been remanded for a much longer period than was usual and memories had of necessity became dim. Nevertheless, the prisoner denied the charge, saying that Brotherton had been drunk and having been turned away from several hotels, had invited Doran and himself to accompany him, implying that the Scotsman was a liar.

The judge himself appeared to be rather sceptical of the Scotsman and made some attempt to test his memory, saying pointedly that it was curious that he should have been in so many pubs on the night in question.

Brotherton parried this and made the rather clumsy statement that he knew his attackers only by the clothes they were wearing…

Mooney retorted that Brotherton had originally been going to give someone else in charge. He also said that the Scotsman had been left in the company of the other man, Gibbon, following the second meeting. However, the latter wasn't called upon to give evidence and the third member of the original trio, Wales, was now dead.

Clearly there appeared to be some anomalies but Inspector Douglas, who had been responsible for the prisoner's arrest, was adamant enough that Mooney had said that he, Douglas, 'wasn't far wrong' and that soon afterwards he had said that it was Doran who had 'put the hang on him' and that he had only taken hold of the man's hand.

Then commenced a vehement attack by Mooney on the inspector's integrity as he hotly challenged the latter to admit that he had came to his cell and said that if he would say that Doran was the culprit, that he, Mooney, would get off.

A firm denial by the inspector.

Mooney refused to accept this; he said that Douglas had came to his cell more than once and also to Doran's with the same question and that Douglas had hit him because he refused to say it was Doran.

His Lordship obviously didn't feel that all policemen were wonderful. He reminded Douglas that he had no right to ask the prisoner any questions and that it seemed as though he had done so.

Another firm denial. No solicitor had been present as there generally would be now of course, should any prisoner request such.

His Lordship remained doubtful and further questioned statements made by the police, directing the jury not to attach much importance to the foregoing, the likes being made by the police to be repeated at the Assizes, adding that though the majority of the police were honest enough, he didn't feel, in sum, that the exact words of prisoners could be remembered precisely.

It really was quite a damning indictment of the police by a judge who appeared at time to be outright subjective. Inspector Douglas and his force appeared to have been left in a rather questionable situation altogether though this did not appear to worry the inspector greatly. The latter had even less cause to be downcast when the jury returned a verdict of guilty and indeed, Mooney had admitted to accepting the stolen sovereign from Doran. The prisoner then pleaded not guilty to a previous offence but this was also proved. If his Lordship had appeared considerate of the prisoner during the trial, this wasn't reflected in the sentence which was one of six years penal servitude.

Beyond a doubt there were some questions left unanswered which a good defence counsel might have asked. But Mooney was undefended and illiterate and his own attempt at playing the lawyer had been unsuccessful. Yet would such a case have got as far as it did in these present times?

19: A PASSING OFFENCE AND ITS CONSEQUENCES

Sam Mooney may have harboured some transitory hope of leniency while the judge found subtle fault with the police at his trial. Fifty-three-year-old Fisher Ashton and his girlfriend Elizabeth Ferguson probably knew they were doomed from the onset.

The twosome appeared at the Cumberland Quarter Sessions in October, 1865 charged with housebreaking in the Keswick area and stealing three pounds in money, a gold pin and other articles, the property of one Ferdinand Cole. A second count charged Ferguson with receiving the goods in the knowledge that they had been stolen.

Ashton was described as a nailer but it seems doubtful if he had practised his trade for a while. Impressions are more of a vagrant, tramping the fringes of the lake district with his girlfriend, eighteen years younger than himself, a disreputable pair who may have first met up along the highway or in some local doss house, both with an eye to the passing chance given their circumstances.

The main details of the offence have a not unfamiliar ring well over a century later. The wife of Ferdinand Cole stated that on 3rd August, 1865, she had been the last to vacate the family home, leaving it locked up prior to joining her family at work in the hayfield. The premises were visible from the field and she saw a man trying the door, thus at times it was obviously unsafe to leave property unattended then as now.

For some unexplained reason she did nothing about her sighting of the intruder but upon returning home about an hour later, she found a skylight broken and one of the windows open. Further examination of the premises revealed the impression of a shoe on the landing soled with sparables. She went through the house and discovered that drawers and boxes had been rifled. Nearly £5 in silver, a gold pin and some farthings were missing. And two large beads were gone from the thrifty lady's workbox. It seemed as though a determined thief had been at work though not a very neat one.

Given that the house was only a short distance from a public turnpike, there was some emphasis on the fact that there were those in the vicinity at the time who could have heard the sound of breaking glass. As matters evolved however, the culprits were to be identified by witnesses as having simply been seen in the area on the day of the robbery.

The network of local roads in those times still being fairly basic and complete with turnpikes, Ashworth and Ferguson were quickly apprehended by an Inspector Rooney. At the local police station they were searched and on Ashworth was found 5½ pence in copper coin inclusive of a marked coin identified by Mrs. Cole as also being hers. On Ferguson's person were discovered the two beads. Not a very large haul as compared to the wife's original list of missing property.

The inspector read a short statement in court allegedly made by Ferguson, implicating her man friend. But now she fiercely defended Ashton saying that the statement was false and that she had been induced to sign it, though by what methods she didn't say. The illiterate woman swore by the Almighty that they were both innocent but to no avail. There was no indication at all as to where the gold pin and silver had gone to and no one sought to ask. But it obviously had to irk the jury considerably that honest hard-working Cumbrians could not go about their business making hay without being preyed upon by such roving parasites as Fisher Ashton and his partner.

Cumbrian courts in the nineteenth century might take some time deliberating the case of a young single mother charged with infanticide and even find her not guilty, just as they would almost invariably recommend such murderers as Cass and Charlton to mercy. Ashton and Ferguson merited no such consideration. There was sufficient evidence to convict them regardless or so it seemed. They were quickly found guilty and sentenced to five years penal servitude and six months hard labour respectively which would put an end to their partnership for some time to come.

At the end of the day, it is difficult not to harbour some sneaking sympathy for this rather abject pair, though there must have been hundreds like them on the roads of Cumberland and beyond in those more wretched times.

20: THE RAFFLES SHOOTING

It would be beyond the scope of this modest work to dwell on more than a minute proportion of all the crimes committed in Cumberland during the sixty years under scrutiny. Many of these were of a mundane everyday kind which would make dull repetitive reading in any case.

Nevertheless, Cumberland was the scene of some traumatic crimes too as already noted in some detail here. It never produced anything quite akin to the Stanfield Hall massacre of 1848 or the Rugeley poisonings of the early 1850s, but the Lancelow Bottom, Embleton and Durranhill murders were horrendous enough as few would deny.

As the 1860s proceeded, the Cumbrian scaffold fell into disuse again but the courts there still continued to do business with the general emphasis on drunkenness, offences against property, common assaults, and theft. Add false pretences, rape, suicide, arson, indecency, using the knife and continuing numbers of young single women charged with the murder of their bastard children, or at best with concealment of their births and a good general picture is afforded of the ongoing criminal scene in Cumberland at that time. Not a very laudable picture though it was often little better elsewhere given the trends of the times. On occasions the number of offences decreased but not too often. Sadly enough, most of those before the courts were still those of the lower orders, though not invariably. Women were in the dock as regularly as men and there were many recidivists of both sexes.

Cumberland was to be ravaged by cattle disease during much of 1866 and at one stage this led to the postponement of the Quarter Sessions altogether but this still scarcely dented the pattern of everyday crime and judicial disposal. From 1865 to 1868 the following is a fairly representative cross section of crime and punishment in Cumberland selected from the court lists of those times. Some of the sentences would be considered outrageous today. Others were scarcely long enough. The law was almost as contrary then as it is now though it probably continued to improve after a fashion bearing in mind that wives and animals at least had had virtually no rights at all a century before. And yet…

In February, 1865, a particularly savage sentence was passed on a twenty-two-year-old man, John Martindale. No matter that he was dying of consumption. He received ten months at hard labour for fraud.

More heartless still was the sentence meted out at the same court on fourteen-year-old Barclay Dean who had stolen a coat and a pair of drawers. He received two months imprisonment with the added proviso that he be whipped a dozen times. This was only for the theft of the coat. It was directed that he serve a further month and receive a further dozen lashes for the theft of the drawers as well.

Less sympathy could be felt at the time for twenty-one-year-old illiterate Isaac Dalton who received a mere eighteen months for rape.

The following April, a nasty piece of work with an appropriate surname, Nicholas Savage, aged thirty-seven years, was given eighteen months hard labour for beating his spouse with a piece of iron at Penrith. He must have hated her: 'I have threatened to have thy blood many a time and finish thee'. The distressed woman had bruises all over her body. A richly deserved sentence. But how many such assaults had gone unchecked elsewhere in the region during the same period?

In November, 1865 there was a case with a difference. A farmer was charged with robbing his maidservant. The list of stolen items was quite impressive given the poverty of many such employees: black kid gloves, black lace veil, neck ribbons, a locket and three brooches, £2.8s.9d in cash, plus two loaves and half a pound of boiled meat!

October, 1866 found an eleven-year-old boy in the dock at the Michaelmas Sessions, one William Sowerby, accused of stealing three canaries. The sentence was a rigorous one. Only one month in prison but with five years in a reformatory to follow. Unfortunately for Master Sowerby, he had offended before.

Paradoxically, when ten-year-old Thomas Neen stood accused of burning down a warehouse the following February, the crime was deemed to have been committed in a spirit of mischief. Thomas was found not guilty and discharged. He was a first offender and it was noted with some pleasure by the court that he had learnt to read since going into custody the previous December.

In October, 1867, a seventy-seven-year-old labourer, Thomas Greenhow, was given seven years penal servitude for stealing four fleeces of wool. Greenhow had previous form and it was possibly intended that he should now end his days in gaol.

At the same Quarter Sessions, fifty-year-old John Mounsey received five years penal servitude for wounding his wife.

In March of the following year, a policeman was fined 10 shillings and costs for being over-zealous while effecting an arrest. The courts didn't invariably give the police the benefit of the doubt as of course we have already seen in the case of Sam Mooney, though the latter still hadn't had the last laugh.

One of the most distressing cases to come before a Cumbrian court was in August, 1868 when a widow, Mary Walker, appeared before the Brampton Bench accused of barbarous treatment of a dog. In a county renowned for hunting, there was nonetheless a surprising amount of feeling for domestic animals. But Walker's treatment of the defenceless animal, passed on by a clergyman who didn't want it, almost defies description. It came into the widow's hands by a roundabout route. She never wanted the creature, deciding first to bury it alive, then changing her mind in favour of poisoning it. When the dog vomited the poison up she poured turpentine onto its coat and set fire to it; there were further atrocities too distressing to mention here. Eventually the animal took off and was put out of its misery with a blast from a shotgun. The shrew's sentence: six weeks at hard labour. She had attempted to flee the county when the offence first came to light but had been brought back.

Another crime involving a dog, which could easily have brought its perpetrator to the scaffold, was the Raffles shooting of January, 1869. It was a crime which even today remains shrouded in some ambiguity and deserves rather more extended scrutiny here.

During the early evening of Saturday, 30th January, 1869, a farm labourer named John Ward was making his way back from Carlisle market to his home at Great Orton on the western side of the city. His route took him via Raffles but the area then was vastly different to what it is today. As locals know, Raffles is now a sprawling housing estate encompassing several square miles. In 1869 it was no more than a small village with a single public house, the predecessor of the present Horse and Farrier. Much of the surrounding region was green fields though served by the same highway as today leading ultimately to West Cumberland and beyond. But obviously the highway was much quieter and narrower in those times.

In those days too, the county had a generous quantity of turnpikes and the Raffles area was appropriately equipped. Ward made his way through the latter encumbrance around six p.m. It lay just beyond the village. He was already more than a mile from Carlisle city centre but some miles still lay ahead of him. He may have regretted turning down a lift in the local carrier's cart but it had already been heavily laden and perhaps out of compassion for the overburdened horse, he had decided to walk the full way home.

As it was, he was not destined to walk much further. He was no more than a few hundred yards beyond the turnpike when a gun went off and his right shoulder was peppered with small shot. He swung round and received another volley in the chest. It was already fairly dark but he saw a short man in what he believed to be a frock coat standing just a few yards from him. The man disappeared and now in considerable pain, Ward struggled to the nearby pub. First aid was administered before he was removed to the infirmary.

In these times the matter might have ended there – a mindless shooting without apparent motive by a shadowy figure who could as easily have jumped into a car and driven at speed down the highway and onto a convenient motorway vanishing into eternity. However, as we have recently seen in the case of Fisher Ashton and Liz

Ferguson, villains could not get away too quickly in an age of narrow roads and horse-drawn vehicles. True, there was a growing network of railways but this mode of travel too was governed by and large by the proximity of railway stations and ticket barriers. Many such crimes were locally orientated in any case as they still are, with attendant motive.

Nevertheless, there was no motive immediately evident in this instance and the criminal had made himself well scarce. It says something for the perseverance and skill of the small local police force that they had a man in custody within three days. He was named as John Little aged thirty-five years, a butcher of Crofton, who was arrested near Wigton and locked up to await questioning while the investigation continued. In this witnesses were to play no small part for though the crime had taken place in the gloom of a winter evening, there was to be no shortage of witnesses of a circumstantial kind. Likewise in those days, it seemed easier to get people to come forward than it is today, though the police were generally no more popular then than they are now with some members of society.

Initially, the investigating officers under Superintendent Taylor had been as baffled as everyone else, with the unfortunate victim being more baffled than anyone. But all roads had eventually seemed to lead to Little. It was true that no one had seen him shoot John Ward but he had been sighted earlier that same day walking in the Raffles area with a dog and a gun. Impressions are of a loner, inspiring much the same doubt and unease as a similar figure might inspire today, strolling around with a double barreled weapon at the ready, even though shooting matches in the area were fairly commonplace. And he had been seen again shortly before the actual shooting, heading in the direction of Raffles. On the other hand, he hadn't been wearing a frock coat. His garb had been more garish: mackintosh, felt hat and a red and green scarf. This was an anomaly which was never fully resolved.

Little himself was admitting nothing but the police continued certain he was their man. Meanwhile, John Ward remained a patient in the infirmary, his condition deemed serious enough to warrant round the clock observation. Under the circumstances, it was felt imperative to obtain his deposition as soon as possible and a J.P. William Foster visited the patient. Little was brought along too under escort, scarcely common practice in these times. But Ward still couldn't identify his assailant. The assault aside, he could recall only height and build, and the frock coat.

Little's hopes must have risen in the light of this.

Unfortunately for the Crofton butcher however, the police had been zealous on other fronts too. Right from the onset, with the unfortunate farm worker removed to the infirmary following questioning and the coming of daylight, Superintendent Taylor and his men had embarked upon a detailed examination of the scene of the crime, presently coming upon a piece of paper smelling of gun wadding. The paper was part of a bag from the local Carrs Biscuit Factory. When Little was arrested the remainder of the bag was found in his coat pocket. And slugs removed from Ward's body matched those found in the suspect's possession. While Little maintained too that he had known nothing of the shooting until the following Monday, he had been heard to speak of it in a pub closer to his home some two hours after the event. The mackintosh, which went a long way towards identifying him, was discovered at his parents home. And what he couldn't deny was that he possessed a double-barreled sporting gun.

When he appeared at the Assizes in Carlisle the following February before Judge Lush the evidence against him was quite damning. There were still anomalies nevertheless. His height and build were never an issue but his clothing was; the various witnesses were far from unanimous in this respect. The victim himself remained sure the man he had seen fleetingly after the shooting had been wearing a frock coat. Others were adamant that Little had been wearing his mackintosh, felt hat and red and green scarf at both times of sighting. But yet another witness claimed to have seen a man with a gun further afield that night by about half a mile; however this individual had been more soberly dressed. The defence claimed that the pieces from the paper bag didn't dovetail properly, that Carrs bags were common to everyone, and that the shot involved was common game shot used by many sportsmen. And what was the motive? Why should Little want to shoot at someone like John Ward, whom he had never met before?

Certainly there were a number of unanswered questions and they were never properly explained away. But many facts remained weighted against Little. No other gunman was ever traced following events of that January evening. Nor did anyone else ever come forward while there were no shooting matches in the area at all that day. Contrary to the arguments of the defence in the shape of the tenacious Campbell Foster, the pieces of torn paper from the biscuit bag fitted perfectly. And Raffles Village itself was not normally a rendezvous for men with guns, however common the slugs fired at Ward might have been, thus affording every likelihood that the owner of the gun and the ammunition in question were one and the same, with the likely assumption that the victim may well have been deficient in his identification due simply to pain and shock and the encroaching darkness.

Then there was the prisoner himself. He didn't have a lot to say and impressions are of a rather introverted individual. But he had already committed himself out of his own mouth by mentioning the shooting the same night of its happening, even while later blandly denying that he had said anything and stressing that he hadn't known of the shooting until the following Monday.

Add to this that there could well have been a motive though indeed, motiveless crimes are not uncommon as we know only too well in these times. But now perhaps sufficient to say that when Little had appeared on his first grand parade of the day in

Raffles, on 30th January, a kind of strolling amateur sportsman with his gun under his arm and his dog at his heels, something happened. All might have been well with his world initially. But then his dog was commandeered by the resident of a local cottage. Whether Little had owed the other man money and the animal had been taken in lieu, or whether he had been ill-treating the creature and it had been taken from him as a consequence of this, or whether the other fellow had simply been the local bully boy, we don't know. But the animal had not been returned to its owner and later that same day, just prior to the shooting, Little was known to have gone to the man's cottage in an attempt to get the dog back but without success. Equally significant was the fact that the taker of the dog was about the same height and build as John Ward.

Be this as it may, the jury took only ten minutes to find Little guilty without even leaving the courtroom. Now it was the judge's turn and he made it quite clear where his sympathies lay. The unfortunate victim was actually still recovering in the Cumberland Infirmary and Mr. Justice Lush sharply advised the prisoner that had John Ward died, then the outcome would have been execution. As it was, while the going rate at that time in Cumberland for using the knife in a fight was no more than six to twelve months hard labour, Little received twenty years penal servitude. Thus even in those days, the potential menace of firearms was recognised.

It is perhaps indicative of the accused man's true guilt that while he had never even taken the opportunity to question Ward at the infirmary, now he accepted his sentence silently and remained quite unmoved. He had not even sought a defence counsel until the day of his trial, when Campbell Foster had agreed to take up the challenge. As matters evolved, this was not destined to be the wizard of the northern circuit's greatest success.

21: THE DEATH OF ABRAHAM STARKIE

Some six months after the Raffles shooting, there occurred another crime in Cumberland rather different to the normal mundane dirge. On the afternoon of 19th July, 1869, the body of Abraham Starkie, a river watcher, was recovered from the River Derwent close to the village of Brigham, near Cockermouth. Starkie's face was severely bloodied with an ugly bruise above his right ear and he had been dead for some hours. Two of his brothers identified the corpse remarking bitterly that the poachers had done for their brother at last. Locals admitted to seeing three men on the river with nets the previous evening but were reluctant to name names, ostensibly lest they might be wrong, but probably because there remained considerable antipathy towards water watchers by many Cumbrians, who invariably saw no reason why ordinary folk shouldn't fish unhindered in the county's rivers and lakes, and because they had no wish to inform on those they knew who did so.

However, someone must have talked because by the following day three local men were in custody: Henry Hodgson and Richard Temple, both labourers aged twenty-five and thirty years respectively and John Moses, a thirty-one-year-old slater. In a way, it was Brocklewath being replayed all over again but in this instance there was already one subtle difference: Moses was also a water watcher, for the Cockermouth Angling Association, and an acquaintance of Starkie.

A great crowd was in court at Cockermouth to see the trio remanded. Moses, a huge bearded man, stared impassively ahead, arms manacled behind him. His two companions looked more troubled. Both were well known poachers with criminal records which had to count further against them. The crowd were generally sympathetic but surprised that Moses should have been associating with men like Hodgson and Temple and seemingly betraying his employers in the process. And who had struck the fatal blow for every indication was that one of the trio had killed Starkie.

Gradually the picture became clearer. There was to be less of the dissimilation evident in this instance as that which had marked the maiden appearance of the Brocklewath Three for Hodgson, Temple and Moses had already all made statements implicating themselves to some degree. It seemed that they had been surprised by Starkie while netting at High Crossay. Temple and Moses had made off but Hodgson had got tangled up in his own net and been left to struggle with the water watcher. Starkie was thirteen stone and in the prime of his life but had more than met his match in Hodgson who was a renowned wrestler. The latter had been further inflamed after Starkie had allegedly bitten his finger and hit him with a stick. Several times they had gone under water but Hodgson still denied ever hitting the man who had nicked him. He was quite adamant that he had never intended to harm the water watcher in any way.

All well and good, but had Starkie drowned after hitting his head on a sharp stone or had Hodgson hit him despite his denials? And why had the threesome all colluded afterwards to hide relevant evidence while Moses had apparently cheated so blatantly on his bosses? These were the unanswered questions which left the issue in doubt. The powers-that-be weren't satisfied. On 28th July, 1869, the trio were all committed for trial for the wilful murder of Abraham Starkie.

Worse was to follow. By an unhappy coincidence, Starkie's fellow watcher, Henry Kendal, died violently in a fight the following January while Hodgson, Temple and Moses continued to languish at Carlisle awaiting their trial. The accused, twenty-five-year-old Wilson Towers, quickly joined the threesome in custody. It is not beyond the realms of possibility that Kendal had died indirectly because of his despised employment and his connection with the late Starkie but this is mere conjecture.

What is more certain is that he had been drinking until the early hours in a pub called the Three Tuns in Cockermouth with Towers and others. A quarrel arose between Kendal and Towers and this developed into a fight out on the street. Kendal was a big man and not one to ignore a taunt or a threat, or he may have instigated the quarrel himself. Like the luckless Starkie however, he was up against more formidable opposition. He went down on the pavement after fighting a mere two rounds and hit his head with fatal result.

Towers was tried the following month but everyone immediately concerned had been so drunk that it was impossible to say whether he had knocked Kendal down or not. The cause of death was given as concussion of the brain with no other marks deemed serious enough to cause death. Towers was thereupon found not guilty and merely bound over to keep the peace. This must have been a considerable relief to Towers and justice does appear to have been done in this instance in a kind of straight up and down way. But there was ongoing tragedy in the fact that Kendal had left a wife and five dependent children while Starkie had been a father of three. Within months therefore, two water watchers serving the same employer were unnecessarily dead as a result of violent confrontation leaving two widows and eight dependent children between them. And there were no state payments to cushion such a blow in those days.

For its part, the bigger trial of Hodgson and Co. was finally about to get under way that same month. Much of the spotlight subsequently fell upon Hodgson who expanded upon his original statement to claim that after a prolonged struggle with Starkie, he had finally pushed the man away and ran off. When Starkie didn't follow he had experienced some concern but was only too relieved to get away. When news of the water watcher's death broke he didn't deny that he had joined with Moses and Temple in hiding nets and articles of his own clothing. A doctor was then called and he confirmed that he had dressed the finger which the prisoner alleged had been bitten by the deceased. The doctor further advised that the bruise above Starkie's ear could have been made by a stone when the latter had fallen down, rupturing a blood vessel within. But there was no evidence to prove that Hodgson had wielded such a stone and one of his buttons had been found attached to a net, confirming to some extent his tale of having been trapped in the first instance.

It was now that the defence moved into top gear. The Perry Mason of the northern circuit, Campbell Foster, was acting for Hodgson and he had obviously striven to do his homework thoroughly. He argued that the scene of the crime was not covered by fishing regulations so Starkie had had no right there. No water watcher was in post at all for that particular district it seemed. Thus what he was saying in effect was that the water watcher had exceeded his remit as some watchers did seem wont to do and had had no right to intervene at all. If true, then this of course did go some way towards exonerating Moses for under these circumstances, why shouldn't he have failed to question Temple and Hodgson's desire to fish that particular stretch of water, even to the extent of joining them for some innocent sport himself without anyone breaking any law?

But the judge held that this wasn't quite true; the trio had been fishing in a private fishery. In a way, he conceded, they had been fishing legally because it had not been the close season, but they had not had the official right to fish and Hodgson ought to have gone along quietly with Starkie. As it was, the water watcher had died unlawfully.

The defending lawyer came back quickly, pointing out the violence meted out to his client; he had had his finger bitten, his throat scratched and he had been hit with a stick. And where was the evidence that he had struck the deceased the fatal blow to the head? Hadn't the doctor also said that death was from drowning whatever had caused the actual blow….?

The court may have been impressed to some degree by such spirited argument which was not without its logic. Indeed, Temple and Moses had already been cleared by this time though indications were that having originally ran off at Starkie's approach, they hadn't considered themselves quite as innocent as the defence would have had the court believe. And, along with Hodgson, they had attempted to dispose of any evidence afterwards. Be this as it may, they were free. Hodgson was less fortunate. He was found guilty and sentenced to five years penal servitude. But given the fear and trepidation he appeared to have experienced before and after his arrest in respect of Starkie's death, he may well have considered himself lucky after all. Compared to John Little's twenty years, he had got off lightly altogether.

It went without saying that the death of Abraham Starkie had still been a very unfortunate event however high-handed the latter may have been. It was not destined to deter poachers from run-ins with water bailiffs in Cumberland in the future. But it would be the last case of violent death on any river in the county ever to come before the courts again.

As for Hodgson, after completing his sentence, he presumably returned to the Cockermouth area, where there is no reason to believe that he was not welcomed back cordially enough, in spite of all that had transpired.

22: THE ARMATHWAITE RIOT

Nationalism is never far away but divergent nationalities have proved capable of living and working together on many occasions without a great deal of friction. Cumberland for its part had long had a large number of Irish among its indigenous population given the West Cumbrian coal trade and the proximity of such ports as Whitehaven and Maryport to the east coast of Ireland. Many Irish had been settled in the county for generations and were as Cumbrian as the host population with little evidence of friction. Most earned their living in a variety of occupations in the more heavily populated areas along with their Cumbrian counterparts, many of the latter with their own share of celtic blood dating back centuries before.

With the advance of the nineteenth century there came additional waves of Irish and others into Cumberland to assist in laying the railways which were being built throughout Britain. It has to be said nevertheless that such employment often tended to attract wilder, more transitory elements, be they English, Scottish, Irish or others, given the rough nomadic nature of railway navvying.

In rude settings often miles from anywhere, small social or personal problems might at times assume mammoth proportions. The only means of settling such differences was likely to be physical, all against a background of unremitting toil only relieved by gambling and heavy drinking. Many railway navvies were even said to work in an inebriated state and their expectancy of life was low.

The practices of certain employers did little to diminish such a state of affairs, nurturing miserable dependence and persisting debt by way of the notorious tommy-shops, owned and stocked by bosses in a variety of industries but with a big majority of such shops on railway sites. Here workers could obtain exorbitantly priced goods on credit, any difference being deducted from their wages or with goods being given at times in lieu of wages. All this was calculated to bring out the worst in many of the navvies, given their habits and way of life, with the English being seen as the most unrestrained of all.

Yet it was still a comparatively minor incident amidst such a setting which was to lead to one of the worst nationalistic riots in Cumberland, the theft of a Scotsman's paltry provisions by several Irishmen on his way back from a tommy-shop. An innocent man lost his life in the proceeding affray and others were brutally beaten. The scene of all this was a most unlikely one, the village of Armathwaite, lying a fairly short distance south east of Carlisle but still remote enough a century and more ago and not too far away from the scene of the notorious Staffield killing of 1856.

Today, Armathwaite is again peaceful enough but in October, 1870 it was in the throes of social and industrial upheaval due to the encroachment of the railway network there. The railways had came on fast from a mere sixty-nine miles in 1830 to fifteen thousand, five hundred and fifty-seven miles in 1870 when the boom peaked. In October of that year the Carlisle-Settle railway line was under construction and Armathwaite was virtually under alien occupation with the track being laid in its immediate environs by several hundred navvies, mainly English and Irish with a smattering of Scots.

Most of the workers were housed in huts in and around the village. Some had their families with them but already there was an element of segregation with the Irish being housed mainly on the outskirts and favouring the New Inn for drinking while English and Scots tended to drink in the Red Lion. There was an element of fraternistion too, though a certain amount of inner resentment did appear to have been building up for some time. This was due to some of the English workforce feeling that the Irish were taking work and money away from them, the Scots tending to side with the English, all against a continuing background of ignorance and deprivation.

After being duffed up and robbed of his groceries early on the Saturday evening of 15th October, the injured man, Campbell, reported back bitterly to his own kind, sowing the seeds of what was soon to come. Word of the assault travelled quickly around the site. With considerable animosity thus further generated, the mood was scarcely very salubrious later in the tap room of the New Inn where a number of English navvies were drinking out of bounds with some of their Irish workmates.

The Campbell episode was on everyone's mind. When an Irishman lost to an Englishman at cards and swept the latter's winnings off the table a row developed even more quickly than normal. The English landlord, Edmond Graham, no lover of the Irish contingent, turned most of them out, adding final fuel to the flames. Between nine and ten p.m. the Irish returned in force, armed with sticks and stones. They surrounded the inn and smashed the windows but the English inside rose in retaliation. Literally under siege they began forcing their way outside, dodging the stones coming through the windows and determined to get the Irish back, both parties being quite heavily intoxicated, the English now being joined by the Scots, including the aggrieved Campbell.

Caught up in all this was an Irishman named Cornelius Cox. A steadier personality than the majority, he had remained drinking in the front room of the New Inn after most of his countrymen had been expelled. Witnesses were to say that he was approached by an Englishman named White who insulted him and knocked him off his chair. He was then dragged into a rear yard and beaten and kicked. Later he was to be discovered behind a wall unable to speak, his head horribly battered. Initially his few companions had fled for their lives, heavily outnumbered by English and Scots. But they did return and sought out Cox, placing him in a barrow and wheeling him through the melee to the safety of a friend's hut. A doctor was called but to no avail. Cox died the following Monday never having spoken again.

Meanwhile the battle had continued, quickly developing into a full scale riot with English and Scots on one side and Irish on the other. The entire area was in ferment. Inflamed by drink, men fought one another until they were battered and exhausted. Fists, sticks and stones were used indiscriminately. One who received a brutal kicking was the unfortunate Campbell. There was damage to local property and locals hid away in fear of their lives. The small contingent of local police could do little. Throughout the night and during most of the following Sunday, the riot continued.

But already, other forces were at work. The whole unsavoury business now became flagrantly political with other players emerging onto the stage. Word had quickly been sent up and down the line of the trouble at Armathwaite. By Monday morning the riot had subsided but now two hundred navvies from further afield marched into the village in military formation. They were armed with bludgeons and led by Joseph French of Warwickshire, a former soldier who had drilled his followers beforehand. With a mind to former resentments, French and his two cronies Joseph Draper and Thomas Jones had determined to use the riot to get rid of the Irish altogether and leave the pitch clear for themselves and their kind.

They marched their men to the house of the site manager, Bell, and told him bluntly that if he didn't get rid of all the Irish, that they would do the job themselves. Bell was angry and inclined to resist but with no tangible support from the under-represented forces of law and order and with fears of further bloodshed, had little choice but to comply. The Irish were called together and advised that they must move. Most were subdued and silent now. They were paid any money still due to them, their belongings were piled into waggons and they all headed for Southwaite Station.

Following this, the situation eased. By Tuesday work had resumed on the railway though both English and Scots were closely watched by the police, finally reinforced and armed with cutlasses. Yet the situation couldn't be allowed to end there. The surrounding area was a shambles. French, Draper and Jones were all arrested and charged with conspiracy. In the event however, they were to be dealt with fairly leniently for they had came later to the scene and it may have been felt that they had even assisted in averting further bloodshed whatever their earlier motives. The law had decided it had larger fish to fry in any case. It had three other men in custody who were soon to be charged with wilfully killing and murdering Cornelius Cox: Joseph White aged twenty-two years, Charles 'Punch' Parker aged twenty-two years and William Caisley aged twenty-eight years. All were English but not Cumbrian, though Caisley remains a name with strong northern connections.

An inquest was quickly convened at Penrith. There were sufficient Irish witnesses to make a murder charge inevitable. The most damning testimony came from one John Forster who claimed to have seen all three men savagely abuse the victim by the light of the public house doors. The threesome all pleaded not guilty and accused the witnesses of lying. This availed them nothing. They were charged and committed for trial at the next Assizes and removed to Carlisle Gaol.

They remained there until February, 1871, a length of time short enough for memories to remain clear and when they came up for trial they could well have faced a hanging jury. But though their defence lawyer, the astute Campbell Foster, was ready to proceed, two vital witnesses, John Forster and Martin Murphy, were missing. It transpired that the police were currently seeking Forster for another matter. Murphy had been seen in Carlisle the day before but had disappeared. Thereupon the Armathwaite trio were remanded back to prison until the next Assizes six months hence.

When they did appear again the following July they were dressed once more in the working attire in which they had been arrested but all looked much thinner and paler. Nevertheless, on this occasion, the trial did go ahead. There was no trouble in producing Forster in this instance; he had been brought from prison. This may have worked to his detriment. The judge was Lord Chief Baron Kelly. With such a surname he might have been expected to look rather more benignly upon the Irish case. Such was not to be. He didn't seem to like Forster. At the very onset he chastised him for using Parker's nickname rather than the latter's proper surname. This was a simple error on the part of a rather simple man who nevertheless stuck firmly by his original story – that he had seen Cox beaten with a shovel and then a metal crook out in the inn yard after Parker and White had dragged him there.

But no shovel was available as evidence. The crook was produced but there were no traces of blood upon it. Martin Murphy was called but again he was missing. This could only assist the three prisoners and the next witness, McDonoghue, couldn't recall the weapon allegedly used. Another witness, John Norris, spoke of witnessing the original assault on Cox by White alone, but one James Nolan deposed that he had seen Caisley kick the unfortunate victim at the same time, while Forster had already stated that the kicking had taken place in the back yard with Parker and White there. However, McDonoghue hadn't seen White, or Caisley, on the scene at all.

It was all very confusing but almost a year had now gone by and memories had to be of necessity rather dim. The defence made the most of this before proceeding to call a number of witnesses favourably disposed towards the accused. The first of these was the landlord of the New Inn, Edmond Graham. The latter had no cause at all to love the Irish now. He had been forced to seek shelter in the cellar with his children while stones rained through his windows and his premises were smashed about him. He spoke very well of all three prisoners. And his sister Margaret was adamant that she had seen White fighting with no one. John Tweddle, keeper of the tommy-shop, agreed that Cox hadn't been the worse for liquor in his experience, but in response to a swift follow-through question from the subtle defence counsel, affirmed the serious harm done earlier to the Scots navvy, Campbell.

All this doubtless made an impression on judge and jury.

The police and a representative of the medical profession went on to confirm the injuries which had caused Cox's death from concussion of the brain. But the defence emphasised the darkness of the evening. How much had witnesses really seen? Obviously Cox hadn't died from a fist blow, but there was no sign of any shovel and the crook also allegedly used had no blood upon it. Forster hadn't even reported the episode. He had gone home, but surely none of the witnesses would have done that if the attack they had seen had been so vicious? There was more in the same vein. Former animosity between Parker and Forster was played upon, And contradictions in McDonoghue's evidence. The landlord of the New Inn had described all three prisoners as quiet men – but the court was reminded that the witness Forster had been brought from prison only that morning; this of course by way of subtle comparison. Couldn't Cox in fact have been struck by a flying stone? Parker had been. Couldn't he have been dragged out into the yard by the Englishmen to revive him? Or couldn't the victim have fallen from the top of the wall he was lying behind when discovered later by Forster and others? In fact, the defence affirmed, no definite proof had been forthcoming.

It was all good courtroom stuff, as effective then as it would be today. It had its continuing effect.

It was time for Baron Kelly to sum up. He gave credit to Forster for his unshaken evidence, but then suggested that he might be holding something back and surely his cowardly conduct must be considered too....? Otherwise, if it was simply a battle between English and Irish then manslaughter had to be a consideration. But if Cox had been deliberately set upon, then it could be murder...

Given all the jury had already heard, the judge's advice scarcely appeared to touch their minds. They were only out for twenty minutes before coming back with not guilty verdicts against all three men, either of manslaughter or murder.

The prisoners scarcely seemed able to believe their ears, nor did those about them. They were discharged and vanished into anonymity.

A nasty business altogether with the unfortunate Cox long since laid to rest in an obscure grave. And yet, some good of a kind may still have came out of it for shortly following the riot and its aftermath, the railway contractors issued a statement emphasising that they had no intention of employing any single nationality on the Carlisle-Settle line and any dissenters had best leave there and then. This appears to have been effective for there was no further trouble and the line as a whole was completed satisfactorily by its mixed labour force with nationalism never being an issue on it again.

Today the railway still runs by Armathwaite, but the riot itself and the wild men who took part in it have long been relegated to obscurity by the majority of Cumbrians and others.

23: SUFFER LITTLE CHILDREN

Infanticide was a continuing blight on Victorian Britain. In this respect Cumberland was probably no better or worse than many another region despite its high illegitimacy rate. But as we have already seen, local courts for their part had long since became generally sympathetic to the stream of poor wretches coming before them at regular intervals, often giving them the benefit of the doubt, Jane Byers being somewhat exceptional with her twelve month sentence of hard labour.

Yet paradoxically, the same courts could bear down extremely heavily when any child died under circumstances which pointed to brutal unmitigated murder, as in the Hagen case, the alleged murderer appearing at the Cumberland Spring Assizes of February, 1873 and netting the first death sentence to be handed down in Cumberland since the case of William Charlton more than a decade previously.

Everything about this case further emphasises the very harshness of the times as they concerned single parents. The victim, eighteen-month-old Joseph Hagen, was the illegitimate child of Ellen Hagen of Cleator Moor. Ellen Hagen herself had surely deserved a better deal from life than the one meted out to her. And yet she had obviously striven to meet all her children's' needs conscientiously just as the majority of single parents did in those times, even amidst the extreme privation of nineteenth century Cumberland and beyond.

At the time of the murder on 7th December, 1872, she had been a widow for almost six years. Her husband had left her with five children now ranging from thirteen years to six years. Eventually she had entered into a relationship with another man but if she had been seeking security and stability she had been disappointed. She had merely been left with an illegitimate child, naming the infant Joseph and giving it her own married surname. Nevertheless, the child was as well loved and cared for as any of her other children, even though the mother had only the tenancy of a small one-bedroomed cottage and made but a slender living selling home-made sweets and other small items off a stall in the local market.

More recently, her late husband's cousin, Hugh Hagen, had taken to visiting her. He was an odious specimen, a stocky forty-year-old bachelor, who had already served a prison term for attempted rape in the Egremont area in 1867. Unable to get his way with the girl concerned, Mary Hanley, he had attempted to drown her in the nearby river and she had been fortunate to escape with her life. For this he had received a paltry two month sentence.

In 1870 he had been arrested following a violent attack upon a girl at a lonely farm at Wythemoorhow. Everything pointed to Hagen as being the individual concerned but the terrified victim had been unable to identify him specifically and so he was freed to roam again at will. As events were to unfold, it was a tragedy that he hadn't been locked away indefinitely at that time.

Why Ellen Hagen tolerated him in her home is uncertain for she must have known of his criminal record. There may have been an element of intimidation for the man has been described as short but well-knit with a persistent gaze. But perhaps the fact that he was of her late husband's family and may have been assisting her financially from time to time could have been a more relevant factor, Hagen having employment as a stonemason. Or she could have simply felt sorry for the middle-aged loner who didn't live far off and tolerated him out of sheet habit, being a basically good-natured woman. He may even have been her lover though this seems doubtful.

The fact remains that she had not been averse to facing up to him either, despite his violent reputation. She had responded quickly and sharply to his derogatory comments about her illegitimate son, to whom the visitor had taken an almost pathological dislike, speaking freely and saying that it ought not to live as it was eating food other children should have. The mother had told him sharply that it was none of his business and there the matter appeared to have ended at that time. But perhaps she ought to have been forewarned given the man's record. As it was, she let the matter pass and he continued to visit as before.

Saturday, 7th December was a cold gloomy day but Ellen Hagen had especial need to mind her stall in the market with Christmas approaching and additional calls upon her purse, her day to day situation remaining precarious to boot. Once again, Hugh Hagen was visiting. He had been paid off that day but appeared unconcerned about the loss of his job. The mother left for the market at three p.m. There was a good coal fire burning in the cottage grate. All the children were at home but Joseph was left in the special care of his eldest half-brother, thirteen-year-old John.

No sooner was the mother gone than Joseph began to cry. Hagen flew into a rage, grabbing the child and throwing it onto the bed in the back room. The eldest boy immediately recovered the infant and took it to his mother in the market where he explained the situation. Ellen Hagen, encumbered with a stall to mind and the need to return home with sufficient money to help feed herself and her children examined the child and felt it was all right. She sent John and his young charge home again, advising the teenager that if there was any more trouble from Hugh Hagen, to fetch the police and leaving it at that.

Back home, the situation settled itself briefly. The infant fell asleep and John Hagen put it to bed. Then the unwelcome visitor became unpleasant again, ordering the young teenager to make himself useful and get out. The youngster resisted, retorting that he was already usefully employed looking after his brother. But he was no match for the older man who drove him out with a poker. Soon his brothers and sisters were also evicted. Hagen was left in the cottage with the eighteen month old infant.

The eldest boy in particular had frightening premonitions of what might now occur. He and his siblings made for the market and brought their mother up to date. It was now dark, adding to the disquiet of the situation. Further delay was out of the question. Quite concerned now and perhaps suddenly mindful of more recent threats by Hagen against the child, the harassed mother left her stall unattended and hurried back. Her home was locked against her but she forced an entry. Hugh Hagen was leaving the bedroom as she burst in through the front door. He claimed that Joseph was outside with the others but the mother saw a foot protruding from beneath a piece of wooden railing lying on the bed. She ran back outside and slammed the door shut behind her, screaming for the police who were quickly on the scene.

They apprehended Hagen and discovered the child bleeding from the nose and mouth but still alive. A doctor was called and felt he would live. For some reason it was deemed unnecessary to arrest Hagen at the time. He were merely required to give his name and address. Giving a false name, Weir, he departed. There had to be some laxity over this, more-so given the fact that within hours the child had died.

Now it was a question of murder. Hagen was arrested soon enough and an inquest held at the local Queens Arms Inn. By this time word of the crime had spread and there was a great deal of anger against the alleged murderer to the extent that it wasn't felt wise to bring him to the inquest. Many locals had considered him an oddity for years and the case of Mary Hanley remained clear in the minds of the majority. The cause of death was assessed as concussion of the brain and Hagen was indicted on a charge of wilful murder.

He was tried at Carlisle before Mr. Justice Archibald. The outcome was never really in doubt. The prisoner stared vacantly before him and had little to say for himself beyond pleading not guilty until Ellen Hagen began to give evidence when he became distinctly emotional, discounting what she had to say and endeavouring to lay hands upon her. This action of itself further damned him in the eyes of the court. Meanwhile, there was evidence of blows to the face as well as to the head of the defenceless child, presumably administered by Hagen with the lump of wooden railing normally used for propping open the cottage door. The child himself had been sturdy and well-nourished and couldn't possibly have died of natural causes.

The jury were out for half an hour, returning with a unanimous verdict of guilty. There was no recommendation to mercy and Hagen was sentenced to death. He remained indifferent, muttering that he knew nothing at all about the child.

There the matter might have ended, with the law taking its full course. No one appeared very concerned to save the despised stonemason. Calcraft the hangman had been notified and the day drew near for the child killer's execution. But it is a sad soul who has no one and then as now, there had been those zealots working diligently on his behalf, led in this instance by one Canon Curry. At the latter's instigation, a number of affidavits went to the Secretary of State testifying to Hagen's shaky state of mind by responsible West Cumbrians who had known him for years, with the emphasis on delusions. This led to Hagen's examination by the medical superintendent of Broadmoor and the surgeon of the County Gaol. Two lengthy interviews resulted in certification of insanity leading to a reprieve on the day preceding his intended execution. The prisoner was removed to Broadmoor Criminal Lunatic Asylum, there to spend the remainder of his days.

A just finale? There were undoubtedly many who begged to differ.

24: FOUR DELINQUENTS

We have reached 1874, with close to half a century having gone by since the trial of fifteen year old Robert Lamb and thirteen year old Joseph Furnace for the theft of linen and a silver watch from the home of a Penrith hawker. Both had had sentences of death recorded against them but even then, Cumbrian courts had became reluctant to hang juveniles. Indeed, most courts in the country had long been reluctant to hang anyone without careful sifting of the evidence before them. Had everyone been hanged who appeared in court in Britain for thieving or any other type of crime in the last century, or even before it, a battalion of hangmen would have been required with the risk of a public uprising. But while theft in particular could still not be tolerated then, there had been another alternative type of sentence available for all age groups and almost as equally effective as the hangman's noose. This was transportation and as we already know, Lamb and Furnace had both been eventually transported, though the thirteen year old was of previous good character.

Now, with hanging reserved essentially for murderers and transportation a thing of the past, how did our courts deal with juvenile delinquents in 1874? In point of fact, punishment for juveniles remained severe enough as has already been indicated in our transitory study of other local cases along the way. In 1874 there still remained a quite unrelenting attitude towards delinquency of any kind and juveniles in Cumberland were not exempted from this. Consider for instance the following sentences meted out to four local youngsters who had committed much the same type of offence as that committed by Lamb and Furnace all those years before.

William Gribbin and William Doran were two boys not yet into their teens who had stolen a number of tumblers and glasses and other small articles from a house in Whitehaven in May, 1873. They had recruited two teenage coal pickers as accessories, fifteen year old Rachel Nesbitt and sixteen-year-old Ann Tummelty, the offences possibly nurtured by the growing poverty in the region.

The foursome all appeared at the Cumberland Midsummer Sessions on 3rd July, 1874, almost a year after the occurrence of the offence. Thus they might well have already spent an extended period in custody in their local House of Correction. Their trial was embellished by an element of humour. Indeed, laughter in Cumbrian courts and others remained common in those times at the expense of the prisoners, regardless of age or crime, and was not necessarily always checked.

In this instance the offended party was a droll individual named John Murray who had been moving his possessions from one house to another. He had moved half of them to his new house in Scotch Street on the Saturday evening preceding the crime and departed, locking the house up. On the following Monday he discovered a window broken and some of his property missing. He quickly made enquiries. A neighbour was found who was quite willing to testify against the juveniles, having seen the boys passing out the articles concerned to the girls on the preceding Sunday through the window. There followed an exchange between the defence counsel and Murray. The latter admitted that he didn't know much about his glasses and pots but surely when a man got a wife, then she would look after the crockery but when it came to locking the door, it depended on who had the key. There was more in this vein, affording considerable hilarity, but it didn't assist the accused.

They did get off the more serious charge of housebreaking as the house had not been occupied. But they were still found guilty of larceny, albeit with a recommendation to mercy on account of their youth. So far so good, up to a point, and nowadays all four might well have received no more than a modest fine and a ticking off in most British courts given that the house had been empty and no one hurt. But this was Cumberland 1874 and the bench was not inclined to be so frivolous. Tummelty already had the reputation of being tarry-fingered. She was promptly sentenced to three months at hard labour. Her female accomplice had no previous form whatsoever but this didn't help her; she too went down for three months. The two small boys received a month's imprisonment apiece. Not such a heavy sentence perhaps, in the opinion of some. But to further deter them for future offending, each was sentenced to no less than twelve strokes of the birch.

All four were of the lower orders though it would still probably have been little consolation to Gribbin and Doran that just a short time later, the headmaster of a swanky school in Yorkshire was cleared of caning the sons of gentlemen until blood came for some petty misdemeanour. When it came to juvenile misbehaviour and corporal punishment in those times, class was possibly of lesser account though the offspring of the poor were still more likely to be dealt with publicly. Cumberland was no exception in this respect.

On the other hand, hard labour and birching still had to be preferable to hanging or transportation irrespective of who the culprit was amongst the youthful fraternity. Slowly but surely, there had been some undoubted improvement on the juvenile scene over the years even while much still remained to be done, both in Cumberland and beyond.

25: FATE OF AN EXILE

It was the Reverend John Ogilvie who was the recipient of a verbal thrust from Dr. Samuel Johnson which has became widely quoted to this day: 'the noblest prospect which a Scotsman ever sees, is the high road that leads him to England'. Johnson may have been speaking with less malice aforethought than has at times been attributed to him in this respect. His greatest friend and champion after all was a Scotsman, responsible in fact for immortalising the remark: James Boswell.

What is true nonetheless is that many Scots did make their way to England to seek work and success in former days and have continued to do so, often ending up in good circumstance, even though the situation could now have been partially reversed with the advent of north sea oil.

On the other hand, one Scot who did make the journey just over a century ago may have pondered Johnson's remark with some irony between his religious devotions. As he sat in the condemned cell at Carlisle in 1876 awaiting the arrival of the hangman, he may well have wished he had never set off down the high road to England at all, though given the very peculiar make-up of the man, who can tell?

James Dalgleish is more or less forgotten now by the great majority but has the doubtful honour of being the first man to be executed in Cumberland since William Charlton. He was also the first of his kind to be executed privately in the county and the only killer in Cumberland to be taken well outside the county to be tried, though he was brought back for execution soon enough under close guard and quickly dispatched at the age of twenty-seven. Yet the question remains – should he have been hanged at all, given that he had almost certainly been suffering from mental health problems and had to be almost equally deserving of consideration for a reprieve as Hugh Hagen.

The son of a shepherd, Dalgleish was a native of Berwickshire and like others of his breed, was imbued with a deep love of learning, despite his lowly background. It was a bright young man of some education who eventually left his native Scotland at the age of twenty-two years to seek his fortune in England but he travelled no further than Penrith where he became a clerk in the offices of the expanding police force. He appears to have had neither kith nor kin anywhere south of the border who could accommodate him but was able to obtain lodgings through his own efforts with a Miss Sarah Wright, then forty-three years old, who kept a small boarding house in Albert Street, Penrith.

There were many such establishments in those days and some none too salubrious but impressions are of a respectable place in this instance, with a homely atmosphere, though fairly small with only three bedrooms. The female proprietor and the taciturn young Scot seemingly took to one another from the onset and he began to look upon the Cumbrian spinster as rather more than a landlady. He settled in at No. 17 Albert Street and never lived anywhere else for the remainder of his life as a free man, an exile without direct contact it seems with anyone back in his native Scotland, but accepted well enough in the small market town by those with whom he had dealings. Yet soon enough there were indications that all wasn't well with James Dalgleish.

Before setting off to seek his fortune in England, he had been employed for several years as a railway clerk near St. Boswells. Here he had been especially well-thought of and came south well recommended by his station master and other local worthies. His career with the County Constabulary moved along similar lines initially. But he failed to achieve any kind of promotion which may have been indicative of itself that he was beginning to falter and left the police office after less than two years to take up employment as a clerk and general assistant to a local spirit merchant, Thomas Lumb. From then onwards, his life and career began to go into marked reverse.

Ever reticent and reserved, he may have been able to conceal more portentous signs at the onset, but it still wasn't long before Lumb formed the opinion that his young employee had mental health problems. On one occasion the Scot had stood on a stool and beat on the ceiling with his hands. And his visits to the doctor became increasingly frequent. He wasn't ailing a great deal: indigestion, a boil on the arm, but appeared convinced that he could die of such conditions, dwelling on death to an obsessive degree and often sunk in melancholia. It may also have been about now that he turned to alcohol as a means of consolation.

Dalgleish worked for Thomas Lumb for almost three years but finally Lumb wearied of his clerk's odd behaviour and he was dismissed. He was still in with a chance; he was able to obtain employment of a similar kind with a man named Hetherington in the centre of Penrith, not far from the premises of Thomas Lumb. However, this employment lasted only a short time. From Christmas 1875 Dalgleish never worked again, becoming dependent upon his landlady who was soon the main butt of his increasingly difficult behaviour.

Such conduct must inevitably have been compounded by the life he was now leading. His own family remained too far off to be of any real assistance since he chose to stay on month after month in Penrith which perhaps by unfortunate coincidence, is said to have had the highest number of licenced hostelries for its size in the county. Much of the Scot's time however, appears to have been spent at his lodgings in Albert Street rather than in any of the public houses. But he still drank and when he had taken drink, was said to be livelier company, being dull and depressed and turned in upon himself when sober and no company at all.

The small boarding house was now full to capacity. Dalgleish shared a room with the landlady's brother, David, and a local watchmaker named Jackson. The two smaller bedrooms were occupied respectively by the landlady's friend, Margaret Youngdale, and the latter's brother-in-law, Jospeh Lambert Proctor, a smooth character who had been a coffee planter in India. No one really knew why he had given up on colonial life but he had returned to England and taken a job at Penrith Gas Works, quite a contrast to life under the Raj. Proctor was later to give telling evidence against the young Scotsman in court, along with Jackson the watchmaker. With all the bedrooms taken, Miss Wright herself had taken to sleeping on a makeshift bed on the parlour floor with her niece, sixteen-year-old Mary Fox.

So many people living in such close proximity was not a unique situation anywhere in Victorian Britain but almost inevitably it bred tension. Yet much of the tension in this instance was almost certainly generated by James Dalgleish. He remained friendly with Sarah Wright's brother and niece but maintained a simmering grudge against Proctor who appears to have had romantic designs on the landlady and who didn't like Dalgleish in his turn. The watchmaker and Margaret Youngdale were uneasy neutrals amidst this acrimony which included Dalgleish's rather despicable treatment of Sarah Wright on far too many occasions. The landlady herself presented well to the world outside and impresses as having been a basically decent woman but perhaps with some penchant for alcohol.

Her feelings for the failed clerk were of themselves complex. She had apparently established a rapport with him from the onset. He would read to her; he was deeply attached to her and this attachment grew increasingly intense, on his part at least., Some time after becoming unemployed he had fallen physically ill, much more seriously than usual, and had been confined to bed. Sarah Wright had at once taken it upon herself to nurse him unsparingly leading to a new kind of intimacy between them. Victorian morality has forbidden any hint of a sexual relationship in accounts of the case at the time, but Dalgleish was later to say that he had loved her and she had loved him and that she would never have taken money from him when he could no longer pay his way. This may have been true. Nonetheless, in his fits of acute melancholia and frustration, he would turn on her and had taken her by the throat on at least one occasion, as though compelled to hurt the one closest to him.

When first thrown out of work, he had been able to pay his way for a time by pawning his few possessions and this helped. But with nothing eventually left to pawn and no prospect of work or simply unprepared to seek such, he had became increasingly pathetic and all the more dependent on Sarah and abusive towards her. Patiently she still bore with him but when he spoke of smashing her brains out it was only a matter of time before she told him that he must leave, whether or not she really meant this. But David Wright defended him anyhow and he stayed. Thus the situation remained unresolved with Dalgleish having now taken to drinking whenever he could borrow or find another means of paying, rendering him the more volatile. And yet he was not said to be a heavy drinker even now. Indeed, brought up a Presbyterian, he actually appears if anything to have begun clinging to religion to an almost obsessive degree, reading to those about him from biblical literature, and to himself, rather than giving himself over totally to alcohol. Meanwhile, however, he also continued to be obsessively jealous of Proctor…

During the early evening of 24th September, 1876, Dalgleish and Sarah were seated in the kitchen of the boarding house. The young lodger could be said to have had a rather better day and was reading 'The History of Joseph and his Bretheren'. Nothing of any consequence happened for some time with life proceeding smoothly enough at No. 17, or so it seemed. Presently the kindly David Wright took Dalgleish out for a drink. They were out only a short time, Wright driving Dalgleish from the parlour afterwards around nine-thirty p.m. By this time most of the residents had retired. Miss Wright and her niece subsequently went to bed on the shake-down but kept a lamp burning.

Shortly afterwards, Dalgleish returned to the parlour and made some comment to Sarah who got up and went upstairs with him. The niece fell asleep but was fairly soon awoken by the sound of a heavy blow. She saw no one else in the room but her aunt who had obviously returned to bed, but whose head was now running with blood. Frantically she raised the alarm. First on the scene was James Dalgleish with Margaret Youngdale close behind. The latter cried out for a doctor and Dalgleish at once said he would go and fetch one. He promptly went racing off to the family doctor's surgery shouting for the medical man to 'come away as Sarah Wright was bleeding and that he had done it'.

It was the senior partner, Dr. MacGregor, who attended. He found Sarah Wright still bleeding but alive on the shake-down. She was in a stupor but an empty whisky bottle under the mattress was of itself significant. Dalgleish was staggering but not intoxicated in the doctor's opinion. However, the situation as a whole was serious enough. Sarah Wright had two gaping wounds on her head and the weapon was quickly found behind the parlour door: a five foot shank topped with a curved blade covered in blood.

James Dalgleish was soon in police hands and charged with murderously assaulting Sarah Wright. He claimed that he hadn't known what he had been doing, remaining excited but not apparently drunk. More tangible pointers to his mental state manifested themselves soon enough in the police station. He was placed in a cell but couldn't rest, pacing up and down; he spoke of the death bell tolling and kept calling out to an imaginary girl whom he was convinced was visiting to keep him informed. He spoke of the place as being crowded out with people. But he was the only prisoner.

Things were soon to get worse for him. Sarah Wright died and he was charged with murder. He was steadier now and made no reply though did presently ask Dr. MacGregor to write to Scotland and bring Dalgleish Senior up to date. Whether or not MacGregor did this is unknown but there is no evidence of any family member coming south at that time. Some may have done so but there is no mention of them until the business was all but over. The police themselves may have informed them of the murder charge but could any of the family have even afforded all the additional expense involved at the time for it was not even intended to try the accused man at Carlisle.

What was intended was a trip further south into Lancashire for about this time, an obscure act had been passed permitting Cumbrians and others to be tried outside their own field of operations with a view to ensuring that they received maximum consideration. Dalgleish travelled south to Manchester in due course with five other local criminals. It was his first trip south of Penrith. It would be his last.

He was tried at Manchester Assizes on 30th November, 1876 before Mr. Justice Lopes. The change of location availed him nothing nor his plea of insanity. The jury were to be less than impressed by Dr. MacGregor's testimony emphasising his patient's low state of mind, or the police account of Dalgleish's hallucinatory episode on the night of his arrest following the fatal attack. They appeared to listen much more keenly to the evidence of Proctor and Jackson, the latter both focusing upon the prisoner's antagonistic attitude towards Sarah Wright during the months preceding her death. Neither was there any definite evidence to prove that James Dalgleish was a very heavy drinker and that the empty whisky bottle found at the scene of the crime had been his, nor that he was unaware of what he had done. The defence could only protest that if Dalgleish had committed a calculated crime, why hadn't he left the house? Why had he gone for help? Words such as depression, dullness and delusion were further bandied about but in vain. The jury were unconvinced, finding the prisoner guilty of murder after retiring for just forty minutes. The judge advised that he concurred with this and promptly passed sentence of death. The entire trial had taken less than a day.

Events continued to move quickly thereafter. There was no intention of keeping the condemned man or any of the other prisoners from Cumberland in Manchester a day longer than was necessary. On 4th December, 1876 they all arrived back at Carlisle railway station. Dalgleish was handcuffed and chained to two convicted burglars, James Clarke of Workington and William Fleming of Wigton. The sorry group were promptly returned to the city gaol.

Hugh Hagen had been despised by the majority of Cumbrians and few had been concerned to see him escape the scaffold irrespective of his state of mind. It had been left to a small minority who would now be contemptuously labeled 'do-gooders' to intervene successfully on his behalf. But now a much larger group of people headed by none other than Thomas Lumb got together at Penrith. In fact there was a lot of sympathy for James Dalgleish there. The bashful, shy young man described as muscular and of moderate height with a fresh complexion and profuse black beard had been well liked by those locals who had known him in happier times. A petition requesting mercy based on the former clerk's odd behaviour and signed among others by business people and various local gentry was now sent to the Principal Secretary of State but without result. Dalgleish was not destined to be accorded the mercy fairly recently afforded to Hugh Hagen. Indeed, it was intended that he be turned off before Christmas.

The condemned man appeared to have already accepted his fate. Tending to blame his past conduct on over-indulgence in alcohol but with a final admission of jealousy too in respect of Proctor, though still denying recollection of the crime itself, he was devoting himself conscientiously to his bible between writing to those he felt close to, especially Mary Fox, who took the magnanimous step of visiting him in Carlisle gaol. We know that he saw members of his immediate family too during this period, without breaking down. But did he still on occasion regret taking the high road to England? Or was he now on a thoroughly religious high as he annotated passages in his bible and spent hours on his devotions in a state smacking of complete mania....?

The ageing Calcraft had finally been compulsorily retired two years previously after forty-five years of hanging and flogging. With the young Scotsman's execution now fixed for 19th December, Askern of York was sent for. There is evidence that he was no more competent than Calcraft on occasions, even while possessed of an excellent opinion of his own abilities which he was known to air to those prepared to listen to the extent of total indiscretion in respect of his clientele.

The morning of the execution dawned raw and cold. A crowd of some eighteen hundred people gathered outside the gaol as the passing bell began to toll at seven forty-five a.m. Dalgleish had been busy with his devotions to the very last moment. Now as he finished singing 'Safe in the Arms of Jesus', Askern and his satellites moved quickly into the condemned cell. Evidently the prisoner was prepared to go quietly and this was a relief in itself. His arms were pinioned and he mounted the scaffold resolutely. The hood went over his head and he died without a struggle at eight a.m.

Outside in the street there was an element of farce. Hushed awe turned to derision as the black flag was thrown loosely over the top of the prison wall, the pulley of the flagpole refusing to work. Those hardier souls who had perched themselves on nearby roofs where they could see straight down in the gaol were especially disappointed, the execution having gone ahead in complete privacy in a secluded yard.

At nine a.m. the body was cut down and buried in lime, close to the remains of Thompson, Munroe, Cass and Charlton. Was Dalgleish as great in his villainy as the foregoing wretches appeared to have been in theirs? Surely not. He was undoubtedly a much sadder figure altogether. And his state of mind still has to remain greatly in question.

26: THE WIDOW'S SECRET

No sooner had James Dalgleish been despatched than Penrith erupted into the news once again with the discovery of a crime of a very different kind. The Kirkbride case, better known as the Penrith Horror, had its origins some miles off at Helton but first coming to light at Penrith, was named accordingly by some zealous reporter and the title stuck. Almost undoubtedly, it was a much more gruesome affair than the Dalgleish murder, tragic and violent though the latter had been, and kept the county and the countryside beyond agog for many weeks.

The Penrith connection had first came about in June 1876 when a forty-year-old widow, Elizabeth Kirkbride, approached the landlord of the town's Griffin Inn and asked if he would store a number of boxes for her until she was established with her son in the Liverpool area. Mrs. Kirkbride, a slightly-built, sharp-featured little woman, well-spoken and not unattractive, was known to have kept a school at Helton some seven miles from Penrith. Earlier in 1876 she had removed to Langwathby with the intention of opening a new school there but she was now so deeply in debt that her creditors had foreclosed upon her remaining assets and she had then resolved to move away and live with her eldest son, John, who had a situation on Merseyside. At that time Mrs. Kirkbride had been widowed some eleven years and had four sons. At least some of this the friendly landlord knew. He took the boxes and stored them in a lumber room at the inn. There they remained until January 1877, unclaimed and all but forgotten.

They might well have remained there even longer but for the fact that one of them began to give off an abominable smell. The box was opened and the body of a decomposing child was revealed. It was wrapped in rags and fully developed and appeared to have been strangled for there was a woman's garter about its neck. It had been dead for a fairly extended period. Further examination of the contents of another box revealed the body of a second child, in a state of some decay but still preserved enough to reveal crude attempts to cut its throat and with damage to a leg and shoulder blade; this apparently as a result of forcing the body down into the box. This second corpse seemed at a rough estimate to have been hidden away for some two years.

The stench had became appalling and those gathered in the lumber room recoiled in horror and disgust while struggling to fight back their nausea. Such was the opening scenario to a case which was one of the worst of its kind ever to hit Cumberland. But there was even worse to come.

Since the preceding June, Mrs. Kirkbride had remained domiciled with her eldest son and his sixteen-year-old brother in rented accommodation at Tuebrook, Liverpool. It took but little time to trace her and she was visited by the police on the Saturday evening following the discovery of the tiny corpses at Penrith. As it transpired she was in the house alone, where she had the sole use of the parlour, her sons living and sleeping upstairs but paying for their mother's accommodation along with their own. For the moment, Elizabeth Kirkbride was able to play for time. She denied everything but agreed to return to Penrith, only requesting that she be allowed to leave a note for her sons explaining her whereabouts but stressing that she did not want to add a great deal of detail to this as she was living in a respectable house. The police agreed. A note was left and the little party went on its way but remained in Liverpool for the moment, where it was intended to begin preliminary questioning.

Not until the following Monday did the landlady, Mrs. Orbeti, miss her lodger, who was given to spending most of her time alone doing needlework. The landlady had especial reason to seek out the widow on this occasion, namely suspicion of theft. In point of fact she had been wary of Mrs. Kirkbride from the very onset when the latter had arrived the previous summer to take up her tenancy bearing only an umbrella. There had been something not quite right about the woman in the opinion of the forthright landlady, the wife of a ship's steward. Elizabeth Kirkbride was obviously well-educated and cultured but had been evasive and ill at ease too. Not until two tin boxes arrived from Aintree did she appear more relaxed, though the boxes had remained unopened until now on the landing upstairs. More recently, the steward's wife had missed a coat and felt that only Elizabeth Kirkbride could have taken it. She suspected it could have been pawned. In that case she was not totally unsympathetic and was prepared to wait until it was redeemed. But a blanket and tablecloth had also gone missing. And now the suspect was nowhere to be found.....

Mrs. Orbeti was not a woman to dither. She waited until the widow's eldest son arrived home for lunch and confronted him with her suspicions. John Kirkbride was concerned and accepting that his mother could be guilty offered some glasses and books as surety, having explained that Mrs. Kirkbride had been called suddenly to Penrith, though he didn't know why? Yet the speed with which he accepted his mother's possible guilt still had to indicate his low opinion of the woman's integrity, whatever he may have thought about her untimely departure. As it was, the landlady wasn't satisfied with the glasses and books. Thereupon John Kirkbride took the immediate step of going to one of the tin boxes, breaking the lock and prising open the lid. He was assailed by a vile smell but attributed this to the dampness of the clothing within the box and did nothing more for his own part, returning to his work and leaving the landlady to claim what she wanted by way of additional surety.

The indefatigable Mrs. Orbeti had the box carried down into the yard and its contents were painstakingly removed and sorted through at great length. Very soon, a discovery was made which resulted in the box being taken to Liverpool mortuary. It was almost unbelievable but the box contained the decomposing corpses of no fewer than three infants, one with a piece of string tied tightly about its neck. All three corpses were at different stages of decomposition but such was the ongoing knowledge of anatomy that it was possible to establish a fairly revealing picture. All three children had been newly born. The best preserved had been hidden away for perhaps five years. The second corpse had no head but could have been there eight years; the third lay among clothing and carpets at the bottom of the box, close to the missing head of the second child, and was estimated to have been there for as long as a decade. An absolutely horrific state of affairs.

Why had these corpses remained undiscovered for so long? Like the remains found at Penrith they had passed through several hands of late in their resting places and had even remained for some time at Aintree Railway Station while Mrs. Kirkbride had been visiting in that area. But while the boxes at Penrith had eventually begun to give off sufficient stench to warrant investigation, without Mrs. Orbeti's quest for compensation, the tin boxes at Tuebrook might have remained closed and ignored indefinitely overall for the simple reason that they were so tightly sealed. Needless to say, the widow's secret was now out and she made a confession of sorts to the effect that the dead children were hers all right, that she had concealed them, but hadn't murdered them. She was to stick by this statement thereafter.

There were those who were astounded that she was in such trouble at all. It transpired that she had been the only daughter of very respectable people and unlike most of the poor unhappy women coming regularly before the courts in Cumberland and elsewhere for concealment and even murder of their offspring, had known wealth and education and some opportunity. Her father, John Hayton, had held a good post with Customs and Excise in Liverpool. Then he retired to live at Helton, near Penrith, where he resided with his wife in comfortable circumstances for several years. Meanwhile, their daughter had made an early marriage to a man named Kirkbride who held a good position in the prison service in the Liverpool area. The couple lived at Litherland Park, wanting for little. The marriage produced four sons and seemed to have been happy enough.

However, the whole scene changed when the husband died. Any income ended with him. The widow moved back in with her parents bringing the two older sons with her. The two younger sons went to live with their paternal grandparents. But Elizabeth Kirkbride's bad luck didn't end there. Soon her father also died and his estate may well have amounted to less than what was first supposed. At any rate, his daughter was fairly soon involved in opening a school at Helton whilst continuing to live with her mother who was to become an invalid soon enough, and destined to run deeply into debt.

Elizabeth may well have assisted in bringing her mother to poverty. However, this was never really suggested and the widow's evident ill fortune had to leave her deserving of some sympathy. But there was destined to be a seamier side to the dismal scenario too, quite titillating in an age of such hypocritical double standards. In sum, Mrs. Kirkbride appeared to have quickly struck up a clandestine relationship with a local man believed to be married, though living as she now did in an exceedingly rural district, she couldn't move too far afield without being conspicuous. This didn't seem to trouble her greatly. The widow took to spending considerable time away from her home at Helton, generally at night. She was often out until the early hours and became a not unfamiliar sight to the local bobby, stealthily traversing the country lanes as she commuted regularly to and from her home. Not only the policeman became aware of her. Others in the neighbourhood were equally observant and felt they knew the object of her journeying all right. But the couple never courted openly and had the babies' bodies not been discovered, the woman and her shady affair would probably have been quickly forgotten altogether once she had removed to Liverpool. As it was, all the original gossip was now reactivated.

Mrs. Kirkbride for her part had now chosen to make a statement which was duly promulgated. Since it does increase our knowledge of both major players apparently involved, to some degree, it is reproduced here in full, being short but not uninstructive. It read as follows:

> 'I want to tell you who is the father of all the children I am here about. His name is Thomas Moss and he is a tea and ham and bacon dealer at Askham, near Penrith. He is the only man I have had anything to do with in any way, and I think it is only right that he should be exposed as it is entirely by his own persuasion that I am placed as I am. He has always promised that he would make me his wife, and instead of doing so, when he was in a position to do so, he married another.'

The bitterness of Elizabeth Kirkbride is all too apparent and who could entirely blame her? The man himself, whose letterheads were ironically inscribed 'Be just and fear not' never did come forward to admit or deny his involvement with the shrewish little woman over a period of no less than a decade, though there were those in the locality who believed him to be involved all right. He merely undertook to have a solicitor in court to watch the proceedings and to represent his interests as necessary. Had Moss been an active accomplice? For some reason, no one seems to have tried to prove that he had even been the shadowy lover. He came over as a thoroughly despicable piece of work but succeeded in remaining totally in the shadows at the time.

Mrs. Kirkbride was much less fortunate. She continued to attract increasing odium by the day. Fairly soon she was brought back from Liverpool to Penrith by train. Travel by rail was of course a much slower process in those days and great crowds were assembled at every station en route, hopeful of catching a glimpse of the perpetrator of the Penrith Horror. There were derisive shouts and crude imitations of children's cries.

Only the previous day, the body of yet another infant had been discovered at the instigation of the woman's younger son, William. He had told the police that he recalled his mother burying something in the garden at Helton some six years previously. The grave was under a pear tree, the body was several years old and there was some talk of it having originally been thrown onto a midden. At the subsequent committal hearing, the above details were recounted with William Kirkbride, like his brother John, having no qualms about implicating his mother. They both appeared to loath the thin-faced little woman for what she had done, and the disgrace she had heaped upon them.

The police had been vigilant too after a fashion, now that the facts were out. They hadn't gone after Moss but were able to produce a former domestic servant of the family, Mary Agnes Forsyth, who spoke of having seen Elizabeth Kirkbride in bed at Helton with a child just over a decade previously. She had heard the cry of a child at the time, but admitted that her memory had dimmed....

Nevertheless, the widow remained in deep trouble. With insufficient will or evidence on the part of the authorities to put Moss into the dock and with herself saying nothing further against him, she was set fair to bear the full burden of guilt. On the other hand, though the emphasis was on infanticide as much as concealment, there still remained the limited medical know-how of the times. For the moment however, insofar as the populace was concerned there only remained the question of where she would be tried? Granted, the first two corpses had been discovered at Penrith and then there had been the find at Tuebrook, but the original births were all believed to have taken place at Helton which in those days lay in the ancient county of Westmorland, close to Penrith though it was. Before a courtroom filled to overflowing, it was decreed that the woman would be tried at Westmorland Assizes, in the town of Appleby.

The trial itself was not long in getting under way on 21st February, 1877. There were only five for trial in the normally mundane county court room, the widow of Helton proceeding another well born individual, twenty-six-year-old William Cranston accused of forgery, who received five years penal servitude. Many anticipated that Elizabeth Kirkbride's sentence would well exceed this and so perhaps did she, seated with eyes cast to the floor, in black bombasine, a veil shielding her face. In the light of the sunshine streaming into the court room, she looked pathetically shabby, a fallen gentlewoman who had known better days.

The sordid story unfolded. The return to Helton after widowhood, the abortive attempt at running a school, old Mrs. Hayton's failing health and eventual insolvency, the decision to remove to the village of Langwathby in Cumberland with the intention of opening another school. But Mrs. Hayton had died and her effects had been sold to satisfy her creditors. Her daughter had then made arrangements to remove to Liverpool and the rest is history. What was omitted was the apparent infatuation in respect of Thomas Moss over a considerable period and the consequences and his seeming act of abandonment and what had really happened to six helpless infants over no less than a decade.

The outcome of the trial proved a pathetic anti-climax. Despite the evidence of the garter about one child's neck and the fairly obvious attempt to cut the throat of another, as almost to be expected, the medical fraternity were not prepared to swear that any of the children had been born alive. We have to remember of course that this was 1877 and medical knowledge still had some way to progress. Therefore Mrs. Kirkbride was tried and convicted on charges of concealment only, like many of her poorer contemporaries. She was ordered to lift her veil and stand up and received a mere twenty-seven months imprisonment. The judge made no secret of his true feelings. Clearly he would have liked to have tailored the sentence to fit the crime as he saw it. But his hands were tied and he had to be satisfied with the delivery of a cutting verbal reprimand prior to the widow of Helton being taken below to commence her sentence.

It was a travesty of justice in the opinion of many. The widow's sentence was indeed light compared to that only recently imposed upon a woman in Carlisle for the theft of a single pair of trousers. Thirty-six-year-old Annie Gilthorpe received twelve months hard labour without any hope of remission of sentence and the prospect of the treadmill. Elizabeth Kirkbride for her part had wantonly concealed the births of six children; many also believed she had murdered them. On balance, she received less than six months imprisonment for each child when the going rate was two years maximum for each concealment proven of itself, even while few courts did go to the limit in this respect as we already know.

Many must have been frustrated and perplexed by the very ambiguity of Elizabeth Kirkbride. A gentlewoman fallen on hard times, yes, that they could accept. But she wasn't alone in that; ill fortune could strike anyone. On the other hand, fallen gentlewomen weren't normally committing adultery for ten years and more and hiding the results in their luggage, with the added suspicion of having taken the lives of their ill-begotten offspring beforehand.

So what was it with Elizabeth Kirkbride? Was she a woman merely seeking some kind of emotional and material stability following her widowhood? One who appeared let down by a suave scoundrel who merely wanted her body and who didn't care very much what happened to the fruits of their adultery, leaving her to get on with the disposal of it with a few cursory words of sly advice perhaps, as the need arose, and the dubious promise of future security. For her lover must surely have been aware of her repeated pregnancies assuming he was one and the same. Or was she a foolish woman who remained infatuated with her man and who was prepared to do anything to hold on to their relationship, keeping him largely in ignorance and taking it totally upon herself to dispose of their unwanted offspring as the need arose, whether or not the infants had lived beforehand? On the other hand, were the twosome no more than the victims of Victorian double standards, frightened to simply air their relationship as many would do today? Maybe, but they were apparently fornicating for more than ten years without any recourse to birth control and the relationship only ended following the arrival and dubious departure of at least six bastard children.

So much has to remain shrouded in ambiguity in this case and we shall never really be any wiser now but one major question remains unanswered amidst so many others. Namely, why didn't Elizabeth Kirkbride dispose of the bodies more efficiently? In fact, it did seem easier to go through the ritual of seduction, pregnancy and childbirth without detection than to actually dispose of an unwanted result, whoever the parent might be, in Cumberland or anywhere else in Britain in those days, whether or not the child was born alive or dead. Needless to say many mothers did come clean anyhow, but others were given to secreting their dead offspring in hiding places as divergent as dresser drawers and coal cellars where sooner or later the little corpses came to light as was almost inevitable. Perhaps so many of the betrayed women simply wanted something to hang on to, whether or not they had killed their bastard children, the maternal instinct overriding the fear of disgrace and punishment. Some may even have subconsciously desired the concealed bodies to be found. But who can really tell?

Meanwhile, Elizabeth Kirkbride disappeared off the scene. Being well-educated and reportedly speaking several languages, she possibly became something of a personality in prison, aiding her survival there. However, given the female psyche, the opposite more likely applied, rendering the widow of Helton a complete pariah among those she must have formerly deemed her inferiors when her husband had been alive and well and serving as a prison officer. Many may well have already given her a rough time while she had been in gaol on remand once her celebrity status diminished, her antagonists including keepers as well as other inmates.

As for Moss, though he had been careful to stay clear of the prisoner throughout the furore, he was not destined to escape unscathed. Though the law had proved unequal to the task of pulling him in, he was judged by his peers and punished almost as severely as the widow. He was completely ostracized. His Askham business was boycotted. He tried to sell it without success and eventually left the area a ruined man. Thus justice of a sort was at least seen to be done all round.

27: THE MAGNATE AND THE CHIMNEY SWEEP

We have already seen how hostile local court audiences could be when they deemed a decision to be wrong, but how swiftly they could show their approval too. This was a not uncommon state of affairs in Britain as a whole in the nineteenth century and before, as indeed, it can still be today. But Victorian courts could be the scene of some hilarity too on occasions, as also noted in passing, with the courts becoming almost akin to theatres. Cumberland in particular lent itself to this sort of thing with its quite unique brand of droll earthy humour. True, this may have verged on the banal and insensitive at times. However, it was also aligned to a profound pleasure in seeing the so-called better people humbled when possible, which many deemed no bad thing.

A classic case of this was that of John Musgrave versus Michael Crawley at Whitehaven Petty Sessions on 26th July, 1877. Musgrave was a man of some position and wealth in the town as well as being Chairman of the Harbour Trustees. The latter was a role which he performed with especial zeal to the extent of patrolling the harbour and putting up notices, warning against the dumping of rubbish in the water or along the harbour embankment. Crawley was a chimney sweep with a record of petty offending but not without friends in the locality among his own kind.

On the evening of 12th July, 1877, around eight thirty, Musgrave and his right hand man, Hodgson, were walking along the waterfront when they observed Crawley emptying a bag of soot over the embankment. Musgrave was incensed. He thought he recognised the chimney sweep from a time when he had employed him to sweep his own chimney but couldn't be certain. At any rate, he proceeded to ask him his name? Crawley gave it, or so he was to maintain. Musgrave then instructed Hodgson to fetch a policeman. No sooner had the latter departed than Crawley took off also, advising that he must collect his tools lest he lose them.

This didn't satisfy Musgrave. He followed the chimney sweep who began to run. Anger mounting, Musgrave also quickened his pace. He was carrying a heavy stick. He struck Crawley across the shoulders, then brought him down with a blow to the head, the impetus of this bringing him down on top of the unfortunate sweep. His prior cry of 'Stop Sweep' had attracted the attention of some who might otherwise have been less observant. Matters moved on from there to the Petty Sessions.

Since Musgrave was so well known in Whitehaven and Crawley had his own friends and supporters, the courtroom was filled to capacity, more-so since the chimney sweep had taken out his own summons against the magnate and was seeking to outdo him. A subscription had been raised for him in the town by a fellow sweep, bringing in sufficient money to pay for an able defence counsel: J.W. Clark of Lancaster. Musgrave was defended by a Mr. Howson who though possessing skills enough, was to prove much less eloquent than the subtle Mr. Clark.

From the onset, Clark provided his own kind of entertainment, set to please the crowd, while also irking Musgrave. It transpired that he knew the latter to the extent that they had been old friends – he now apologised but felt in sum that he was compelled to do his duty and appear for a humble young man of Whitehaven, a chimney sweep. Loud laughter filled the court. Crawley may have been badly used by Musgrave and of lowly status but humble he had never been, given that he had several past convictions and was no stranger to that very courtroom.

As it was, he played the injured party for all the role was worth, advising peevishly of the week he had lost off work following the assault. He spoke of having gone three times to the infirmary but that there had never been a doctor available. He hadn't noticed the gentleman's stick at the start, but his shoulders had felt it!

More laughter and the tale unfolded in full.

Clark made a suggestion implying that Musgrave might now be conscience-stricken if a fine were too small?

The magnate made no reply to this but the laughter continued unchecked.

Glibly the chimney sweep's lawyer noted the apparent feeling in Whitehaven that his client might not get a fair hearing today but he was sure that he would. He had once been before a court himself and that had been far worse and so his old friend shouldn't feel too badly.

Crawley was at pains to let the court know that he had borrowed money to get a summons, that he hadn't known of the subscription then. He had heard that Musgrave was taking out a summons against him and had simply made up his mind to do the same.

Witnesses were called who testified to the blows received by the unfortunate Crawley. Asked if a particular blow was hard or soft, the first witness said she didn't know as she hadn't felt it!

Further laughter, the crowd appearing to find the whole business hilarious. And yet Crawley obviously had been quite badly-used by the irate magnate.

The sweep appeared to be winning though. When his friend James Sharp was called to confirm the assault, the best Howson could do for his client was to query waspishly off Sharp if he expected to get anything from the subscription fund.

Amidst more laughter, Sharp retorted blandly that he didn't know. Would in fact such a question have ever been tolerated in a court in these times?

Not to be outdone, Howson proceeded to advise the bench of Crawley's previous convictions, some fourteen in all.

The sweep butted in to affirm that he didn't have as many convictions as that.

Howson tried again, speaking of the notices prohibiting the dumping of rubbish which at times had been deliberately flouted. He argued that Crawley had given a false name to his client. Evidence of the sweep's dishonesty surely? He further felt that Crawley had been influenced by others in taking out a summons against Musgrave.

The magnate had became so indignant that he made matters worse for himself. Called to give evidence he said that he had hit the chimney sweep all right, but had been sure the latter had been resolved to hit him. He made it known that he would do the same again under the same circumstances with no indication at all of regret.

Clark quipped that he hoped he would be fined more each time then. It seemed unlikely that he and Musgrave would resume their former intimacy in the light of all this.

The magnate was still unrepentant. He admitted to felling Crawley but emphasised that it was a matter of getting in first.

The bench were unimpressed. They fined Musgrave £4, a considerable amount of money in those days, with loud applause throughout the court.

Crawley didn't get off totally. He was fined ten shillings and costs for dumping his soot. But beyond doubt it was his day. Justice could probably be said to have been done against initial odds, leaving aside the sweep's blatant unconcern for the environment, while the public had had a first-rate time with Victorian justice having proved to be not totally weighted against the underdog.

28: STARVATION OF A CHILD

Just as several obnoxious episodes dealt with in these pages have been the result of heavy drinking, so others have involved the deaths of children. Some of the latter could have happened anywhere. The death of little Sarah Crosby at Lamonby probably was the result of parental incompetence and instability, irrespective of the confusion surrounding her final demise. There were plenty of flawed parents in Britain overall; indeed there still are. The Hagen tragedy for its part was a prime case of murder out of mind but such a crime was not confined to Cumberland either. And the Kirkbride case, more complex though it was, had its origins outside the county.

But Cumberland did have more than its share of vulnerable girls and illegitimate births which made for regular ongoing tragedy within its boundaries as already noted. Such crimes unfortunately continued to be compounded by an archaic poor law and the sheer grinding poverty of the times, even as the century moved into its ninth decade. The case of Sarah Jane Lees illustrates this better than most, resulting in a verdict which would appear to indicate that the court was especially aware of all the foregoing dynamics.

Sarah Jane appeared at Carlisle Assizes in January, 1880 following the death of her child in a rural area of West Cumberland the previous October. The twenty-year-old domestic servant was single, semi-literate and unsupported, a not untypical example of the kind of poor wretch being arrested year after year in Cumberland and beyond and charged with the wilful murder of their illegitimate offspring, only to have the charge usually watered down to one of concealment. But in this instance there could be no question of concealment. Sarah Jane's child was one of those which had definitely lived. For sixteen months she had actually supported it, getting on with her humdrum life and the additional duties of motherhood, with no apparent hope at all of any ongoing support from the child's father.

Now however, it was alleged that the mother had deliberately neglected the legal duty placed upon her to provide for her child's needs which included the provision of food and the child had died. The prosecution had built up a quite formidable case against her. Given that she was being tried for manslaughter there wasn't any question of her facing execution in the event of a guilty verdict. No woman had ever been hanged in Cumberland that century and there did appear to be a reluctance to hang them there in any case. But she was still in trouble and being of obviously sound mind she couldn't shelter behind a defence of insanity. Yet even now, there was some perceptible feeling for her as there was for so many of her kind. She had no one to defend her but Lord Justice Brett instructed a lawyer by the name of Dickinson to take up her case.

There was nothing particularly sinister about Sarah Jane Lees. She was just another victim of circumstances. She had given birth to her illegitimate child in the summer of 1878 and there must have been some support at the onset for the infant had thriven well enough. Perhaps she had been in the workhouse then where at least there were rations of a sort. But in the summer of 1879 she had again been making herself available for work. A major obstacle had been the child, debarring her from most domestic employment. The only alternative was to work in the fields but this paid no more than 6s. a week. However, she had little choice. She went to live with a Mrs. Middleton near Gosforth who was also agreeable to catering for the child at an overall cost of 4s. a week. But this left little spare money and mother and child soon moved in with a Mrs. Carrol who charged 2s. a week, or 10 pence in today's currency.

This latter move proved a retrograde step. Mrs. Carrol already had four children, three of her own aged eleven years, nine years and five months respectively, plus someone else's child of nursing age which she professed to look after. She provided some food for Sarah's child but could not promise that such would always be available. Nor was she always available herself. Care of the younger children generally appeared to be left to the eleven and nine year olds while she and her lodger went away to work all day in the fields, it seeming perfectly acceptable for such young children to be left in charge when they ought really to have been in school.

Three months later, Sarah Jane Lees returned with her child to Mrs. Middleton but a drastic change was noted in its condition. It was sickly and wasted and within three days it was dead. The mother was apprehended while at the doctor's seeking medicine. She cried out and accused Mrs. Carrol as being equally to blame upon being advised of her child's death.

In court, a dismal picture emerged of a deprived child but of an unjust and inequal society too. The woman, Carrol, spoke of the girl leaving food for her child when she could afford to do so from her weekly pittance while she herself provided bread and milk in the evenings. But indications were that the eleven and nine-year-old were all too often away playing when they were expected to be looking to all three dependent children's needs. It was interesting nevertheless that the child most deprived of food had been the prisoner's child. The other two children appeared to have been thriving well enough. And Sarah Jane had complained to Mrs. Middleton that one of the Carrol girls had been cruel to her child. Yet still she had rejected Mrs. Carrol's suggestion that she and the child go into the workhouse, while also declining to take her infant to the doctor's, but this was simply because she had had no money.

The doctor, when he was finally called, found the child to be very weak. Shortly afterwards it died, he believed for want of adequate nourishment. Witnesses spoke of the mother at one time cursing the child in her frustration and wishing its breath had been stopped and shaking it. It did seem a very bad case of neglect but who overall was to blame? Could Sarah Jane herself be held fully responsible for a state of affairs which clearly reflected so badly on Victorian Britain as a whole, and which would continue for some time yet.

The jury had little doubt in their minds. Without specifically blaming anything or anybody and having heard the defending lawyer out, they promptly returned a verdict of not guilty and the mother left the court.

29: AN EVIL ACQUIREMENT

The Sprunston Farm murders of 1881 are of particular interest in that we have seen some disturbing parallels in our own times. They also led to the only death sentence ever being passed on a female in Cumberland throughout the nineteenth century and beyond. And that female was only fourteen years old.

When Mr. and Mrs. John Palliser of Sprunston Farm, Durdar, acquired teenager Margaret Messenger as a servant and nanny to their three children, Margaret, Mark and Elsie, early in June, 1881, she came well recommended. Described as a 'strong-looking girl with an intelligent appearance' she was the second eldest in a family of six, the youngest being but two years old. Her family were hard-working respectable people; her father was the foreman of a local chalk works in the Wigton area. Her mother spoke of Margaret as being well used to children and of having brought one up, presumably one of her own younger siblings. Both parents recommended her to the Pallisers. Less was made of the fact that she could be of sullen disposition on occasions. She appeared to fit well into her new home and was only reprimanded once, for teasing her charges. The farmer and his wife may well have felt that they could have chosen much worse. Unfortunately, all was to change within just a few weeks, leaving the family bereft and devastated.

The scene of the crimes lay some six miles west of Carlisle in the vicinity of Raughton Head and the Pallisers had been there for three years, previously living in Westmorland. Both their younger children had been born at the Durdar farm. On 25th June, 1881 the first tragedy occurred. Messenger had care of two-year-old Mark. She cried out that he had been drowned in the farm well and carried the child's dead body back to the house. Perhaps surprisingly, she invited no suspicion whatsoever. Her word was believed to the extent that there was but a cursory enquiry and a verdict of 'accidentally drowned' was returned. When Messenger remarked almost blithely that they wouldn't need to clean little Mark's clogs any more no one appeared offended. Nor did she invite criticism for having been in any way negligent in her supervision of the child.

The parents, though not unnaturally grieved at the loss of their only son, still in fact trusted their teenage servant sufficiently to leave her in charge of their two surviving children when they departed for Carlisle market on 2nd July, no more than a week after Mark's death. They merely cautioned her to be vigilant and leave other work aside with a view to giving additional attention to four-and-half-year-old Margaret and the six-month-old baby, Elsie. It might have been more appropriate for Mrs. Palliser to have remained behind, given recent events, at least for the moment, if only to afford her eldest child some continuing emotional support following the death of her brother. But she carried on as normal and the result was double tragedy.

Within hours of the couple's departure, Messenger was making further outcry. Apparently the baby was missing. The hired lad, George Haffen, was working in a nearby field. He heard Messenger raise the alarm and the sound of a child screaming. He hurried to the scene and little Margaret Palliser told him that a man had taken Elsie. Margaret Messenger confirmed this but Haffen felt that they were having him on and returned to his work. Perhaps the lad wasn't too bright but both he and his employers had erred now. Haffen might just have saved the infant's life had he investigated the situation there and then. But like the Pallisers, and others, he had failed to appreciate the evil of the girl acquired so innocently at the hiring fair less than a month previously.

Presently it was close to break time and Haffen cast his eyes back towards the house. To his surprise he saw the nanny carrying the inert body of a child. He raced to a neighbouring farm, genuinely alarmed now and alerted the farmer's wife there, a Mrs. Storey. She was quickly on the scene. The child was little Elsie and the woman made some attempt to revive her, the body being still warm, but it was too late. Messenger stood calmly by. She had spoken of finding the child face down in a bog with a stone upon its head and indeed, its mouth was full of soil.

The parents were sent for, and the police. The former arrived back fairly quickly but were too shocked to make much of the situation. It was left to Mrs. Storey and her husband to delve further into the affair at that stage. The bog mentioned by Messenger was close to the well where Mark had died. The farmer went there. There were footprints all around it and a huge stone. Storey wasn't satisfied with Messenger's story, no doubt recalling the recent death of the first child. He challenged her bluntly and she burst into tears and said she would tell the truth.

By the time Superintendent Sempill arrived later in the afternoon, the Storeys were convinced that they knew who the killer was. But in fact Messenger had already told a number of contradictory stores: that a man with a straw hat had taken the child away, that she had been sitting outdoors with the child and fallen asleep and awoken to find it gone and had then found it near the well. Presumably the older sister had been primed to say that a man had been involved but no more was made of this. There was no need. Messenger was now to reveal that she had acted alone and that no one else had helped her. But she didn't reveal the reason why…?

Sempill was especially interested in the bog and the footprints around it. Casts were made of the latter and Messenger's clogs were taken away for closer inspection. The footprints were found to match the clogs. There were no others. The stone alleged to have been on the baby's head was almost as big as a man's head. Elsie had obviously been weighted down and suffocated in the mud. It was one of the most horrible crimes recalled by anyone in Cumberland, the murder of a child by a girl little more than a child herself. And Messenger was also to admit that it was she who had put Mark in the well.

At her trial in November, 1881 she pleaded not guilty to wilful murder but remained quite composed throughout. The whole sordid story was told yet again to a crowded court – it had already received wide coverage in the press. It was a comparatively short trial and the prosecution could offer no reason for the killing of two innocent children. The defence was equally impotent. The jury took only ten minutes to find the prisoner guilty but recommended her to mercy on account of her youth. Thereupon the judge sentenced her to death, having indicated in his summing up that he too had felt her to be guilty all along and there were many among the public who would doubtless have been pleased to see her atone for her ghastly deed, young though she was.

But the death sentence proved to be a mere formality in this instance. Though there had been no mention of insanity to date, it must have remained a matter of prime consideration in Messenger's case, even while it had still been deemed irrelevant in the case of James Dalgleish no more than five years previously. Fairly soon, Dr. Orange of Broadmoor was called in to interview the big strong-looking girl from Wigton, who had kept in regular touch with her family and developed into a chatty letter writer. She was a model prisoner, polite to all those about her, enjoying her food and sleeping well.

Perhaps realising that it was in her long-term interests, she proceeded to make her fullest confession yet to the visiting psychiatrist. She appeared to have seen most of those about her as spies or enemies but ever cautious in her speech, afforded the doctor no tangible motive for killing the Palliser children themselves. She was nevertheless deemed a candidate for either Broadmoor or Parkhurst and promptly vanished from public sight.

What of the actual diagnosis here? In some respects, big Maggie was not unakin to others of her class in those times. She had, it appeared, been a maid of all work to her younger siblings, bringing up one child in particular virtually single-handed, and may never have experienced a real childhood. She had then been rudely parted from her natural family at an early age to cater for other children, not even her own flesh and blood.

Thus there may well have been an element of emotional deprivation to begin with, albeit which most of her kind simply had to contend with. In this case on the other hand, mental illness undoubtedly had to take precedence. Could Messenger have been the victim of a personality disorder, or worse, paranoid schizophrenia? Dr. Orange's report is not available to us but the latter possibility does appear the more feasible. Unfortunately however, any diagnosis had came too late to save the lives of two defenceless children. In our own century and not too long ago, we have of course seen Messenger's likes before the courts, presenting symptoms just as ambiguous for offences equally as tragic. Hopefully, such cases may continue to remain at a minimum. Certainly they can occur in any place or in any century but whether we do have any more answers now than we had in Cumberland back in 1881 must remain questionable.

30: BENEATH A HEAP OF STONES

When sixteen-year-old Lucy Sands disappeared on the Thursday evening of 1st December, 1881 there was no furore. She had been with sixteen-year-old Jane Shannon and fifteen-year-old Margaret Cranney on a visit to Maynard Harrison, son of a manager at the West Cumberland Ironworks at Northside, Workington. Seventeen-year-old Harrison had taken the three girls on a tour of the ironworks and then into his parents' garden for some fifteen minutes. About eight forty five p.m. Lucy left them, saying she had to meet a local boy, Billy Wilson. Presently Cranney drifted off, leaving Shannon alone with Harrison with whom she was having a relationship. Then she too departed, it appeared around nine thirty p.m. and joined up again with Cranney, leaving her boy friend headed in the direction of his own house.

Later, a local woman, Hannah Gibson, was to claim that she had seen Lucy standing alone around nine p.m. on the fatal evening, in the vicinity of Harrison's house. As matters evolved, there was in fact to be a lot of uncertainty about precise times and deeds and utterances. But what was certain thereafter was that Lucy Sands was never seen alive again after being sighted by Mrs. Gibson, except by the person or persons who murdered her.

Meanwhile however, no one thought to report her missing. Lucy had lived with her grandmother, Sarah Stewart, a church cleaner, in Christian Street, Workington. The latter remained oddly silent though at the onset, may simply have been relieved to be done with her granddaughter. She had taken the orphaned girl and her younger brother in to live with her some years previously. Lucy had proved flighty and increasingly uncontrollable. Mrs. Stewart was to say that she had thought her granddaughter had gone elsewhere to work, the girl having already been in service in Liverpool, and that she had found a husband. By that time she was grief-stricken and probably regretted not having gone to the authorities in the first instance. But it was then too late. As it was, any possible clues had became virtually obsolete when the girl's body was finally discovered early the following March.

The corpse might have remained hidden even longer but for a roadmender who had begun operations on the Northside highway close to Workington Bridge Railway Station and not too far from the West Cumberland Ironworks. Requiring material for his task he went to a heap of stones by the roadside and removed several of them, then recoiled in horror at the sight of a human foot. He promptly raised the alarm. The stones were cleared away. The corpse which was to be identified as that of Lucy Sands was revealed, laid straight out with the hands by the sides and the head turned to the left. Since there were no boots on the girl's feet, these were already beginning to rot away. But wounds were still just discernible on the head and face.

A full-scale enquiry ensued following identification and it did not take the police long to focus their full attention on Maynard James Harrison. The body had been discovered on 1st March, 1882. Harrison was questioned closely within days. He confirmed that Lucy Sands had visited him with Jane Shannon and Margaret Cranney on the evening of her disappearance but denied seeing her again after the trio had all gone. He spoke of reporting a faulty furnace to his father before going to bed at ten thirty p.m. and of not being out of the house again that night. He afforded a full description of the victim's clothing on the fatal evening, including her navy blue stockings. Superintendent Taylor of Cockermouth at once picked him up on this – how had he known the colour of the stockings? For in 1881, dresses were still below ankle length. Harrison quickly explained that he had playfully grabbed the victim by the leg while they had all been in the garden.

This was all well and good but others questioned were saying contradictory things, or advising of dubious remarks the young man had made to them before and after the discovery of Lucy's body. Some of these things appeared exceedingly suspicious. The police became convinced that Harrison could be the killer. On 9th March, 1882 he was arrested and charged on suspicion of having wilfully murdered Lucy Sands. He burst out crying and said he needed to see his mother but she wasn't at hand. When she did appear, the situation was put to her, and to her husband. Maynard Harrison's bedroom was searched. A six-chambered revolver was discovered and a pair of carefully washed blue serge trousers. These articles were taken away for further examination while Harrison remained in custody.

The inquest on Lucy Sands was moved from the Bridge Railway Station to the Green Dragon Hotel, Workington, close the victim's home, on 14th March, 1882. Ironic how most inquests continued to be held at inns and hotels when there still remained so much drunkenness in Victorian Britain, the cause of so many crimes. In this case, a number of facts emerged which had first been uttered in drink. However, the latter was seemingly not the prime force as it had been in other Cumbrian killings. The background dynamics here were much more complex. Harrison himself was present at the Green Dragon, looking much more self assured and detached by this time, of average height, slim, fair-haired and not unattractive. He listened carefully to the witnesses.

The first to be called was the then seventeen-year-old dressmaker, Jane Shannon. She confirmed the visit she, Margaret Cranney and Lucy Sands had paid to Harrison on 1st December, 1881 and of events then, prior to Lucy's departure. It was to Shannon that the prisoner had presently mentioned that the missing girl was in Preston, and then Liverpool. More recently, since the discovery of the body, he had spoken oddly, advising her that she must say that he grabbed Lucy by the leg on the night they were all last together. Shannon didn't seem to grasp the possible reason for this and it was to transpire that she had seen him do no such thing.

Margaret Cranney hadn't a great deal of importance to offer for her part, beyond confirming the visit to Harrison on 1st December, concluding in the garden and Lucy's subsequent departure. She said that she had seen Harrison 'swinging Lucy about'. Hence he might of course have glimpsed the colour of the girl's stockings then. But she made no mention of Lucy having been grabbed by the leg.

Jane Shannon, as Harrison's ongoing girl friend, had continued to see him and appeared privy to his more personal side. She admitted knowing that he had possessed a revolver, and a knife, but still seemed to feel he was innocent of any offence. What she and Cranney were both definitely agreed upon however, was that neither of them had actually seen Harrison enter his home on 1st December, 1881 after taking their leave.

Billy Wilson, a local marble mason, caused some of those present to look further askance at Harrison and the two girls when he swore that he hadn't seen Lucy Sands for a week prior to her disappearance and that she had never promised to meet him on the night of 1st December. He was able to prove that he had been in other company on the night in question.

The inquest continued, with a stream of witnesses going on to speak detrimentally of Harrison. Two teenage girls, Alice Atkinson and Liz Smith, formerly employed as house servants by his parents, spoke of the youth arriving home during the early hours around the time of the killing and endeavouring to get into his bedroom via the wash house roof. Others of his peer group were still more damning. One of them, Thomas Rosser, alleged that Harrison had drunkenly confided, following the discovery of the body, that he was last with Lucy that night. Harry Mainprize, a young apprentice, spoke of Harrison recently saying that he had arranged with Lucy that she should stay on after Shannon and Cranney left. To another teenager, Henry Kerr, he had seemingly divulged shortly after Lucy's disappearance that she was in the family way and had gone to Preston, appearing to know something others didn't know. To yet another youth, Tony Daglish, Harrison had allegedly said: "Poor bugger, she's gone the road that a good deal such as her would go". If true, not much evidence of genuine sympathy and even less respect for the victim as a person, whether or not he was directly implicated in her demise.

Yet it had already been queried if one person could have committed the crime anyhow? It was felt that the body might well have been dragged some distance to its eventual resting place beside the main road, with fairly considerable effort being required to heap the stones about it. Harrison had also been proved a liar in that Lucy hadn't been pregnant, nor was there evidence of sexual violation And there was ambiguity as to what weapon had been used to perpetrate the evil deed, given the extent of decomposition and the fact that no weapon had been found. Fast Maynard wasn't out of the wood yet however.

The inquest finally drew to its close. It had gone on for nearly nine hours. Outside the hotel hundreds of local people awaited the findings. Others had been packed inside the building. The verdict was one of wilful murder against some person or persons unknown. But it was stressed that the police were to make further enquiries and there was no question of Harrison being released. The crowd applauded. Workington it should be said, had grown greatly from the early nineteenth century when the population had stood then at less than six thousand and had taken in part of Harrington, due in no small part to iron and steel. But the population there and in outlying towns and villages was still small and concentrated enough to have remained intimate with local affairs and there was anger and indignation over the whole Sands business.

All three girls: Sands, Shannon and Cranney had already came in for considerable criticism for their conduct on the evening of 1st December, 1881. In Cumberland or anywhere else in Victorian Britain, it just wasn't considered proper for three teenage girls to be carrying on as they had been doing then, even though such conduct might be deemed more acceptable in these times.

Nevertheless, there was still considerable concern over the fate of Lucy too. There may also have been some criticism of the girl's grandmother for not reporting her disappearance in the first instance. But all in all, the local public sympathised with Mrs. Stewart and the victim to some degree. A flighty girl had came to grief but she hadn't deserved what had befallen her. Opinions remained mixed but many appeared sure that they knew who the culprit was: Maynard James Harrison, the wayward spoilt offspring of parents who ought to have kept him under greater control.

At the onset, it must indeed have seemed to many that the suspect would quickly be exposed to the extent that he would be brought fully to book and despite his youth, even go the way of Thomas Munroe. But though Harrison was soon remanded again following a hasty court appearance, it became increasingly apparent that there was a dearth of evidence to link him positively to the crime. Lucy Sands had died as a result of blows to the head; this was definitely established. It was considered that she had been placed beneath the heap of stones either after she was dead or shortly before. But it still remained uncertain as to what had caused the fatal wounds, revolver, knife or otherwise, even though the suspect had possessed both the former. And the place of death itself was still unknown. To date, any evidence against Harrison had to be very much circumstantial, still heavily dependent on careless talk and chance sightings. And by this time he was capably defended. His parents had seen to that. From now onwards the police would have an uphill struggle.

They did persevere. Harrison appeared in court again at Workington on 31st March, 1882 and there was further protracted examination of witnesses. The prisoner had already threatened the youth, Mainprize, as he had been led back to the cells the previous Saturday, seemingly angry that the latter had spoken ill of him then without justification.... For some reason, most of Harrison's peer group appeared to dislike him.

A much more damning testimony came from yet another acquaintance of the prisoner's: Evan Jones. He stated that on the day Lucy Sands' body was discovered, he had gone for a drink with Harrison and the latter's aunt in a local public house. Jones remarked that it was strange the body should have laid so long on the public highway. To which the prisoner had apparently said knowingly that he knew the body was lying there all along. And indeed, the victim's hat had been discovered weeks earlier near Harrison's garden, though it might have been left there early on the fatal evening of course, by the girl herself. Ever there were such contradictions and uncertainties. Her footwear meanwhile never had been discovered. And no one questioned could suggest why it had gone missing in the first place?

The prosecution also produced a young woman, Dorothy Grant. She claimed to have met Harrison out on the road between Workington and Harrington on the evening of 21st December, 1881. Harrison had spoken ambiguously of a girl having had her boots and hat taken off by two men but there was the suggestion that the witness could have been drunk. However, her husband, William, confirmed the tale. This again was damning enough evidence after a fashion.

Sam Lees testified that in late February, 1882, Harrison had shown him a knife with a nine inch blade and spoken of making a mess of anyone who tried to assault him. Then finally the proceedings were adjourned again and the suspect was taken back to the cells.

By the time he appeared again on 7th April the rumour mill had gone into top gear, to the effect that he had made a full confession. Hundreds had again gathered, spilling out beyond the small local court room. They were destined to be disappointed. No confession had been made. Indeed, the entire proceedings on this occasion wore a distinct air of anti-climax.

The two teenage servants, Atkinson and Smith, had been recalled again. Alice Atkinson testified that she had definitely seen the prisoner out on the wash house roof in the early hours requesting to be admitted. But she couldn't fix a date. Elizabeth Smith was equally vague. She had seen Harrison out on the roof but couldn't confirm that he had ever asked them to let him in. She seemed to recall that he had only waved his hand. Another small discrepancy perhaps, but important enough for the defence solicitor, Paisley, to seize upon. Nor would Smith confirm that she had seen any blood stains on the prisoner's blue serge trousers, which hadn't in fact been washed until the following February. With the witness Henry Kerr's reliability having also been brought into question, the prosecution's case was looking decidedly weak by this time. Harrison was committed for trial at the forthcoming assizes nonetheless, Shannon and Cranney being jeered and hooted as they left the building. All in all, no less than thirty-three witnesses had been called.

Came the grand finale. Some were still anticipating a full trial and a conviction. Yet perhaps it didn't come as a total surprise when the teenager was discharged by a grand jury at Carlisle on 18th April, 1882. There was simply insufficient evidence to proceed further with any certainty at the time and no one else was ever charged.

So who really did kill Lucy Sands? Was it the works manager's scapegrace son? The police evidence against him was far from wanting. He had attempted to get Jane Shannon to lie in his defence. He had no tangible alibi and had been seen abroad in the early hours around the time of the victim's disappearance on several occasions, which may have included 1st December, 1881. Likewise he could well have arranged to be with Lucy Sands after Shannon and Cranney had gone for the story she had told about meeting Billy Wilson had proved to be a total falsehood. And hadn't she been seen in the vicinity of Harrison's door some time after her supposed departure, while he himself had gone on to make mindless statements about her before and after the disappearance, including the disclosure that he had known she was under the stones all along.

Especially intriguing was the statement by Dorothy Grant, that she had met Harrison on 21st December when he had spoken of a girl having had her boots and hat removed by two men. Was he referring to Lucy Sands? If so, he appeared to know something of what was later to be revealed, even while at that time, the girl's body was still entombed, indicating that he might well have worked in partnership. It wasn't particularly difficult to pinpoint a motive either. Lucy had had the reputation of being a loose girl but could merely have been a tease and might well have died protecting her honour.

Yet there were questions to set against all the foregoing too. In an age when young people were usually expected to grow up rather more quickly, Maynard Harrison clearly remained an immature personality, as well as a braggart and a know-all. His grandfather and father were both respectable people who had attained positions of responsibility in the workaday world of West Cumberland. But Maynard was described in court as imperfectly instructed. He obviously hadn't made much of his education. He had gone early to sea but hadn't stuck it there. At the time of his arrest the only work he had been able to find was labouring in a local steelworks. Over-indulged to begin with, and drinking too much, he might simply have talked himself into trouble with half-baked unsubstantiated utterances and indeed, we already know that Lucy wasn't pregnant. Nor, as already indicated, might she have been quite so loose as Harrison had made her out to be, bragging at one stage to Mainprize of arranging for the girl to stay behind 'so that he could have a damned good ride out of her before she went away to Liverpool', but panicking when eventually confronted by the police and prepared to use anyone to get him off the hook.

The couple could well have been alone together on the evening of 1st December, 1881, when she could have lost her hat. Harrison might well have been out on the wash house roof afterwards. But what did this prove? There was no evidence to confirm the hour or date Lucy Sands had died, or where she had died. Opinion had it that she could have been murdered in a dark gully in the nearby Northside Hills and transferred manually to her final resting place. But if so, could Harrison, a youth of poor physique, have dragged or carried her back any distance on his own, after supposedly killing her, even though she was fairly small, a mere five feet and one inch tall. Two men might have done so, as had already been suggested at the inquest, leading some to suppose that Harrison could have operated in partnership. But what real evidence was there of this, Dot Grant's testimony being insufficient of itself and afforded little lasting credibility, though some might argue that it merited rather more scrutiny at the time.

Had Harrison even the nerve to go to extremes? All indications are that he was a rather pathetic individual altogether, not particularly robust or popular with his peer group, with evidence of a marked inferiority complex. Hence the revolver and the knife, and his need to talk big in front of the opposite sex and others. And yet, he never weakened under police pressure to the extent that he made any kind of detrimental statement either...... And that pressure was probably quite considerable at the onset, without any access whatsoever to a solicitor then.

But who else could have been the killer if not Maynard James Harrison? To better ponder this a study of the immediate area of the crime has to be relevant. Today the Northside highway is a fast modern route in and out of Workington, carrying motorised traffic to and from the north west. The site of the heap of stones is overlooked by a housing estate spread out over the Northside Hills. The former West Cumberland Ironworks half a mile up the road have long gone along with the adjacent railway line and the Bridge Station. Only the River Derwent remains much as it was on the lower side of the highway. Traffic aside, the place is fairly tranquil and pleasant.

In 1881 it had to be different. The road was busy enough then given that the ironworks, railway station and docks weren't too far off, but it would probably be less well maintained, with a greater abundance of casual pedestrians. It must also have been lonelier and darker at night and that particular stretch of highway had an unpleasant reputation, even while many had little choice but to use it. About the time Lucy Sands vanished, a man had tried to drag a girl into the gully opposite the heap of stones but had been interrupted and dashed away into the darkness. Another girl had been raped in the same vicinity shortly afterwards.

Thus while still allowing for other possibilities, Lucy could just as easily have been the victim of a local deviant perhaps, as she hurried back home towards Workington town centre following a covert half hour with Harrison, traversing the dark stretch of road with its bushes and trees and brooding mass of high ground on one side and the river on the other. It isn't difficult to imagine her being grabbed and pulled into the gully by some crazed individual, beaten lifeless then entombed under the stones which were painstakingly built up around and over her, affording the culprit an integral three month span to get clear. For good measure her attacker had possibly taken off her boots and thrown them into the nearby river, her hat having already been left at Harrison's.

Here we may again be into the realms of assumption. But who else was there? There were vague references as to a Nordic-looking sailor, seen in the vicinity at the time of the girl's disappearance but the latter never became a tangible reality. Local tramps came under the spotlight for a time but they too were eliminated. This again left Maynard Harrison. Mr. Justice Cave may well have had his own doubts about the teenager's innocence for he instructed the grand jury very carefully, that if Harrison was acquitted at a subsequent trial, that he could not be tried again but that if he was acquitted by them at that time, should further evidence be uncovered, that he could still be tried at a later date. The result was that the grand jury found no bill against Harrison and he was acquitted and discharged. However, no further evidence was ever forthcoming.

The case of Lucy Sands continued to be talked about for years afterwards in the locality. The victim's grave in St. John's Churchyard, Workington was visited regularly by members of the public who often brought flowers. The girl's ghost was even claimed to have been seen over ensuing years in the vicinity of the heap of stones where a tree was planted and named after the victim. The entire affair had seized the imagination of the public given all the macabre details surrounding it. Today the grave is untraceable and the stones and tree are gone along with other trappings of the times. It is still possible to find plenty of people in Workington and beyond who know the case, but no one is really any nearer to solving the riddle of who killed the teenager who paid so dearly for her frivolity, and who must have been in a state of sheer terror at the end.

What the case does illustrate above all else are the persisting moralistic tenets of the time. Harrison appears to have made himself scarce after his final court hearing. But Shannon and Cranney were less protected and had continued to attract the prevailing contempt of other West Cumbrians, rude and hard-drinking though many of the latter still were in the early 1880s. Only a short time before the acquittal they were pelted with turf at Frizington by a hostile mob and had to take shelter in a hotel for several hours. While Harrison was apparently sneaking back home via Dalston after the final hearing, they were booed and jeered again. Possibly they continued to attract this kind of odium for some time to come.

31: THE MAD BOMBER

It was a tranquil summer evening in June, 1882 when the Brown family retired to bed at their home fronting the green in Dalston Village. The place was as quiet then as it often is today, very much larger now, but still lying comfortably away from the western suburbs of Carlisle, with some miles of rural countryside further dividing it from the more volatile urban regions of West Cumberland.

The Browns were a family not unrepresentative of those living out in the rural regions of the county at that time. Indeed, their likes are still around today, law-abiding and uncomplicated. Head of the household was Mrs. Mary Brown, widowed for several years, who had been sharing her home for some time with her sister and niece, though the mainstay of the family was Mary's son Thomas, a time-served clogger and member of the Carlisle Rifle Corps.

The family occupied a terraced house not dissimilar to those on either side, with one exception; Mrs. Brown and her sister were sleeping in a room situated above a grocer's shop which lay below part of their premises, operated by a Mr. and Mrs. John Bell. Around two fifteen a.m. Mrs. Brown was awoken by the sound of something falling onto the bedroom floor. She sat up in bed and observed a small metal object with a fizzing tube attached, giving off clouds of smoke. It could only have been thrown through the open window.

Immediately panic-stricken, she called out for her son who rushed into the room and at once grasped the reason for his mother's agitation. Without a moment's delay he seized the offending object and threw it down the stairs. There was a terrific explosion. The entire building trembled. Doors were blown off their hinges, windows were shattered and the ceiling fell in. But thanks to the young man's presence of mind, no one was hurt. Had he not acted so promptly lives might well have been lost. The missile had been filled with tonite, a highly explosive substance, and timed to go off within minutes.

At the onset, the police were baffled. The Browns were a family with no enemies that anyone was aware of. All a bemused Thomas Brown could belatedly suggest was that the Fenians might have been after his rifle but this had to be mere idle conjecture and so much nonsense. There had never ever been a Fenian within many miles of Dalston. The men in blue were on firmer ground however, following an interview with the grocer John Bell and his wife Martha.

It seemed that the Bells did have an enemy in the form of John Bell's twenty-seven-year old brother, Joseph, who blamed Mrs. Bell especially for thwarting him in his wish to emigrate to America. A recent letter from the Liverpool area where the man had been working on the Mersey Tunnel went some way towards throwing light on what was an ugly situation. The letter, addressed to John Bell, was dated 22nd May, 1882 and read as follows:

> Dear Brother,
> I write these few lines to tell you I received a letter from America, and there was no pass, as you have written to him and told them I was both lazy and drinking. I want to know what good it has done you for telling such lies. What you think you deserve for it. I mean striking square with her for what she has done. It shows you are guilty in not answering the letter I sent you before. I think you have a very nice wife for to hinder your brother from going to America. The fagot, she should be gibited. I'm not working, nor does not intend to in this world. I've not worked since the letter came. This is the last letter I send to you. If you are going to write soon and give an account of yourself, why you have done it, it would be the best job you ever did for to send eight pounds to carry me out to America. No more at present from your brother.
>
> "Jos Bell"

John Bell never had responded to this letter, any more than he had responded to the one preceding it. But the tone of menace in the recent epistle was unmistakable. The police proceeded all the more quickly with enquiries in the Liverpool area, even while they felt they now had a good knowledge of the man they were seeking and the background to the situation as a whole.

From information provided by John Bell, it had emerged that the suspect was a native of Broughton in West Cumberland where he and his siblings had been brought up. But whereas the family as a whole had had the reputation of being conscientious and industrious, Joe had came to be looked upon as a misfit. He had worked as a coal miner in the past but taken to drifting, eventually surfacing on Merseyside. Here he had obtained lodgings at the home of his sister in Birkenhead and now rather surprisingly, took up as a labourer on the Mersey Tunnel and stuck the job for an extended period. But here too he had had access to explosives and the type of device which had wrought such havoc at Dalston, it already being assumed that Mrs. Brown's bedroom window could have been mistaken for part of the grocer's accommodation.

What did emerge in particular was Joseph Bell's great preoccupation with America. Beyond doubt he looked upon it as the proverbial land of milk and honey. A relative, Uncle Joe, had promised him assistance to get there. However, as the foregoing letter indicates, his sister-in-law wrote, spiking his guns and his brother had after a fashion, colluded. As a result, no pass ever came, though it had been earlier promised.

Enquiries on Merseyside established that Joseph had been telling many of those about him of the pass to America. He seemed to have all but convinced himself that the pass was as good as his. When he finally received word to the contrary it was all too much.

Only semi-literate himself, he called his niece to him and dictated his poisonous letter of 22nd May. He gave up his job and reverted back to his former lifestyle, hanging around in idleness, though didn't leave Birkenhead at once. However, as day succeeded day and no reply came to his letter, he finally did leave the area, having been heard to curse Martha Bell roundly and say that she might prepare for another world.

This was on 17th June, 1882. There followed the Dalston explosion three days later and the intensive police follow-through, leading to the suspect's arrest in Whitehaven on 23rd June where he had been preparing to embark on a boat back to the Liverpool area. It was another commendable effort on the part of the forces of law and order who had normally far fewer means at their disposal in those days, to effect such a speedy arrest.

Joseph Bell was detained pending further enquiries and finally appeared before local magistrates on 12th July, 1882. By this time a considerable number of witnesses had been located who were able to testify to his having been in the Dalston area just prior to the explosion. Bell seemed relaxed enough. But he did challenge the authenticity of the police evidence, accusing one Superintendent Thornborrow in broad Cumbrian: "Thou is a most notorious liar, man, thou is!" Some echoes of the brazen Thomas Sowerby of twenty-two years previously perhaps? There was more in similar vein: "Damn, I would speak a laal bit of truth if I was thee."

None of it did the prisoner any good. The police continued to steadily build up a case against him and when he eventually appeared for trial in November, 1882 he was as good as convicted. It was established beyond doubt that he had arrived in Whitehaven on 18th June where he called on his cousin, Henry Riley. The latter testified that they had gone to St. Bees to seek the prisoner's sister but she had moved to service elsewhere. That same evening, Riley saw Bell off on a train bound for Maryport. This was Sunday. On Monday, 19th June, the day prior to the explosion, the prisoner was seen at the Crofton toll bar, a mere four miles from Dalston, by a Mrs. Pigg. He told her some vague story of having been robbed, of that he was going to America – the continuing preoccupation with the new world remained a striking feature. Two hours later he approached a local man, John Jacques, closer still to Dalston, and asked him for matches, though he wasn't known to smoke. That same evening he was seen but a mile from Dalston by another witness.

But then he disappeared totally for forty hours. He wasn't seen again by anyone until seven a.m. on Wednesday, 21st June, 1882 when he surfaced in a stable in the Maryport area, speaking of having came from Newcastle more than sixty miles to the east.

Needless to say, it was still a case of circumstantial evidence. He had been charged with feloniously and of malice aforethought attempting to kill and murder John and Martha Bell by means of an explosive at Dalston on 20th June, 1882, but had pleaded not guilty. And indeed, no one had seen him hurl the device through the window. He had also spoken of having spent his time with a girl following his leave-taking of his cousin on 18th June, drinking and lying in hay lofts, providing his alibi confidently.

But it took little time to demolish most of this. Too many people had seen him in the Dalston area just prior to the crime and he had been alone then, speaking freely of America and easily identifiable. Nor did any girl ever come forward to confirm his alibi. Equally damning was the contraption which had almost wiped out the entire Brown family. It was a cartridge no more than three inches long and an inch wide but containing sufficient tonite to wreak total havoc within a confined space, the whole capable of being activated within three minutes by a live fuse. Such cartridges had been accessible to Joseph Bell during his stint as a labourer on the Mersey Tunnel and in fact the fuse from one of them was found in the wrecked Dalston building. A burn had also been found upon the prisoner's finger which could well have been caused while he was lighting the fuse attached to the cartridge. He had also spoken out rather too freely with threats against Martha Bell beforehand and to one of his sisters had said ambiguously that he hadn't done it, but that he knew who did... Who else could it have been but him?

We can easily concoct our own picture of events during the hours in question. Probably Bell made his way to Dalston in easy stages after leaving the train at Maryport. He could well have walked all the way there. The walk would not be beyond the energies of a fit young man of twenty-seven years, additionally fired up by a pathological desire for revenge on those he felt had wronged him, the cartridge concealed in his pocket, harmless without the attachment of detonator and fuse, the latter by themselves in another pocket. After meeting several people as he drew closer to Dalston, he then presumably decided to go to ground completely before and after the deed. It would be easy to conceal himself in a barn or a wood as needs be and it is also known that back in Whitehaven on 22nd June, he pawned a revolver and cartridges. Perhaps the latter had also been intended for use at Dalston.

Undoubtedly a dangerous young man who ironically enough, was only saved from execution by the timely intervention of Thomas Brown that summer evening who for his part could well have died along with his innocent kith and kin. A sentence of twenty years penal servitude was handed out as a fitting alternative. Bell was seen to peer angrily about the court before he was taken down. His sister-in-law may nonetheless have wished that transportation was still the norm for such offending. Indeed, she was still not out of danger.

Fifteen years went by and in September, 1896, Joseph Bell was released on a ticket of leave. He returned to his place of birth in West Cumberland but was soon complaining of police intimidation and applied for a pardon to allow him greater freedom of movement. Spearheading support for this was none other than his brother, John, still in the grocery trade with his wife at Dalston.

To the convict's disgust, no pardon was forthcoming. He took off anyhow without notifying anyone, making his way to Dalston and paying a short visit to his brother and sister-in-law who greeted him tentatively. Joseph refused the offer of a meal and was soon on his way again. Upon parting with his brother out on the Carlisle road, he showed him a loaded revolver and spoke menacingly of Martha. It was evident he had forgotten nothing and learnt nothing.

John Bell hesitated only a short time before going to the police. Joseph Bell was arrested on 2nd January, 1897 and charged with changing his residence without prior notification and carrying firearms with intention of murder. He blustered and said he only wanted the revolver to carry when he went to America. He wasn't believed. His licence was revoked and he was returned to prison to complete his twenty year sentence though within five years, would be totally free.

The grocer and his wife must have felt decidedly uneasy. A dangerous man had been sentenced, released on licence then returned to prison. But once his full sentence had been served, he couldn't be arrested and tried again until he did more harm. And this seemed highly likely. The couple may even have regretted what their rather narrow-minded action had brought about all those years ago. But now they could only wait and see. In this respect the British law hasn't changed a great deal. We have had similar situations within our own present day social system. In the former mad bomber's case however, he must have finally decided that twenty years was penalty enough for no more was ever heard of him. Nevertheless, the entire situation could so easily have had far more tragic consequences than it did.

32: A CONGLOMERATION OF VIOLENCE

The small township of Caldbeck, situated cosily on the eastern fringes of the Lake District, would seem a most unlikely setting for a violent death. With its ancient church, solitary pub, general store, neat rows of cottages and well maintained cricket pitch, it gives the impression of having remained virtually undisturbed for countless numbers of years. Many visitors see it simply as a peaceable kind of community which in fact it is, where one can spend a pleasant hour just wandering about, or enjoying coffee and cream scones in one of its small restaurants before moving on elsewhere.

Yet only in the last century, Caldbeck was an entirely different place with mines in the surrounding hills, mills, breweries, numerous shops, an abundance of pubs and a rough vibrant population within and around which included John Peel and his offspring. The scene of our unnatural death in this instance was the bobbin mill situated just beyond the township in a shadowy wooded ravine known as the Howk, traversed by the famous 'cold beck' which had given the nearby centre of population its name centuries before and which also drove the great mill wheel.

In these times most of the mill is a ruin though recently there have been belated moves to restore it. In 1882 it was fully operational and had been since 1857, owned by a local gentleman, John Jennings, but now managed and administered by members of the Brownrigg branch of the Ashbridge family, who when Jennings eventually died at the turn of the century, took the mill on and ran it in their own right for some years. The main product had long been bobbins for use in the textile trade. But the mill also turned out clog soles, pick shafts, wooden dolls – in fact anything commercially viable. At times close to three score men and boys were employed there, dependent upon trade, but the mill was often a dangerous place. Its early labour force was said to have had a predilection for strong drink. It was on fire several times and in 1863, one of its young employees was caught up in a machine and badly injured.

Yet still it survived. Payment was based on result and a man or boy had to be working virtually non-stop from dawn to dusk, just to produce enough of the main product to earn subsistence wages. But given the economic climate of the times there was generally never any shortage of labour. Such was the setting when Alexander Aitken approached the manager, Thomas Ashbridge, in the early summer of 1882 for a job. Though Aitken was a qualified bobbin turner, the manager was reluctant to take him on, knowing him to be of a bad-tempered quarrelsome nature and he had enough to do keeping others among his unruly workforce in line. What finally decided the manager to give Aitken a chance was a good word from one of his established turners, fifty-two-year-old Anthony Proctor, who knew Aitken personally. Thus though he was also aware that Aitken was a restless individual who tramped about the countryside regularly and might well let him down soon enough, Thomas Ashbridge decided to start the man, though he could probably have done without him.

At first all went well. Proctor and Aitken worked together, with Proctor doing the fundamental work on the bobbins before passing them over to Aitken to be finished off. But on the morning of 1st July, 1882, the two men were observed to be quarrelling. Indications were that Aitken wasn't happy with Proctor's standard of work which rendered his task harder. In the crowded dusty room where both men were located, they shouted at one another across a lathe and Aitken struck out at Proctor. He followed this up by going around to Proctor and confronting him. Proctor, not a man to stand idly by, picked up the huge wooden clamp with which he held the bobbins and hit Aitken several times over the head with it. His son John went to assist him. Amidst the whirring belts, he dragged Aitken away from his father and the unguarded machinery. Aitken fell backwards and struck the back of his head on an iron headstock. But his head was already covered with blood from the blows of the wooden clamp. A man, Richard Dixon, shouted: "Don't kill the man!" Proctor retorted: "He struck me first". Aitken seemed muddled but then gathered himself together and offered to fight the Proctors outside, one at a time, but they declined.

The mill's working day had been severely disrupted and the exasperated manager had had enough. He hadn't wanted to take Aitken on in the first instance and proceeded to see him off the premises. He may have advised him to see a doctor. The injured man was certainly seen some time later in a public house in the locality with his head bandaged. But then he vanished completely from the Caldbeck area and wasn't seen again until 5th July in Eskdale. By this time he was noticeably ill. The following day he was admitted to Bootle Workhouse. On 8th July he died. An inquest was held and cause of death was established as 'a collection of pus or matter on the membrane of the brain'. Further enquiries led the law to Anthony Proctor. He was arrested and appeared at the Carlisle Assizes in November, 1882 charged with unlawfully killing Alexander Aitken.

What the prosecution sought to prove was that Aitken had died as a result of the injuries inflicted by Proctor. The latter had inflicted several wounds; this was not disputed. Richard Dixon was called as a witness to this. But in the prisoner's defence it could be claimed that there was also the blow Aitken had sustained to the back of his head after John Proctor, the son of the prisoner, had dragged him away. Following this he had been dazed, scarcely surprising since he had hit his head on a block of iron after falling hard upon it. The pus had been located below a cut on the head; this cut had been inflicted by Proctor Senior. But was the fatal damage anything at all to do with this?

The very character of the deceased had to weigh in the prisoner's favour. He was well known as a mercurial individual given to quarrelling and mouthing threats. Anthony Proctor had spoken up for him in the first instance and persuaded the sceptical mill manager to take him on. Alexander Aitken had repaid his benefactor by striking him. What sort of man was that? There was the setting of the affray too - a crowded workroom filled with heavy lethal machinery and belts, some of the latter almost a foot wide. The deceased had been dragged away by the prisoner's son and he had then fallen and hit his head to the extent of becoming obviously dazed, against a protruding iron headstock. A plan of the mill was produced for the court's further edification.

After all the evidence was heard there was still an element of uncertainty. But Mr. Justice Day made it clear that he felt there were insufficient grounds for a conviction. He directed the jury to bring in a not guilty verdict. They did so and a relieved Anthony Proctor was discharged. Some might have said he was lucky, others that he scarcely deserved to be in court anyhow. There were few men of his kind who wouldn't have hit back under the circumstances, in Cumberland or anywhere else in those unsophisticated times, against such a setting. But a man had died and then as now, justice had to be seen to be done.

All this notwithstanding, 1882 had still been a violent year insofar as Cumberland was concerned. Aitken's death and its aftermath had been nothing compared to the antics of the Dalston bomber. There had also been the sordid Lucy Sands enquiry with all its implications of very recent savagery. 1882 could possibly have seen several hangings in Cumberland had Thomas Brown not intervened to throw Bell's infernal contraption downstairs, and had a case been proved against Maynard Harrison, with a death sentence in fact passed on a third man from the same area as Harrison, for a crime so foul that perhaps the least space devoted to it the better, though it does merit some mention.

Hugh Grant was a twenty-one-year-old soldier from Workington. His family were rather better off than some in that they could afford to keep a servant, though given what many servants were paid in those days, this really meant little. When Grant was in his late teens he seduced his parents' maid, a local girl named Mary McGowan and she bore him a son. The couple were eventually married in December 1881 and in the summer of 1882 a child, Eleanor, was born, but the marriage had never been happy and the couple were living apart by March, 1882. The failed husband had plenty going for him physically. He volunteered to join the army and was immediately accepted. But army life didn't suit him it seemed and by September 1882 he was back in Workington. At a loose end, he didn't rejoin his wife but returned to the home of his parents and sister.

Here he was to be rudely reminded of his marital responsibilities by his mother, who advised him of his wife's intention to take their two children and enter the workhouse, ever a symbol of stigma. Obviously the feckless West Cumbrian hadn't been facing up to the fact that he had others to think about as well as himself and this was possibly his wife's way of getting back at him. At times Grant could seemingly be placid enough, smoking his pipe and playing the model son, but this latest news brought out all the worst in him. Bolstered by drink he raced to the McGowans home a short distance away where his wife and children were living and proceeded to beat his wife and knock his father-in-law down, though indeed he received almost as good as he got in part for his wife hit him with a poker and a tea tin.

But then in a blind fury he grabbed his infant daughter and swung her round, either by the legs or by her clothing, like some kind of rag doll. She hit her head on some boarding and ended on a hen house roof in the back yard. The infant's head was so shattered that she only lived a short time afterwards. Even before the little girl's death however, Grant realised the magnitude of his action. He returned to his parents' home, crying out for God's forgiveness and speaking of preparing for the rope.

At his trial a few weeks later, there was some dispute as to what the two main witnesses had actually seen but his guilt was in little doubt and he was sentenced to death following a fairly quick verdict of guilty, though with a recommendation to mercy. Grant was a very unhappy young man indeed by this time, and his family with him. He appeared to hold out little hope of a reprieve but already the anti-hanging lobby was swinging into action. In the Carlisle Patriot of 10th November, 1882 there appeared a plea on behalf of the condemned man, noting that there had been no recommendation to mercy for instance, in the case of George Cass, twenty-two years earlier, so that the jury must have felt that Hugh Grant, in sum, must have merited some consideration. And hadn't an evil man like Joseph Bell recently got off with twenty years penal servitude…?

Such pleas were often quite simplistic but in this instance, the plea didn't quite ring true. There had been a recommendation to mercy in the case of Cass, though it had availed him little. And Bell had been responsible for no loss of life whatsoever though he might easily have been of course, and then he would almost surely have been hanged.

As it was, the abolitionists appeared to be fighting a losing battle. Grant's crime had aroused a great deal of local revulsion and he was listed to hang at Carlisle on Monday, 13th November, 1882. However, it then transpired that Marwood the hangman had other business. The very next day, with the scaffold ready and waiting and with his wife and sister having already visited him for what they anticipated would be the last time, Grant's death sentence was commuted to penal servitude for life.

Thus by a combination of luck and a kind of twelfth hour conversion on the part of the powers-that-be, the drunken irresponsible parent had been snatched from the path taken by Pearson, Thompson, Munroe, Cass and Co. Rather surprisingly it was reported that there was some general satisfaction in Workington after all, following word of the reprieve. Cumbrian public opinion did appear to be gradually getting softer, but Grant's crime has to remain one of the most sordid and violent of its kind in the county.

33: AN INFAMOUS TRIO

A local case which invariably continues to receive a regular airing is that of Anthony Benjamin Rudge, John Martin and James Baker, who murdered Police Constable Joseph Byrnes at Plumpton Village just north of Penrith on 29th October, 1885. As late as October 1938 it was the subject of a popular play at Her Majesty's Theatre, Carlisle. It has been served up afresh in the local press many times. It is one of the cases invariably chosen for inclusion in any book or presentation on local crime and criminals. And until fairly recently at least, it was said of anyone reaching impressive longevity in the Carlisle area that they showed Rudge, Martin and Baker the way, as it was said of this writer's own great grandfather who died in 1957 aged ninety-five years. No Cumbrian crime before or since has merited such notoriety or interest, even while it has long since slipped from national attention.

Why the continuing local absorption with three villains, whose kind are scarcely unique?. They only came to Cumberland in the first instance to steal from their so-called betters. They weren't very clever in their attempts to shake off their pursuers and were all caught in less than two days and hanged ignominiously at Carlisle following a short trial. Perhaps it was the sheer ruthlessness of the trio while they were on the run in the county, their total disrespect for life and limb, their particular determination to brush aside the forces of law and order at any cost, which fascinated a primarily rural population, many possibly feeling during the short period of time involved, the doubtful thrill of being at actual risk themselves, with such a fascination following on during succeeding years in the locality. But who can really say?

Of greater pertinence, the actual handling of the affair by the powers-that-be was a shambles. Though much was made of the bravery of the policemen involved, and the civilians who had a part in the final dramatic capture of the trio, and rightly so, the fact remained that lives were put needlessly at risk and the victim himself need not have died had different tactics been employed. Before the end of it all, a fourth man was able to slip away almost without question it seems, who might have been able to throw much more light on questions which were never really asked at the time.

It all began on 28th October, 1885, on a clear moonlight evening at Netherby Hall, the country seat of the Graham family, some two miles outside Longtown close to the Scottish border. Just a few years ago, in 1989, diminishing family fortunes resulted in the house being sold by Sir Charles Graham, but a century previously the Grahams had still been affluent enough. At that time their kind had lived at Netherby some three hundred years, being immortalised at one stage by Sir Walter Scott in his poem: Young Lochinvar. There had been a number of notables in the family, the best known of these in the nineteenth century being Sir James Graham, a capable administrator and parliamentarian. He had died in 1861 and been succeeded by his son Frederick, a less colourful character, but who along with his wife, Hermione, had proved popular enough.

The couple were still enjoying their inheritance in 1885 and were regularly in residence at the Hall.

It should nonetheless be said that the Grahams were never as wealthy or renowned on the Cumbrian scene as such families as the Howards of Naworth or the Lonsdales of Lowther Castle. Netherby Hall itself was no more than an ornate country mansion in comparison to many great northern residences. It also lay off the beaten track and it remains a mystery as to why it was singled out for a grand jewel robbery in the first instance, given that there was not a vast amount of jewellery to steal anyhow. Someone may have talked, giving an exaggerated picture to the criminal fraternity further south. But more of that anon.

What is certain is that around eight p.m. on the evening of 28th October, 1885, a maid went to the bedroom of Lady Graham on the first floor of the main wing of the house. Her errand was trivial. She quickly returned downstairs where Sir Frederick and his family were at dinner. No more than ten minutes later, another servant tried the bedroom door and found it locked. She raised the alarm. It was found impossible to force the door and entrance to the bedroom had to be made via one of the windows utilising a ladder. A garden seat was found beneath the window which had been used to support a shorter ladder, taken from the estate farm. The gas lighting in the room was blazing and it was soon discovered that jewellery worth around £250 was missing, not a gigantic haul needless to say, but sufficient to result in an immediate call to the police.

The electric telegraph was quickly brought into play, already noteworthy in helping to track down the Mannings of Bermondsey as far back as 1849, following their slaying of Patrick O'Conner. It had also proved useful locally over ensuing years in a number of cases including those of George Cass and Elizabeth Kirkbride. Superintendent Sempill of Carlisle, whom we have already met in respect of Margaret Messenger, was promptly able to instruct Sergeant John Roche and Police Constable Handley to go in the direction of Kingstown, lying just outside Carlisle on the road from Longtown, where it was assumed the burglar or burglars might be intercepted.

No sooner said than done, but at Kingstown there was then a quick change of plan. Handley was sent back to watch the railway station at Carlisle while the sergeant called upon Constable Jacob Johnstone, the local beat bobby at Kingstown, to assist him. Semphill's assumption quickly paid off. No later than ten thirty p.m., some yards along the road from Kingstown, the police sergeant saw four men in the moonlight coming from the direction or Longtown. Three of them wore long dark overcoats and hard hats. The fourth wore lighter-coloured attire, but all looked suspiciously out of place. Roche challenged them to his detriment. He was quickly covered with revolvers by the two older men of the group, later to be identified as Rudge and Martin. They opened fire, shooting him in the arm and following through with a beating to the head before making off down the road in the direction of Carlisle with their two companions. Johnstone began chasing them, followed by a badly shaken Roche. The former was gaining ground when he fell, shot through the chest. Roche now concentrated upon his colleague, helping him back towards his house. Thereafter, the two policemen were out of the chase.

Handley, sent off earlier towards Carlisle, hadn't got very far. Less than a mile down the road, just short of the then hamlet of Moorville, he stopped when he heard shots and a cry of pain, clearly audible in the still night air. He immediately grasped what might have happened. Handley was no coward but felt he required assistance, being alone without any weapon but his stick and no means of speedy communication with his superiors. He improvised, going to nearby houses and enlisting the support of two local men, Armstrong and Hetherington. He is said to have asked Armstrong to bring a loaded gun but there was no gun and it was three unarmed men who faced the foursome approaching them from Kingstown, shortly after eleven p.m.

In these times, civilians would never be recruited in such a manner or placed in such grave danger. On the contrary, they would be warned off and categorically instructed not to have a go. Policemen too would never approach criminals they knew to be armed, in such a way. But Handley knew no better. Such was the policeman's lot in those days. He was expected to get his man regardless. All this against a backdrop of some general hostility. For though policemen had gradually won some public respect, they still weren't too popular either, in Cumberland or anywhere else in Britain.

The nation hadn't wanted a police force to begin with. Finally introduced in 1829 in London, and though quite remarkably successful, the force was still low in numbers everywhere, poorly paid and often in danger, with poor backing from the courts. Only the previous year, at Hensingham in West Cumberland, P.C. Alexander Forbes had been shot at twice while pursuing one William Domigan across a field. Domigan, claiming to be drunk, and frightened, following recent religious riots in Cleator Moor, had taken to carrying a gun and a police uniform had apparently been just too much for him.... His sentence, though charged with wilfully and feloniously shooting with intent to kill, was a paltry three months in prison and a surety of £100 to keep the peace. Other such examples were not uncommon locally. This at a time when forgery and robbery by a postman could still draw a sentence of five years penal servitude.

Thus it was possibly with no illusions about the policeman's general standing but with some personal zeal and professional pride nevertheless, that P.C. Handley confronted the foursome in the moonlight. He spoke first to the younger man of the group, who proved to be Baker, and to the man in light clothing, who claimed to have been assaulted back along the road. Handley wasn't satisfied and stated that he must detain the latter. The man at once pulled out a revolver and pointed it at Armstrong while Baker covered the policeman with a similar weapon and Rudge and Martin stood ominously by.

It was all too much for Thomas Armstrong. His nerve went and he suggested that he and

Handley and Hetherington get to hell out of it as none of them were armed. Thinking on his feet and looking death in the face, Handley agreed. He and the two civilians withdrew and the four villains went on towards Carlisle without further argument. Handley had shown more common sense than either of his fellow policemen. He could just as easily have died that night along with his two pressed volunteers had be persisted in trying to make an arrest. As it was, the police had now had the first indications of the kind of ruthless miscreants they were up against. But little was seemingly learnt from the foregoing encounters by those directing the operation.

Several hours passed. The local police simply didn't have the resources to mount a gigantic manhunt and had the gang now chosen to split up and melt away into the surrounding area for a time, they might well have got away altogether, as indeed one of them eventually did. For the moment however, as was soon to be revealed, they all stayed together, three of them next being seen by the level crossing keeper at the Dalston Road crossing close to Carlisle city centre around two thirty a.m. Looking out of his shed he observed three men headed towards the goods yard.

The threesome were trespassing; Strong the crossing keeper may have known nothing of the event at Netherby and its fairly immediate aftermath but was still concerned enough to report the three strangers to P.C. Christopher Fortune when he came past shortly afterwards. P.C. Fortune knew enough to realise who the interlopers might be. Without a great deal of thought for his personal safety he caught them up. Scarcely had he challenged them when a fourth man suddenly appeared and that was the last Fortune remembered. He was knocked unconscious and came to his senses at the bottom of the railway embankment. Fortune was so badly beaten that he never fully recovered. But he could just as easily have been dead. According to later evidence, it seemed that the unfortunate policeman had been left lying across the railway lines where the next train could have cut him in two, until Baker had suffered a sudden change of heart and gone back and tumbled him down the embankment.

Thereafter we hear no more of any fourth man. He must have left the group and got well clear to the extent that he was never traced, though several earlier witnesses had had a good glimpse of his face in the moonlight. The others continued on together. The south must have appeared all the more alluring from whence they had all came and to date they had still killed no one and still had the Netherby jewels, even though they had left a bloody trail behind them. According to James Walter Brown, in his short but pertinent narrative, they were next seen between three a.m. and four a.m. in one of the railway goods yards by some workmen. Then they vanished until around seven p.m. that same day when they were seen at Calthwaite Railway Station, more than halfway from Carlisle to Penrith.

Presumably they had taken time out to catch up on some sleep, possibly in an isolated barn during the daylight hours. Needless to say, they must all have been exceedingly hardy ruffians. Initially they had apparently walked all the way from Netherby to Kingstown in less than three hours with their mysterious companion, before brutally dealing with the police officers barring their way. But as was later revealed at their trial, they then realised they had another obstacle to contend with of a different kind. This was the River Eden with its solitary bridge on the road directly before them leading straight into Carlisle and the southern highway beyond. The bridge in those days was much quieter then than it is today but was still a key route and almost bound to be watched by this time. Thus they reasoned and rightly. Deciding a boat would be a better alternative, they therefore struck off through the area to the left of the bridge taking in a large tree nursery en route with nothing to light their way but the moon. They did find a boat but it had no oars. Nothing daunted, they retraced their steps all the way back to one or other of the two railway bridges further up the river at Etterby, a distance of some two miles, which weren't watched, and are assumed to have crossed there illegally.

By two thirty in the morning they were certainly within the boundaries of Carlisle, close to the city's railway station. They might well have hidden themselves away in a waggon and rolled safely out of Carlisle had they not been seen by Strong the crossing keeper and confronted by P.C. Fortune. Following this the fourth man presumably left them but the threesome had succeeded in remaining free a further fifteen hours. During the latter part of that time they must have walked at least a further nine miles to reach Calthwaite, with little if any access to food or drink.

But now they acted more carelessly, though none of them had scarcely went out of their way to practice concealment during the earlier stages of the police attempt to apprehend them either. They asked at the small station if there was a train south. They were advised to the contrary so made their way along the nearby road to Plumpton, some two and a half miles away, making no attempt to seek cover. Perhaps they were under the illusion that back out in the countryside they were safer. Nothing was further from the truth. By this time they were headline news for miles around and the station master at Calthwaite immediately telegraphed details through to his counterpart at Plumpton, who contacted the local policeman, Joseph Byrnes. The latter at once headed for the Pack Horse Inn at Plumpton, which lay on the main road to Penrith and the south.

What followed was an unnecessary tragedy. Given the treatment already meted out to Roche, Johnstone and Fortune and the lucky escape of Handley, Hetherington and Armstrong, it must have been evident to those at higher level that they had a violent gang of criminals on their hands, all in possession of firearms, who probably wouldn't hesitate to kill if cornered. But if there had been a gradual dawning of the dangers facing police officers or anyone else approaching the Netherby burglars, then warnings to stay clear of them couldn't have been issued very emphatically. Nor was there evidence of any kind of back-up support, such as the militia, or any apparent intention of calling upon such. Byrnes went straight in, armed with only a truncheon. He met Rudge, Martin and Baker shortly after they emerged from the Pack Horse. He was shot through the head and thrown over a wall, being discovered around one and a half hours later, bleeding to death. He died shortly afterwards.

Such a lack of tactics was to be demonstrated again almost thirty years later in the same district, while the hunt for the delinquent soldier, Toplis, was in progress. However, no policeman was killed then, and a plan of sorts was eventually formulated. Other officers have died in shooting incidents over succeeding years, but most of the latter have been caught up in the unexpected. All in all, the death of Joseph Byrnes had to beg of some serious explanation, even in those less genteel times, but none was ever forthcoming. Was Byrnes simply a foolhardy individual inculcated with the notion of doing his duty regardless? Maybe. On the other hand, was he insufficiently instructed to begin with? The latter possibility does appear worthy of serious consideration.

The remainder of the saga remains almost equally as controversial and it is remarkable that more lives were not lost. The threesome were captured within hours but by a group of civilians. A police constable, James Patterson, saw the trio walking along the railway line towards Penrith shortly after ten p.m. He alerted his Superintendent then went out alone to seek the villains. Perhaps fortunately for him he failed to find them, but then alerted Christopher Geddes, a Carlisle goods guard. Geddes kept a close eye on his train and actually saw the threesome scrambling into a waggon as the train moved out of Penrith. Once again the telegraph was brought into use and a crowd of railwaymen assembled at Tebay. Here the trio broke cover after being located in the now stationary train. They ran for it. Rudge was knocked down by an engine driver, Robert Wills, and secured. A revolver was found in his coat pocket and the stolen jewellery in the nearby river Lune, thrown there by the fugitive. Martin had made off in the opposite direction but he was felled by a porter brandishing a brake stick. An engine driver, William Parker, tied his hands. Even then, Parker was at considerable risk for while he made to seize Martin, the latter, possibly the most ruthless of the trio, reached in his pocket for a revolver. But he was dazed and Parker was a strong man.

Baker got as far as Lancaster on another train. At Oxenholme the train was searched by three police officers but without result. The train set off again and was searched in vain at Carnforth. It transpired that the third member of the trio had been moving from waggon to waggon while the train was in motion, his profession as a cat burglar standing him in good stead. But at Lancaster he was stranded in the early hours and made the mistake of approaching a railway guard, Henry Cooper, and asking him about a train for Crewe. Cooper recognised him and made what might be best described as a citizen's arrest. By late afternoon that same day, all three criminals were lodged in Carlisle Gaol.

The behaviour of the railwaymen was brave and patriotic. Yet with the benefit of hindsight, it could be deemed foolhardy too. And yet, without them, would the trio ever have been arrested and the murder of the unfortunate Joseph Byrnes avenged? None of these questions were asked at the time. In fact, it is doubtful if they have ever been asked. The prevailing mood was one of euphoria. The villains had been caught, Lady Graham had her jewellery back. All was well again on the Cumbrian scene.

The trial of the three men which commenced on 18th January, 1886, and ended two days later was to afford a rather different picture. Though Superintendent Sempill received praise for skill and judgement in his handling of the case, the state of his officers scarcely bore this out. Sergeant Roche, one of the biggest and smartest policemen in the force, if James Walter Brown is to be believed, had been rendered virtually immobile. His companion, P.C. Johnstone, shot in the chest at point blank range, remained so shattered that he had to give his evidence seated in a chair. The unfortunate P.C. Fortune had received no less than nineteen wounds to the head and was never again fit for work. Byrnes of course, was dead.

More was learnt of the unfortunate policeman's demise from Baker, who had talked afterwards in prison. Byrnes had approached the three villains and they warned him off but he was insistent upon taking at least one of them into custody. Insofar as they were concerned he had had his chance. He was shot through the head like a dog. Rudge, Martin and Baker were not unlike many professional criminals. They didn't like the police but weren't necessarily concerned to kill them or anyone else unless they were thwarted or cornered. Then it could be different. All considered, it is remarkable that the railwaymen, so intent upon having a go and not discouraged from doing so, didn't suffer their own toll of casualties. But perhaps the threesome had became a trifle more weary by the time they reached Tebay.

The evidence against the three men in the dock was quite overwhelming. They weren't denying much of it and the outcome of the trial was almost a foregone conclusion. Before the jury retired, Rudge actually confessed to the murder himself in an attempt to absolve his two companions but to no avail. The verdict of wilful murder was reached in just sixty-five minutes against all three and they were sentenced to death.

It emerged that they were all criminals of some standing. Anthony Benjamin Rudge, the oldest at forty-five and the most literate of the trio, spent some time prior to execution penning an account of his past experiences in prison, a copy of which is in local police archives. It reveals an embittered albeit far from unintelligent individual who might have done better in life with some appropriate guidance. But though he described himself as a dog trainer, it is doubtful if he had ever followed any kind of gainful employment for long. Also known as William Walsh and William Fennell, he had served two lengthy sentences of penal servitude and was suspected of shooting a policeman at Leek earlier in 1885 while resisting arrest.

John Martin, aged thirty-six, of Irish descent, had an equally staggering criminal record going back to when he was fourteen years old and had recently been wanted for questioning in respect of the murder of a police inspector in Romford. He was a semi-literate brute of a man who gave his occupation as that of cigar maker. Martin was allegedly the member of the gang who had shot Joseph Byrnes while the other two held him.

James Baker, twenty-nine years old, described as a cabinet maker, was a less violent individual but an accomplished cat burglar with a string of convictions. It was he presumably who had scaled the ladder and entered Lady Graham's bedroom, purloining her jewellery with such speed while his accomplices kept watch below. Of the threesome, he was the only one with a wife and a home, though the wife too had a criminal record and was well known to the police in Bethnal Green where she and her husband had owned a greengrocery shop.

All were well-made, strong men, in the prime of their lives and of not unhandsome appearance. But their foray into Cumberland spelt their end. For their initial wrong-doing there they would still have gone away for a long time but a man had also died and that man had been murdered in particularly brutal circumstances. Whether he had been a policeman or not was irrelevant given the background dynamics. Rudge, Martin and Baker were all hanged together in Carlisle Gaol on 8th February, 1886. The prevailing piety of the time demanded that some attempt be made to save their souls beforehand and the prison chaplain had got to work. His attempts were not without some result apparently, though it is hard to believe that such ill-conditioned rogues as Rudge and Martin were especially concerned about their maker.

This still left the matter of the fourth man. Who was he? The trio maintained that he was someone they had picked up in Longtown who had agreed to show them the way and no more than that. But he had had a gun in his hand at Kingstown and had been present when P.C. Fortune was beaten senseless. At the trial, some vain attempt was even made by the defence to blame him for the Byrnes murder. Nevertheless, it seemed sufficient in and around Carlisle that the supposed prime movers had been caught and not a great deal was apparently done by those concerned to run the missing man to earth.

Yet mightn't the mysterious fourth man have been the master mind behind the whole expedition? It emerged that the day before the burglary, the trio had arrived by train at Gretna bearing housebreaking equipment. They had already been burglaring further north and it might be argued that they now intended to make a grand foray against many of the large houses in the border area after taking in the Longtown coursing. But why make immediately for Netherby Hall. Why not Gretna Hall, or Kirkpatrick Fleming's Mossknowe, or Eaglesfield's Springkell, all lying fairly conveniently nearby and possibly offering richer pickings? Mightn't the fourth man have been a local crook with inside information, however misguided, as to the value of the Netherby jewels, able to lead the southerners straight to m'lady's bedroom window following some last minute plying of local natives on the day by the trio themselves? A villain equally as ruthless as they with a thorough knowledge of the entire area, guiding them as far back as the Carlisle goods yard, but with the acumen to slip away now that the going had got really bad? We shall never really know now of course, as is the case with so many old crimes, but the mysterious stranger might just have been able to resolve quite a few unanswered questions.

As for the police, in spite of all the high talk in court, they did come out of it all rather poorly, suffering reversal after reversal, with civilians finally effecting the actual arrest. They had proved capable of sterling work in many cases, local and elsewhere. But desperados like Rudge, Martin and Baker were an entirely different proposition to the Raffles gunman or even the mad bomber of Dalston. The trio were ruthless criminals from a totally different mould, bungling though their attempts were to escape.

The police did their best. Superintendent Sempill himself was said to have scoured the countryside all night in his pony and trap. But dedication and bravery wasn't enough. Those in command just weren't geared up to staging any kind of tactical search, or schooling officers on the ground or anyone else, in the art of protecting themselves. A proper understanding of fundamental human behaviour also left something to be desired. And there weren't enough police personnel in Cumberland or anywhere else anyway, as already observed.

The situation has to be rather different in our own age with a greatly increased police presence everywhere, equipped with helicopters, fast patrol cars, radios and mobile phones, with first class communication too between every police force in the country, and with some emphasis on psychology. On the other hand, criminals have became more sophisticated too of course....

What of those among the key players in the drama who survived? The majority passed into obscurity as so often happens. But we do know that P.C. Handley was eventually promoted to station sergeant at Carlisle, and that Johnstone and Fortune, though exceedingly badly used by the villains, lived on for a considerable number of years afterwards. Christopher Geddes, the railway goods guard who had given such an impressive account of himself in the arrest of Rudge and Martin, was invited to join the local police force and did so. However, he couldn't have been a success because for some obscure reason he was later asked to resign, while still living longer than anyone else involved, surviving beyond the Second World War. Meanwhile, a neglected memorial stone in Plumpton still marks the spot where P.C. Byrnes died in the call of duty on that eventful evening more than a century ago.

34: DEATH BY THE MILESTONE

As the Victorian era progressed, there were still plenty of tramps on the roads of Britain though if anything, their numbers were generally linked to the vagaries of the economy. Never was this more evident that during the years following the trade depression of 1883 when wages slumped and unemployment rose particularly sharply. Many took to the roads again in search of work. But there had always been a minority too, who tramped because it was a way of life they preferred. The same applies today. Somewhere between these two stools fell William Hunter.

Hunter was a Glaswegian but had came soon to England where he settled in Salford. Trained as a blacksmith's striker he followed this employment for some years in Lancashire but then took up a wandering way of life, initially to escape the responsibilities of maintaining his wife and child. Over the years he was several times in the hands of the police for petty offending and went to prison on one occasion for assaulting a policeman. He was also charged with not maintaining his wife and family, having briefly returned at one stage to his wife and fathered another child, but kept moving, travelling where work might be, yet slipping increasingly into the ways of a seasoned roadster.

September, 1887 found thirty-two-year-old Hunter in Cumberland where he had been for some months previously, a man of average height, passably good-looking, with an incipient moustache. With him was the woman with whom he had been travelling for some twelve weeks, Mary Steel, a shoddy, coarse-featured woman from Ayrshire. Echoes of Fisher Ashton and Liz Ferguson perhaps. Ashton, it may be recalled, had been a nailer turned tramp and opportunist thief, accompanied along the roads of Cumberland some twenty years previously by his girl friend, less literate than he was, but here the comparison ended.

Between the fifty-three-year-old Ashton and thirty-four-year-old Ferguson there had apparently been considerable attachment and a kind of dogged loyalty on her part. Hunter and Steel however, were on very bad terms. She had voiced her desire to leave him earlier in the relationship and this wish had steadily gathered momentum, given his volatile temperament and the sheer wretchedness of the life they were leading. Yet Mary Steel was no more reputable than Hunter. She had had six illegitimate children and four of these were still living. Three were with her mother in Scotland, but the youngest, three-and-a-half-year-old Isabella, remained with her, an additional source of friction between herself and the former blacksmith's striker. The child was given to crying and whining which irritated Hunter. He came to see the infant as a drag on their journeying about the countryside and began to undertake what he felt to be necessary acts of physical chastisement and correction.

It hadn't always been that way. When the couple had first met in a Dumfriesshire doss house during the early summer, Hunter had appeared to accept the little girl and the threesome had set off south, over the border and into Cumberland. Their wanderings had taken them over much of the northern area of the county without any kind of legal intervention. But the previous month, a lodging house keeper in Carlisle had taken Hunter to task for physically chastising the child and had reminded him that there were laws to protect children. Mary Steel hadn't been very kind to her daughter then either and indications were that such treatment was nothing new. Hunter had responded with a mouthful of verbal abuse and the couple had been asked to leave the premises.

They returned westwards, as far as Workington, where Hunter had been given the opportunity of a day's work in a steel plant, but his prime attempt to earn money in West Cumberland had amounted to singing in the streets. The couple began wending their way towards Carlisle again, via Maryport and Aspatria, still with the child in tow. By 7th September they had reached Wigton, tramping all the way. They stayed the night in a cheap lodging house and the following morning, set off on foot on the final leg to the border city, a distance of some eighteen miles.

Matters now appeared to have came to an irrevocable head between the couple. Hunter had proved an especially poor provider. When his pockets were turned out later by the police the contents were evidence as to just how poor he was: two pawn tickets, a pipe, an empty tobacco tin and a catapult. This and his uneasy temper had finally left Steel thoroughly disillusioned. Though of limited intellect she had finally taken a decision and decided to return with her child to Scotland. But Hunter refused to be shaken off and it was the unfortunate child who was caught up tragically in the final scenario.

After a few miles they halted and Isabella began to cry. The mother threatened her with her clog. Hunter chose to hit her with a stick. Yet paradoxically, he then gave her a piece of bread and mended her boots, which he had earlier begged for the child. Such was the make-up of this man, carrying the little girl at times, then giving her a hiding to stop her crying, tramping to avoid taking responsibility for his own children.

Just short of Raffles the couple halted again, the city itself within their sights. But what could it offer them short of the workhouse? Isabella began crying again. Anger, born of frustration, seized Hunter. He kicked the child and she fell down and cried no more. Steel cried out: 'you've killed my bairn!' But Isabella wasn't quite dead and a panic-stricken Hunter rushed to a nearby house for water to revive the infant. It was too late. Death came and the wretched man ran into a field, pulled a claspknife from his pocket and slashed furiously at his throat. But though he bled profusely and lapsed into unconsciousness, he failed to sever the vital artery.

Thereafter, events moved fast. The police were called out from Carlisle and entered upon the tragic scene. Hunter was taken to the Cumberland Infirmary where he lingered for some days, but lived. The child was taken to the local inn, the mother babbling profusely. A subsequent examination revealed that the infant's body was a mass of black marks around the head, back and arms. Indications were that she had been continuously beaten for weeks previously. The mother was to admit this.

By the following November, Hunter was well recovered and able to stand trial, his former girl friend having turned Queen's Evidence. He pleaded not guilty to murder and there was some suggestion that manslaughter could be a consideration. But medical evidence clearly indicated that injuries to the head and neck could well have caused death. Hunter claimed that he kicked the child and she fell against a milestone. But the milestone he referred to was some yards away from the scene of the final abuse. Mary Steel was thoroughly castigated by the defence as an unreliable witness, given her own background and way of life. But the bruises discovered upon the helpless infant were clearly etched upon the minds of those concerned. William Hunter was found guilty of wilful murder and sentenced to death. Steel was packed off on a train to her home in Old Cumnock immediately afterwards, primarily for her own safety.

Hunter was an exemplary prisoner while continuing to maintain that he had inflicted no more chastisement upon little Isabella than he would have inflicted upon his own child. He was hanged in Carlisle Gaol on 15th November, 1887. Few appeared concerned about his end but it is perhaps indicative of the murderer's make-up that he stuck to his views on child care to the end and left a brief statement completely exonerating himself.

35: TRAGEDY IN DENTON HOLME

Denton Holme has its origins in the 1850s when local working class housing was finally beginning to improve, an inner suburb of the old border city of Carlisle with streets of solid terraced houses once largely occupied by artisans and their families, many of whom worked in nearby factories. Most of the original factories have now closed or changed their focus and the type of resident has undergone some change. There is more traffic but the area still remains a fairly quiet backwater where little untoward generally occurs. Early in 1888 however, it was to be the scene of one of the most horrific murders ever committed in Carlisle, proving that nothing is ever quite as it seems.

On the morning of Saturday, 21st January of that year, Mrs. Dodd of Westmorland Street knocked on a door some yards up from her own to rouse her neighbour, Mrs. Jane Glaister. Receiving no reply she departed but became uneasy in her mind, her errand having not been a happy one. The previous evening Jane Glaister had asked Mrs. Dodd to give her a knock around seven a.m., the latter being a shopkeeper in the street and generally abroad early. For Jane Glaister intended to leave her husband the following morning. This was a far less common occurrence in Victorian Britain than today needless to say. But the wife was firmly resolved. A carrier was due later in the morning and she hadn't wanted to be late receiving him.

There were various items to go all the way to her father's home at Silloth where she intended to take up residence with her younger children aged two years and two months respectively. She had prevailed firmly upon her neighbour, the nearest thing she had to a friend, to ensure that she was up in time. Mrs. Dodd had agreed, not liking to refuse, even while she knew that the younger woman's husband was bound to be distressed. Yet she may still have sympathised with both the Glaisters, being fully aware of the reasons behind the intended parting.

At one time, any kind of break-up would have been unthinkable. The couple, both natives of the Silloth area, had been married for a number of years; they were still comparatively young in 1888, Richard Glaister being thirty-five years old and his wife thirty-three. Married at Abbeytown, they had lived there for some time afterwards. The future appeared assured. Richard had been a commercial traveller with a London firm of drapers and well thought of. But then he had sustained severe head injuries in a road accident. He recovered after a fashion but appeared to have completely lost his confidence and was unable to continue in his former situation. His father-in-law had helped him out financially at Abbeytown following this, then set him up in a drapery business closer to Carlisle, in the village of Scotby. But Glaister failed at this and in 1887 he and his wife and family moved into one of the small terraced houses in Westmorland Street, close to a jam factory in the heart of Denton Holme, a presentable but inconspicuous property, cheap to rent, probably the best they could aspire to under the circumstances.

By this time the marriage had gone into a complete decline. Richard and Jane Glaister had two children when the moved to Denton Holme and were presently to have another but the latter did nothing to sustain their relationship. The couple had no friends in the city. Jane Glaister had a brother, William Messenger, who was in the drapery trade in the city centre. But otherwise, there was only Mrs. Dodd. This contact had simply came about through the fact that the younger woman had taken to going into the latter's shop for odds and ends and when she had been confined with her last child the previous year, Mrs. Dodd had assisted. But generally the Glaisters kept themselves very much to themselves.

One of the persisting problems in the marriage of late had been Richard Glaister's total lack of will to seek work. After failing in business at Scotby he seemed to have given up completely. By this time the oldest child was being cared for by the wife's parents at Silloth and the older couple may also have been keeping the couple and their two younger children. Jane Glaister hadn't spared her husband verbally. He had threatened her in return but she had never taken his threats seriously. Finally she had decided to leave him and go with her remaining children to Silloth. She had advised her husband of her intention and confided everything to Mrs. Dodd. The carrier had been hired and the wife appeared to be in control.

Needless to say, nothing is ever clear-cut between any couple at such a time. Only the previous day they had been out together, getting the baby vaccinated and calling in on William Messenger on the way back to Westmorland Street. Even at that late stage, the frustrated wife had admitted to Mrs. Dodd that she would have stayed with Glaister had he shown any evidence at all of wishing to seek work. But no such evidence had ever been forthcoming. Notwithstanding, on the Friday evening of 20th January, 1888 he was still able to go out for a drink and returned fairly sober. But unbeknown to everyone, he also posted two letters to the East Cumberland News.... Jane Glaister called on her friend that same evening for a candle. She was never seen alive in the community again.

After receiving no reply to her knock the neighbour returned several times and knocked again without result. The carrier met with the same response. Mrs. Dodd became increasingly concerned with premonitions that all wasn't well. Finally she sought out William Messenger. The services of a local joiner were enlisted. He broke into the house. An appalling sight met his eyes in the first floor bedroom facing onto the front street.

Jane Glaister lay on her face halfway out of the bed, an arm and a leg trailing uselessly over the side; she wore only a slip and a skirt. There was blood all over the bedclothes and a cursory examination revealed that the woman's throat had been cut. She was quite dead. A further macabre touch was added by the sight of the two-year-old child playing with her mother's toes.

Richard Glaister was huddled up at the head of the bed, clutching a bread knife in his right hand. His throat was also cut but much more severely than that of his wife to the extent that he had almost decapitated himself. While William Hunter the child killer had failed to end it all by the same means the previous year, Richard Glaister had succeeded only too well. Could he have been influenced in his means of suicide by the action of Isabella Steel's murderer? We shall never know. But yet another knife was found under the mattress. Clearly he had meant business way and beyond that of Hunter, though the baby sat near his bloody corpse quite unharmed.

A crowd soon assembled, standing outside the small terraced house and gaping, as humankind is wont to do on such occasions. Of course they could see nothing, but they muttered among themselves and gazed up at the bedroom window and at the authority figures coming and going. Then finally they grew bored and departed.

Some time afterwards an inquest was held. More was revealed then of the unfortunate pair. William Messenger confirmed his brother-in-law's unhappy accident and the help afforded him afterwards by the family. A next-door neighbour of the couple, John Bell, spoke of hearing a woman's cry of 'murder' around seven forty-five a.m. on the Saturday morning followed by gurgling noises. But he admitted that he had done nothing and gone off to work. Bell came in for some criticism at the inquest but to be charitable to him, he may not have appreciated the extent of the assault at the time. He admitted that he suspected some kind of violence but thought that Jane Glaister had came round. Afterwards he was so upset that he had moved house.

Bell's testimony did at least establish what time the unfortunate woman had actually died. But greater evidence of the evil intended by Richard Glaister came from the editorial side of the East Cumberland News in the form of two letters which they had received on the day of the killing. The first was dated Tuesday, 17th January and is reproduced in full:

> Sir – kindly ask Mr. Messenger of Cow Lane, Silloth and Mrs. Glaister of Lesson Hall Wigton to see the letters. Then you will get full particulars of our end. It's been her cursed temper and her tongue that has caused this affair, to say nothing of the use of her hands. She has been killing me by inches and driven me distracted and ruined my business; but it's all over now, and may God have mercy upon our souls, protect our dear children, and keep them from harm.
>
> May this be a lesson to all to live happily together; forgiving and forgetting, not to be continually upcasting everything and instead of making houses happy, trying to make them miserable. Many in Scotby can tell what my fate was, and how, at the last she acted as she said knavishly with Dobinson and

Son, against my wishes, and even got a solicitor to assist her to do it, whilst I for peace had to hold my tongue.

Send a copy of your paper to Copestake and Co., of London.

Yours truly,
"R. Glaister"

The second letter was shorter but in similar vein. The date was significant. The wretched man may still not have quite made up his mind, holding the first letter over, but by Friday he appeared fully resolved and his wife was doomed.

Westmorland Street, Friday Night.

Dear Sir – I've lived as long as I could, and no longer than I could for peace in this world. I now fly to the next to get peace and rest for my poor shattered head and mind. Had I only had peace and kindness at home all would have been well; but only to get worried and cursed and sworn at, battered and all kinds of threats is more than I can bear. May God have mercy upon my soul. I may part with my loving children, but death will only do it. God knows it and into His all merciful hands do I commend my soul and hope and trust that my father-in-law and my mother will see that they are not abused now that Janie and I are gone.

"Believe me, yours truly"
"R Glaister"

Obviously a mind at the end of its tether and Jane Glaister had paid a heavy price for castigating her husband and planning to remove his children from him. A verdict that 'J.E. Glaister was wilfully murdered by Richard Glaister and that Richard Glaister committed suicide while in a temporary fit of insanity' was recorded. Rather a different verdict to the one recorded on Jane Davidson twenty-seven years previously. No mention of self-murder here. But then times and thinking had moved on since then however slowly. And the background dynamics had to be vastly different in the Glaister case anyhow. Even so, the verdict still didn't ring quite true. Richard Glaister had obviously been mentally troubled for much longer than the ten minutes or so it had taken to murder his wife, whatever the powers-that-be might say, though it was still questionable if he had ever been completely insane.

Mentally stressed, yes, and in these times a period in a psychiatric hospital might have wrought some benefit in someone like him. But though Garlands Hospital had been open for business since 1859, the so-called mad doctors there were still lacking in any great treatment skills in 1888. Hospitals like Garlands had gone up all over Britain in the nineteenth century. But they were more akin to depositories for those with a wide variety of mental and personality hang-ups than highly specialised nerve centres. Built to accommodate society's mentally vulnerable and others in the wake of industrial and sociological transformation with the emphasis on saving money, they had rapidly represented a growth industry though no more than that. Not for some years to come would there be any significant change in thinking or treatment on the mental health scene in Britain.

On the other hand, Richard Glaister may have undergone a complete personality change following his accident, or suffered an element of severe brain damage. If that was the case then anything approaching a cure would be doubtful even today. But constant nagging and haranguing wouldn't have helped either, whatever his mental diagnosis. Jane Glaister can perhaps be forgiven to some extent, brought financially low as she had been, humbled, concerned for her own and her children's future, impatient with a man once such a competent breadwinner who now refused to bestir himself. Any sympathy on her part must have been long gone, along with any attempt to understand the complexities of the human mind. However, the spin-off to this had been tragedy of an almost barbaric kind.

The following Tuesday morning, the corpses were removed from the house in Westmorland Street and placed in two hearses. Attended by a huge crowd of people, the cortege went no further than Citadel Station where the coffins were loaded onto a passenger train bound for Abbeytown. Once at Abbeytown, both were borne to the churchyard there and buried a few yards apart, the vicar having obviously decided to admit a suicide to hallowed ground though he need not have done so.

With both parties dead and buried there could be no sensational trial and the Glaister case was therefore fairly soon forgotten. Denton Holme quickly reverted to its normal unremarkable state. Not for more than half a century would it again merit dubious fame of sorts, as the home of pretty Margaret Cairns White, who met and married Hitler's Englishman, Lord Haw Haw, hanged for treason in 1946. But such a claim to notoriety was again transitory and short-lived.

36: AN UNCERTAIN VERDICT

On Sunday morning, 2nd June, 1889, twenty-six-year-old William Kerr left his home in Dalston to go on a pub crawl. Though the product of a respectable Protestant family and still living at home with his widowed mother and sisters, Billy Kerr does not appear to have been one to observe the niceties of Sunday, preferring a pint of beer to a pew and not averse to his own company.

A Cumbrian born and bred, Kerr had served his time as a blacksmith in the Carlisle area and been known as a pleasant and willing apprentice. But then he travelled away to work on Tyneside where his fondness for strong drink may have taken root. When he returned to live back at home again and take up work locally in his trade, he was certainly to become known as a fairly hardened drinker. Yet he still wasn't unlikeable either, a man good at his job, respectful to women and loyal to his family. He wasn't the prototype of the standard Cumbrian: sturdy, fair and ruddy cheeked. The opposite applied; William Kerr was slightly built and wiry if anything, with a dark complexion, black moustache and small matching beard. But though of Latin appearance, his name was local enough. There had been Kerrs on both sides of the border for centuries, alternatively spelt Carr on the English side, and his roots went some way back in the county. Yet his appearance was still to be later remarked upon almost musingly in the local press.

But this was in the future. For the moment, Kerr's mind must have been free of any thought of impending trouble or attendant publicity. Since he started out around eleven a.m. he may well have been without a very full stomach, ever a mistake prior to heavy imbibing. But the excursion commenced pleasantly enough as the little dark man plodded along the winding road from Dalston to Durdar through farming country, a distance of several miles. The weather was mediocre but the scenery no doubt compensated and by the time Durdar was reached, it was time for the first pint of the day and perhaps some bread and cheese. Indications are that several pints were consumed by the wanderer at Durdar before he then made his way through the fields and across the river to the village of Cummersdale. In fact he didn't arrive at the local there, the Spinners Arms, until early evening. By this time it had begun to rain but he was not entirely soaked so could well have sheltered somewhere en route.

Be this as it may, it was later in the evening when our man left the Spinners Arms and made his way down the short stretch of road leading to the main Carlisle/Dalston highway. To date he had moved in a several mile circle and now turned left, back towards Dalston, still reasonably sober, but now the Admiral Nelson Inn beckoned and he turned inside about nine thirty p.m. The latter hostelry, now long gone, was just around the corner from the Cummersdale turn-off and here Kerr stayed only a short time and drank two pints of cheap ale. Back outside, around ten p.m., he met an acquaintance, William Graham, who walked with him a short way towards Dalston. Graham was to be an important witness later in that he claimed to have found the young blacksmith sober.

It was a totally different state of affairs three quarters of a mile up the road at the then small hamlet of Lingley Close Head. William Kerr arrived at the public house there, the Horse and Farrier, around ten thirty p.m. William Graham had left him further up the road. If he had been sober then, Kerr didn't appear sober now. Unable to gain entry to the Horse and Farrier which had closed for the evening, he was seen by two witnesses from within the pub to stumble and go down on his knees upon the wet ground outside. He raised himself up, threw a stone at the front door and went off at a run towards Dalston. Obviously the worse for drink in the opinion of the twosome who observed him.

Chance is a peculiar thing and if another individual had not also taken off from base earlier that day, then the blacksmith would never have ended up as he did, in the condemned cell at Carlisle. Sebra Troughear was a totally different type of person to Billy Kerr. She was fifty-three years old and had spent most of her life in domestic service. A small, not unpresentable woman, she was unmarried and for the past two years had been housekeeper to a Mr. Walter Mitchinson of Lingley Close Head, about one and a quarter miles from Dalston on the Carlisle side. Distances and venues being so important in this case, they are given in some detail.

Miss Troughear left Lingley Close Head at around two fifteen p.m. on 2nd June, 1889, while Kerr may have been leaving Durdar. She walked to Dalston and out beyond it for a further mile to the home of a friend, Mrs. Strong of Hawksdale. She had both tea and supper with her friend and left to return to Mitchinson's house some minutes after nine p.m. that same Sunday. A girl named Armstrong saw her passing through Dalston shortly after ten o'clock that evening, heading back towards Lingley Close Head. She was never seen alive again in public.

Where was William Kerr now? We left him running from the forecourt of the Horse and Farrier Inn at Lingley Close Head in an inebriated state about ten thirty p.m. At around eleven fifteen he was met by two farm workers, Richard Bell and John Ward. They were returning from an evening out in Dalston and going to their homes situated along the Carlisle/Dalston Road. Both knew Kerr and hailed him and he responded in kind. But it seemed apparent that he was somewhat inebriated as he continued on his way towards Dalston.

Bell and Ward proceeded for some five hundred yards and more to Lingley Close Head and almost fell across a body lying by the side of the road in the darkness, no more than one hundred and fifty yards from the Horse and Farrier. Caught considerably aback, they knocked the landlord up and all returned to make an investigation utilising a lantern. The body was that of Sebra Troughear. Her clothing was disarranged. Her legs were fully exposed. It seemed she had been sexually violated. The woman was dead though her mouth and eyes weren't completely closed. Her body was still warm in parts. She didn't appear to have struggled too hard.

Meanwhile, the young Dalston blacksmith was still making his unsteady way home. At about midnight, he was met about one hundred yards from his mother's house by a farm servant, Joe Watson, and the latter's friend, Henry Marrs. Watson and Marrs were both to testify that Kerr was very drunk and that his clothes were wet and dirty. Yet he was able to speak with them too, advising of his earlier trip round by Durdar and Cummersdale and that he had got none of the heavy rain. Shortly afterwards, he was home and in bed, Marrs having seen him to his house.

At Lingley Close Head it was a different state of play. The police were making a thorough examination of the body and the area immediately surrounding it by the light of the pub lantern. The woman lay on her back, staring upwards. There was blood on her left cheek but no wound to accompany it. Some of her attire was found nearby: skirt and bonnet, as well as false hair and an umbrella. More ominously still, there were knee marks in the soft ground between the legs, and a heel mark. Bell and Ward were still present, claiming to have seen no one except Kerr on the quiet road between Lingley Close Head and the outskirts of Dalston that night. The police listened, and then they acted.

William Kerr was arrested at home shortly before daybreak. He had been in a deep sleep and didn't want to accompany the officers concerned. But the details were spelt out to him and he quickly realised he had no choice. Very soon he was on his way to Carlisle for intensive questioning. It had been a simple rural arrest. From the onset, Kerr had maintained his innocence, claiming never to have met Sebra Troughear or to know who she was. But the police were nothing if they were not persistent. They might be at a disadvantage in tracking down such villains as Rudge, Martin and Baker but could not be faulted in their methods of gathering clues and building up a case right away at a time like this; even while forensic detection was as yet still in its infancy. They might work at a basic level, but they worked thoroughly. On the other hand, they weren't infallible either of course.

It was noticed immediately that the suspect's coat and vest were hanging over the remains of the open kitchen fire to dry – both garments were very wet. His trousers, even more relevant as evidence, were folded over a rail at the stairhead; they too were wet, and caked with mud about the knees. His boots too were recovered and found to be plastered with mud. All the foregoing were taken away to be examined in detail.

At the police station, Kerr broke down but maintained his innocence, describing his pub crawl of the previous day with some clarity, but adamant that he had never encountered the dead woman. Then he quietened down, enquiring dully how long he was likely to be in custody? The station sergeant spoke of it being a week at least – a gross miscalculation indeed, as matters evolved. Kerr remarked that it must mean murder if the woman had been found dead, going on to suggest that drink must be to blame for the mess he was in? The sergeant made some show of agreeing, but refused to commit himself further.

An inquest was quickly held with the result that there was deemed ample evidence to send Kerr to the assizes on a charge of wilful murder with malice aforethought, the press providing full lurid details to the extent of all but convicting the man in the minds of the public before he was even tried – such being the manner of reporting in those days as we have already seen; a not unfamiliar state of affairs in our own times either of course.

But certainly the evidence was sufficient, or so it seemed.... Not only had Kerr been abroad in the area at the time of the crime with no one else having been seen there, but he had had two fresh abrasions on his face and had rubbed off the accompanying blood when his attention had been drawn to it. Likewise the victim had had blood on her face, but no wound. So whose blood was it? Blood grouping was still unknown in those days so full proof was lacking but many had already drawn their own conclusions. Even more damning was the vomit which had been found on both Troughear and Kerr; the vomit had been put under a microscope and the same chemical characteristics had been revealed. There was also the mud on the knees of Kerr's trousers; in fact the marks on the ground between the deceased woman's legs proved none too legible as it had been a wet night but marks there had been. The victim had also had a bruise on the right hand side of her head which could have been caused by a heavy blow. Couldn't this in its turn have been administered by the Dalston blacksmith prior to the rape taking place? And to heap even further odium onto Kerr, it was now being alleged that he had criminally assaulted a deaf and dumb girl at Dalston the day prior to Sebra Troughear's death. But still William Kerr maintained his total innocence and his family were all standing by him.

The trial at Carlisle on 12th July, 1889 drew a fairly small crowd initially. Rather odd perhaps, considering the magnitude of the crime and the publicity which it had generated. But it was market day after all and once the early business had been got through, the public gallery filled up quickly enough, with those present destined to experience maximum sordidity and drama. Right from the onset, it appeared that allowing for some slight anomalies, William Kerr would be found guilty, with the police proceeding to bring more evidence still against the swarthy little man whose Latin attributes afforded one particular journalist more than cursory attention. This latest evidence took the form of a number of red threads from the victim's petticoats, which had been found on the trousers of the defendant. Other detrimental evidence continued to be the victim's vomit, allegedly discovered on Kerr's coat and vest, plus the fact that the mud on the knees of his moleskin trousers was different to that onto which he had been seen to stumble outside the Horse and Farrier. And there was clear evidence of rape, with the victim having sustained an internal tear of three quarters of an inch. So it went on. Slowly but surely, the prosecution produced their witnesses and hammered home their case. The outcome appeared a foregone conclusion.

Nevertheless, the case was not to prove quite so clear cut. The defence went on to argue that anyone in Kerr's advanced state of intoxication would surely not be able to rape anyone. Certainly some witnesses had testified as to how drunk he had appeared to be around the time of the crime, even while William Graham had testified to his sobriety outside the Admiral Nelson. The mud on his trousers could surely have been picked up anywhere as he stumbled drunkenly about; the woman herself might well have vomited, but so might Kerr in his drunken state, argued Shee for the defence. Meanwhile, since the victim had definitely died as a result of suffocation, two currants having been discovered in her windpipe, this surely rendered the blow to her head as of no great significance? It was put that she might just as easily have incurred this as a result of falling onto the road prior to Kerr passing by or while being carried from the scene of the crime on a ladder. Much too was made of the fact that the red threads were not discovered for several weeks afterwards. Mightn't they have got onto the prisoner's clothing at the police station after his clothing had got mixed up with that of the deceased woman's? The defence had something to say about the blood discovered on Kerr's clothing too. It transpired that at the police station after being arrested, he had spat blood, the implication being that he could have hurt himself earlier while stumbling about, thus getting bloody along the way. And in fact he had had blood on both his waistcoat and trousers, along with other kinds of stains, though the latter were not specified. The blood on Sebra Troughear's face was given no great airing, as though it were of minor importance now. This in the main was the case for the defence.

Nonetheless, Mr. Justice Stephen was having little of this. He placed particular emphasis in his summing up on the fact that half an hour could not be accounted for by the prisoner between his appearance outside the Horse and Farrier and his meeting with Bell and Ward, who themselves had alibis sufficient to keep them clear of suspicion. And certainly Sebra Troughear had died within that half hour for her body had still been warm in parts after its discovery. The judge questioned Kerr's level of intoxication too, feeling that he had got drunk rather too quickly after leaving the Admiral Nelson.... If anything, the cold air ought to have surely sobered him? Here his Lordship might well have been amiss in his thinking. But he was probably right when he suggested that some men's beastial passions were more likely to be aroused when drunk...?

There was more in this vein. All in all, an adverse summing up which reflected perhaps to some degree at least in the jury's verdict of guilty of murder, brought in after only ten minutes and with no recommendation to mercy. Kerr appeared to accept sentence of death stoically enough. But then as his sister shrieked in anguish from the gallery, he took a silk handkerchief from his pocket and gave it to a friend, saying: "Give this to my sister and tell her that I die an innocent man". A touching gesture of itself calculated to stir the hearts of his audience.

In fact, William Kerr escaped the scaffold. He was to have hanged on 25th July, 1889, but the anti-hanging fraternity were soon labouring on his behalf. The glaring press coverage may even have worked in their favour, more-so given detrimental details of the two women involved, for of course there had also been the charge of assault on the deaf and dumb girl. The latter charge had quickly came to little, it transpiring that the mute was well known locally for her promiscuity. But it was now also divulged that Sebra Troughear was in sum, rather less respectable than she might have been, having given birth to two illegitimate children in the past. This may not have been very fair copy but it might also have assisted Kerr's supporters in a subtle kind of way. Certainly the number of those signing petitions in support of the condemned man now quickly ran into four figures. Many in Dalston itself signed. But this could also have been indicative of normal mood. Beyond doubt, there did remain many in Cumberland, as anywhere else in Victorian Britain, who still favoured the drop for killers such as Cass, Hagen, Hunter and others. But Kerr was rather different. He did obviously engender a sneaking kind of sympathy in many local quarters. Rape was not entirely uncommon in Victorian Cumberland and was generally treated with revulsion. But many now appeared to feel that though Kerr might well be guilty enough, he had possibly been no more than a man who drank too much and who had simply got himself into an appalling mess, whether or not his unfortunate victim had been rather less respectable than she first appeared, many Cumbrians being no strangers to drunkenness and its complex effects.

There was general satisfaction in the locality when the condemned man's sentence was commuted to penal servitude for life, but this was soon replaced by an even lighter sentence of fourteen years penal servitude. Public opinion aside, the legal arbitrators had quite evidently been debating long and hard on the case of William Kerr behind the scenes. The death sentence had been imposed in the first instance on the basis that Kerr had been found guilty of raping Miss Troughear, that she had consequently died as a result of the rape, and so it must have been murder. But there had already been at least one precedent indicating contrary thinking. In Manchester, a man named Parton had recently had his sentence of death commuted when it had been ruled that the victim he had rendered dead with chloroform prior to intended robbery had not been deliberately done to death. Such a case and its outcome may at least have had some bearing on legal reasoning. At any rate, back in Cumberland, William Kerr's life had now been spared, the original verdict in effect deemed questionable.

Here it is perhaps timely to note just what penal servitude involved, for we have already encountered others in these pages who have received it. It was scarcely a soft option but an improvement on hard labour which normally took in the treadmill, oakum picking and solitary confinement and was calculated to break the hardest spirit. By comparison, penal servitude might often involve a greater spread of more useful activities both inside and outside the prison. A prisoner could be given the opportunity to practice his trade, providing he had one, and there was always the incentive of a ticket of leave. On the other hand, any British prison was still a grim place to be in the late nineteenth century and someone like Kerr would no doubt find it hard to bear being a convict, more-so given the comfortable happy home he had came from and the opportunity to roam at will. But at least he still had his life, and his family could perhaps anticipate having him home again in a decade.

Even now, Cumberland was not destined to hear the last of him for in 1891, still protesting his innocence, he succeeded in bringing his case to the attention of the judicature again. But the latter, appearing to feel that enough had already been done for him, dismissed his appeal and he returned to prison and comparative obscurity. Meanwhile, the body of the unfortunate Sebra Troughear continued to decompose in Dalston churchyard.

Could Kerr have been innocent? It is true that no one saw him commit any crime. No weapon was ever traced to him. He didn't attempt to make off across the fields afterwards, continuing shakily along the road to Dalston in the darkness as though nothing were amiss and speaking with several potential witnesses on the final leg of his journey. The heel mark noted at the scene of the crime was discovered not to be his. He doggedly maintained his innocence to the end.

In these times, forensic testing would serve to eliminate any doubts prevailing. Notwithstanding, there still seemed some evidence against Kerr as already outlined. Yet some of the pleas of his defence counsel were far from invalid either and one does tend to wonder if such a case ought ever to have came to trial at all at the time? Really, if he had died on the scaffold in 1889, who knows but what he might well have became much better remembered than he did, eventually achieving the status of a kind of nineteenth century Derek Bentley or James Hanratty?

However, without forensic evidence we can never be sure now. What is more certain is that if Hugh Grant was one of the most sordid criminals to occupy the condemned cell at Carlisle as a result of his excessive imbibing, William Kerr had to be the most wretched, with a question mark still hanging over him regardless for if he wasn't the culprit, who was? And the harmless woman who died in what was known at the time as the Dalston Road murder was definitely one of Cumberland's most tragic victims.

37: CUMBERLAND'S LAST HANGING

The crime perpetrated by twenty-three-year-old Joseph Wilson in 1892 has little to commend it to posterity. The man himself is notable mainly because he was the last condemned criminal to be hanged in Carlisle Gaol. His hanging was also the last in the whole of Cumberland. On both these points alone, he does merit some additional attention. Yet there was rather more to the man and his crime too.

The previous decade had seen a disturbing increase in the number of those being tried and sentenced to death for murder in the county as already noted. Margaret Messenger, Hugh Grant, Anthony Benjamin Rudge, John Martin, James Baker, William Hunter and William Kerr, of these seven, four had been hanged, with Hugh Grant having been fortunate to obtain a reprieve at almost the eleventh hour. Joseph Bell and James Maynard Harrison might just as easily have found themselves in greater trouble too. Had Bell succeeded in his twisted plan, he would almost surely have hanged in 1882. Harrison's fate in the event of a guilty verdict is more questionable. He was very young after all. But Thomas Munroe had been hanged in 1855 while still in his teens. Cumbrian courts had softened to some degree since 1855. But they could still be ruthless too, as was evidenced in the case of Joseph Wilson, who given his state of mind, was another who should probably never have been hanged at all.

In the meantime, from 1889, there had been a lull in capital crime in Cumberland. There had been a similar state of play following the rash of killings in the early 1860s. No more than pure coincidence perhaps for there was still continuing crime of a lesser kind: burglary, poaching, indecency, child neglect and bigamy. And a serious shooting incident at Stanwix in 1890. But by and large there were no spectacular crimes post 1889, and court lists were less than they had been in previous decades. This had to be due to the changing social scene to some degree. There was continuing unemployment but those who did have work were often earning rather more and there were better social amenities by way of greater numbers of schools, libraries, reading rooms, theatres and restaurants, Cumberland not being greatly different to many other regions in this respect, and now well served by both road and rail.

The gaol at Carlisle was itself coming under increasing scrutiny by the authorities and its usefulness queried? Opened in 1827 to serve the whole county, it was quickly in full swing, Fox and Tinnaney being hanged there together that same year. It was to remain well used over succeeding decades catering for all manner of criminals. But by the late 1870s it was no longer the preserve of the local authorities, having been taken over by the government. By the early 1890s there was a whole lot of new thinking on prisons and prisoners in vogue. As the century edged nearer to its close, it had became prison departmental policy to site prisons away from the centres of cities and towns where most of the population still resided, just as many of the Victorian lunatic asylums had been sited in the surrounding countryside decades before, Garlands being a prime example.

Carlisle Gaol was even more badly situated than some of its kind, now being overlooked by high buildings on the Victoria Viaduct. It was also close to the railway station with all its smoke and steam and the gas works were also close by. For Carlisle Gaol, the writing was finally on the wall.

Yet it would be some years yet before it did close and it was still a hanging prison when Joseph Wilson arrived there under heavy escort in January 1892 from Millom, having taken a gun and blasted almost half his landlady's head away. Even now, the reasons for the killing are obscure. But there were those at the time who queried Wilson's sanity and given the great inroads subsequently made in the fields of psychology and psychiatry, perhaps we are rather closer in these times to reaching a more balanced conclusion, which evaded the Victorian court at the time. If only there had been more public interest in the case in 1892, the prisoner might still have escaped the gallows. But Wilson was a nonentity and a nonentity he has remained. Like many others convicted of murder in the county in Victorian times, he wasn't even a Cumbrian, though he would be in these times given more recent boundary changes.

Joseph Wilson was born in Barrow when it was still part of Lancashire. His father was a hawker and there were a number of children in the family, three with incomplete palates, though all grew up worldly enough. If there was anyone tainted it was Mrs. Wilson. At the time her third son Joseph was born she had been a prey to delusions and epileptic fits and the father, William Wilson, had taken to locking her in the bedroom when he went out on his rounds. He also had a cousin in an insane asylum but there was no other evidence of insanity in the family.

Joseph grew up undersized but wiry. He was swarthy and we are reminded to some extent here of William Kerr though Joseph Wilson never grew a beard as Kerr did, preferring a walrus-like moustache. Commonplace features and a low forehead gave him a dull look. He had been sent to school but learnt little and at the time of his trial and execution, remained illiterate. But he was capable of hard work: his first job at fifteen years was labouring on the railway, then the family moved to Kendal and the skinny youngster assisted his father at hawking for a time. Finally, of his own free will, he moved to the Millom area. At Haverigg, now best known for its Category C Prison, he obtained work as a quarryman.

Lodgings were no problem. For some years he had known a householder in the area, Richard Crossman. Crossman had became a widower fairly early but after the manner of many left in such circumstances in those days, had married a younger woman, who had taken on his own children and borne him five more by the time Joseph Wilson moved in with the family in the spring of 1891. A friendly affable woman, Marion Crossman was still only in her early thirties and pregnant again that year. Wilson was the tenth member of the household in an overcrowded terraced cottage, but treated like all the other offspring.

The older members of the family were all working and the household was better off than some, given the economics of that particular area. Richard Crossman liked to indulge himself leisurely in shooting game during his spare moments and kept a gun in the house for this purpose, a double-barrelled breach-loading weapon. This was generally stored for safety in the master bedroom along with the necessary cartridges when not in use. The fact remained that guns and other weapons were not at all uncommon in much of rural Cumberland in the last century, a throwback perhaps to more turbulent times, though the county was not alone in this. Unfortunately however, there remained the minimum of emphasis on the safe-keeping of such articles.

As for Joseph Wilson, he knew of Crossman's gun. But to date he had never been known to handle it or afford evidence of any kind of aggressive or macho behaviour. Quite the contrary; he was popular with all the young Crossman children and was not averse to baby-sitting. He had gone on to get engaged to one of the older Crossman daughters and had begun buying furniture. The engagement had soon been broken off but in spite of this, Joseph still remained one of the family. Come new year's eve, 1892, he went with Richard Crossman and his wife to a neighbour's house where they drank and intended to see the new year in. But Joe was home by midnight, arriving back alone and going straight to bed, albeit not noticeably the worse for drink or difficult in his behaviour.

The following day was a holiday for most of the community. Richard Crossman rose early to catch a train to an older daughter's home some miles away. Whether the impending tragedy might have been averted had he remained at home will always be questionable. He did appear to have some influence over his young friend and lodger, but who knows? What is more certain is that he noted the gun standing in its usual place in a corner of the bedroom and had no reason to believe that it would be moved. Some cartridges were also in a box in a nearby drawer.

Marion Crossman was also up and about early and embarked on a tour of several nearby houses to enjoy a new year drink. It was all commonplace and harmless but to one neighbour she made a remark of some significance which was never gone into in any detail at the subsequent trial, to the effect that Joseph had made a comment to her earlier and that she was thus avoiding him. When he appeared on the scene again around eight thirty a.m. she hid in a neighbour's coal hole but he saw her. She emerged and they laughed together and Wilson had a glass of beer with her. It transpired that he wanted his breakfast and she went off to prepare it. Wilson was heard to say: 'Someone else will have their breakfast in two hours'. Just short of two hours later Marion Crossman was shot in the head, her husband's gun having previously been observed in the kitchen by one of the family, though who had brought it down?

Another family member had been sleeping in the parlour. The sound of the gun awoke him. He jumped up and was appalled to see his stepmother lying on the floor with a sizeable portion of her head blown away. Close to the body was Joseph Wilson. He was laughing and dancing and mouthing rapid sentences: 'I shot her very well' and 'I might as well do it as be done'. And more damning still: 'I put a second cartridge into the gun in case I should not succeed in hitting her with the first'. It should probably be stressed that this was as his utterances were written down afterwards. Joe Wilson could scarcely have made himself understood so perfectly and succinctly. He was of undoubted limited intellect and would normally have spoken in broad dialect, like George Cass and Joseph Bell and others whom we have met in these pages. But he had taken Marion Crossman's life it seemed and the implement of death was close by him. And this was a man who earlier that very morning, had been playing with the youngest child of the family.

His arrest speedily followed. On the way to the police station under escort, he continued to burble, though who was to make much sense of the whole gruesome scenario? Wilson had already admitted to shooting a woman who had previously shown him nothing but kindness. Now the police were treated to such comments as: 'You need not be in such a hurry, I don't mean to run away' and 'I made a bloody good job of it. I'm happy, she's happy' and 'I'll most likely get my neck stretched for it.' All this from a man who didn't appear deranged, who wasn't drunk. And not until almost the end was he to express any regret.

He lay in Carlisle Gaol until his trial the following March, a model prisoner. Appearing at the Assizes he pleaded not guilty to wilful murder. Essentially, the defence was one of insanity. Much was made of the family history, the incomplete palates, the epileptic mother, the father's mad cousin. But the prosecution was quick to come back with the argument that incomplete palates scarcely constituted insanity, that many families had been known to contain at least one mental case, that delusions and epilepsy were not so uncommon and that none of the foregoing need lead to murder.

A key witness was the Medical Superintendent of Garlands Mental Hospital, Dr. Archibald Campbell. Ironically enough, within just a few years, Campbell was destined to be on trial himself at Carlisle following a murky episode within the hospital, found mad and sentenced to Her Majesty's Pleasure. But in 1892 he was still an authority in his field and there to be listened to. He felt that the prisoner was a poor specimen, mentally and physically, with a mind below average and that such individuals could be the product of a parent insane at the time of pregnancy. And yet he didn't feel the subject had been sufficiently researched to allow him to state this as a definite fact.

Other witnesses didn't have a specific opinion either. Richard Crossman, now sadly widowed for the second time, simply couldn't bring himself to speak ill of Joseph at all, remaining amazed if anything that such a mild-mannered lad could do such a thing. Other family members were also remarkably charitable.

The prisoner sat through it all, subdued and benign in the dirty suit of clothes he had been wearing at the time of the killing. He had claimed that he couldn't recall all the circumstances of the incident but appeared indifferent to his situation irrespective. It did emerge that no one had ever seen him bring the gun downstairs but he had admitted to the shooting from the onset and there was no other suspect. Neither was there any question at all of him having been drunk. The jury were only out twenty-three minutes before returning with a unanimous verdict of guilty, but with a recommendation to mercy given the prisoner's previous good character. The Haverigg quarryman received the death sentence unmoved.

Almost at once, the anti-hanging fraternity swung into action with a petition and a number of meetings in Carlisle and other places sufficiently heavily populated within the county. It might have seemed that they had a good case for commutation of Wilson's sentence. Here was a normally placid young man who had killed his benefactor's wife for no tangible reason and had danced and jibed afterwards. He had consumed some alcohol beforehand but a very negligible amount. Surely there had to be something seriously amiss with the prisoner's mind whatever the medical fraternity thought, affording every reason to spare his life? At a period in Cumberland's history when the law had seen fit to spare a drunken reprobate like Hugh Grant and look favourably upon the case of William Kerr, surely Joseph Wilson had to be in with a similar chance? Such was the reasoning.

But perhaps unfortunately for Wilson, he had lived and killed in one of the more isolated areas of nineteenth century Cumberland. Haverigg was seventy miles from Carlisle alone, and a considerable distance too from such busy towns as Workington and Whiteheaven. True, communications had greatly improved locally over the decades but they still hadn't done a great deal to put places like Haverigg on the map. Little county-wide publicity had been engendered at all. And while the man had been tried at Carlisle, his trial had still excited none of the interest stimulated by those of Grant and Kerr with their more questionable facets. To the majority of Cumbrians, Wilson was just a distant simpleton who had shot a harmless woman in a fit of pique and deserving of all he got. At the eleventh hour, some fresh attempt was made to determine the quarryman's state of mind so obviously some doubts must have remained at higher level. Dr. Campbell was replaced by Dr. Nicholson of Broadmoor and Dr. Brayne of Woking but though they deemed Wilson of limited intellect, they questioned if he could be labelled insane.

Time had ran out for Joseph Wilson. After the doctors were done he had a visit from two brothers and a sister but failed to sustain any kind of reasonable conversation with them. The trio quickly departed but did leave a new suit of clothing for their brother to wear at his execution, evidence of some ongoing concern for respectability within the family. The condemned man died at eight a.m. on 23rd March, 1892, having slept well the night before and enjoyed his breakfast of porridge and milk. There was no more than a thousand outside the gaol on the morning of the execution, evidence in itself perhaps as to how little interest the prisoner's crime had generated. But indicative too perhaps, of the fact that private executions as a whole were beginning to excite far less mass morbidity and attention than public executions had done. And after the passing bell had ceased to toll, the crowd melted quickly away.

Wilson died, still claiming that he couldn't recall all the circumstances of the crime but that he preferred death to penal servitude, a riddle to the end. After all these years, what can the armchair criminologist deduce from the Haverigg killing? A clue of sorts may lie in Marion Crossman's giggly behaviour on the morning of her death. She could still have been an attractive woman; there is no reason to doubt that, even while she had borne five children and was expecting another. Scarcely into her thirties, of warm friendly disposition, she may well have given her limited young lodger unintentional signals to the extent that he had became totally enamoured and possessive of her. Early on new year's morning as we know, he had said something personal to her but what he had said was never revealed specifically given the prevailing morality of the times. However, it was enough to drive her into the coal hole later and after her death, the bottoms of her legs were found to be badly bruised. Had the rejected one kicked her in a kind of maniacal frenzy some time before?

Wilson said something else immediately after the killing indicating a marked obsession with his victim: 'The first person who enters the house to touch her, I'll shoot'. Everyone thought the undersized limited lad harmless prior to the appalling crime except perhaps the elder daughter of the household. She had been engaged to him and then rejected him, after possibly detecting a darker side. Could he have carried the seeds of mental instability after all, as Campbell had as good as said, and snapped when he came up against emotions he didn't know how to handle? We can't really be sure, but whether mentally troubled or not, it does seem clear that Joseph Wilson was a very odd personality and much more lucid killers had been spared the drop in more recent years. Sadly enough too, though it wasn't mentioned at the time, he had of course taken the lives of two people because the pregnant victim's child died when she did. It was a tragic state of affairs altogether.

But Joseph Wilson's main claim to fame would continue to lie in the fact that he was the last man to be hanged in Carlisle Gaol and the whole of Cumberland. Not too long afterwards, the gaol itself was officially condemned as unsuitable. By 1922 it had became cheaper to intern Cumbrian offenders in such prisons as Durham, where murderers could also be hanged as required. Later that same year, the gaol had closed for good. By 1933 it had been demolished. It was probably not before time.

38: THE LIFE AND DEATH OF A MISFIT

We began with the case of a degenerate poacher who committed a heinous murder. Subsequently, amidst a medley of other reprobates, we have encountered those who took innocent lives in the course of their poaching activities. Their cases have not been amongst the most scintillating presented here. The perpetrators were either drunk or macho in the main with an element of provocation involved at times. On the other hand, there were many more of their ilk in Cumberland who simply treated poaching as a way of life and a useful sideline, though harmed no one at all in the process; their kind are still around in the county today to some degree.

Our narrative concludes with details of yet another convicted poacher, and his end, but one who was rather different to John Pearson, William Graham and Co., and who had other illegal strings to his bow including alleged highway robbery. John 'Bant' Pattinson was possessed of many shady traits though would probably have balked at taking a life in the course of his exploits. His tragedy is that he could have done so much better. He was brighter than the average and had not been without opportunity. And yet he manifested some similarities to the likes of John Pearson too, and other wretches whom we have encountered in these pages. It does not seem unfitting that we should end with an account of this misfit though indeed, to the forces of law and order, he was probably no more than a squalid nuisance.

His victims may well have seen him rather differently. He must have upset quite a lot of people in his comparatively short lifetime, particularly those whom he physically assaulted or robbed. Also those whom he thwarted during attempts to catch him or get him convicted. He had the last laugh in any number of situations which could have worked to his detriment. Ironically enough however, he has also had the last laugh in death for though apparently once a big enough fish in a little pond, and well reported in many respects, we have no idea now of how tall he was or what he looked like or how he dressed or spoke. Even his last given address is ambiguous. In 1894, the year of his death, he was said to be living in Barleystack Lane, Rickergate, Carlisle. But Barleystack Lane was such a slum, even by late Victorian standards that it had largely been cleared of residents before the end of the 1880s. If Pattinson was still living there in 1894 then we might assume that he was squatting, or had lied about his address as he had lied about other things as a matter of course, even preferring to adopt a false name on the most trivial expeditions.

What appears certain is that he was born in March 1855 and spent most of his life in Carlisle and around it. His parents were said to be respectable working people and there is no reason to believe that he was not 'well brought up'. He was put to the trade of tailoring and completed his apprenticeship. He married and had children. Ostensibly, he had made a good start for a Victorian working class lad. But already it seems, he wanted less and less to do with hard work and respectability. Increasingly he must have begun to neglect his trade and family, having developed a taste for poaching with its element of excitement and fast returns. When he wasn't poaching he was into other dubious activities, between imbibing in the numerous drinking dens in and around Rickergate and Caldewgate. He was generally known as Bant, a titular substitute indigenous to Cumberland. A man is known by the company he keeps so they say. Bant obviously preferred to associate with those of shady habits like himself, notably Chitty Brocker, who was destined to drown on a poaching expedition in 1890.

But Blocker's death was in the future and Pattinson got clear of the affair in any case. Somehow, he appears to have evaded any kind of custodial sentence until 1877 when he went to prison for drunkenness though he was probably well known to the police prior to that. Over ensuing years he went on to amass various convictions inclusive of unlawful wounding and malicious damage and assaulted the Chief Warder of Carlisle Gaol on one occasion while serving a sentence for beating up his own wife, Sarah Jane. Definite echoes of John Pearson here. At times he would bang on the gaol door in English street late at night to cause annoyance to the keepers inside when he wasn't inside himself, enjoying yet another tilt at authority while the worse for drink.

Though devious in some respects, Pattinson still gives every evidence of having been a gregarious creature within his own chosen peer group and enjoying the limelight as a whole. And yet when it came to poaching, his first love, he was not averse to working secretly and alone. Probably the man and his exploits were blown out of proportion by the media of the period to some degree. But he is said to have had his own method of catching salmon well perfected and there is no evidence to dispute that, creeping to the river banks under cover of darkness and gaffing those fish which lay close by. Many of the latter had a tendency to be diseased but this was of no consequence to a man like Pattinson. He would give them a fresher look by smearing them with blood from the local slaughter house and then hawk them from door to door in Carlisle. Almost invariably he sold the lot to unsuspecting householders.

But he wasn't averse to operating during daylight hours either, again along by the banks of the Eden and its satellite rivers, though also with some support on such occasions. He is said to have had a dog trained to carry salmon across the water to associates on the other side at such times, the fish tied to the animal's back. And pursued once by frustrated water bailiffs straight to his home, he apparently threw the fish he was carrying into his wife's washing tub where she was occupied then made to be about normal household business. Sarah Jane did nothing. The house was searched from top to bottom but no fish were ever found and the bailiffs left in disgust. When not poaching salmon, the reprobate might be poaching game, at which he also excelled.

Such people generally have little to commend them to the vast majority. But it is an undeniable fact that the British have a weakness for characters inclusive of some within the criminal fraternity, providing the latter are not too odious and possess the wit to outsmart the establishment and seem to uphold the underdog in the process. Indeed, we have seen evidence of that several times within these pages, no one loving a character better than the Cumbrians even to the extent of some of them cheering when such a specimen as William Graham escaped the drop. It is regrettable but Pattinson probably did enjoy some measure of popularity amongst ordinary local folk given certain of his exploits. He also proved to have the ability to impress some of his 'betters' too it seems and this of all places was in the courtroom. Though successful enough as a poacher, he was still caught on a number of occasions for that also just as he had been caught for other things, suffering as he did from over-exposure in a small city and its rural environs. But often in court he would eschew the services of a solicitor, preferring to defend himself and was so astute and articulate that he was known to get off at times, or at least obtain bail, whereas others of his kind might often be less fortunate and spend weeks inside awaiting trial, or even months.

And no one could ever say that he didn't stretch himself to the utmost. At one stage, we are told, he joined the Cumberland Militia and proved a natural, joining in all the activities and winning prizes on the sports field. The army apparently understood Bant just as Bant understood the army. He served with overall distinction and eventually became the regimental tailor, never once infringing army rules and regulations, at least none that anyone was aware of. Our man was nothing if he wasn't adaptable. Loath to practice his trade at all as a means to making an honest living, he was nevertheless a very good tailor by all accounts. It had been useful to him in the militia. But it was also useful to him in prison for he used it to make himself fairly indispensable and comfortable while serving out his sentences.

All in all, a talented misfit with arrogance for anything who lived life as he wished to live it, associating with those with whom he wished to be with it with and probably continuing to enjoy a measure of good-humoured tolerance from those who did not have to contend with him at close hand. The stark reality was rather different needless to say. Pattinson was totally self-centred with a definite penchant for violence. His wife was thoroughly sick of him and in these times would probably have left him long since but she also had children to consider. He was drinking as hard as ever and was short of money but still had no wish to earn an honest living. At the time of his thirty-ninth birthday he was waiting to go on trial yet again, for an alleged offence of being implicated in the theft of a watch and purse from a drunken cattle drover. However, he had obtained bail while his two co-defendents remained inside; he didn't appear in the least concerned to change his way of life and was confident that he would get off when he eventually appeared at the Assizes. But as events transpired, he never faced another judge. At least not on this earth.

On the Wednesday afternoon of 24th March, 1894, Pattinson spent some time drinking locally with two of his cronies, John Gill and John Smith, from the Caldewgate area of the old city. The trio drank steadily but moderately, none being too flush with money, before returning to their homes. An aimless sort of day insofar as it compared to that of many of their fellow citizens, but one to which the threesome were accustomed and not unreconciled.

Shortly before eight o'clock that evening Gill and Smith sought out Pattinson at his home. The three Johns all wanted to make some money in a hurry. For all his bravado, Pattinson was taking no chances with the latest case pending against him. In this instance he had decided to hire a barrister but such people were no cheaper then than they are now. Gill and Smith were clear of criminal charges but their leisurely lifestyle still required funding. The result was that they all decided to try for some fish in the River Petteril but far enough away from the city to avoid unwelcome attention. The stretch of water they settled upon was close to Wreay, off the Penrith road.

None must have been sorry to depart from the Pattinson domicile, given Sarah Jane's stony silence. As it was, they were all adequately fortified. Pattinson had half a bottle of port wine; Gill and Smith had a bottle of rum between them. They set off down Botchergate and up past London Road Terrace, unchanged from the time of William Charlton's arrest more than thirty years previously. Soon they were out in the country, the great sprawling Harraby housing estate being a thing of the very distant future. They made slow progress thereafter and it was almost eleven o'clock before they reached their destination.

Alas they were due for a disappointment. The fish weren't running their way at all that night. In disgust they finally set off homewards around midnight but the fields were dark and they were quickly lost. They came to a fence and Pattinson climbed over it. Seconds later he let out a shout and vanished completely. Only then did Gill and Smith realise that they were standing on the edge of the huge Newbiggin Quarry, which was sixty feet deep. They rapidly retraced their steps and eventually found their way to the Golden Fleece Inn, sited close to the present Number 3 junction of the M6 motorway.

There were few late travellers at all in those days. The road they were on was designed essentially for horse-drawn traffic and most folk still went to bed early. However, the two luckless poachers were eventually able to rouse the landlord of the Golden Fleece, William Garnett. Probably reluctantly, they agreed to a policeman being called and P.C. Illingworth of Wreay attended, arriving at the inn by the usual means of travel in those days – the bicycle, still actually in vogue for country policemen more than fifty years later, senior officers generally continuing to travel by gig, until the advent of the motor vehicle.

Illingworth instigated a search with the aid of lanterns. Pattinson was discovered lying in the quarry. He was sprawled across a heap of sharp stones with a huge cut across his head running deep into the skull. He was quite dead. A search of his pockets came up with the remains of the port wine still intact in its bottle, and two keys. He was penniless, which mightn't have caused him a great deal of embarrassment, though he would no doubt have regretted leaving the world with half a bottle of port wine unconsumed.

Where better a place to hold the inquest than the nearby Golden Fleece Inn? It took place there the following Friday and was of short duration, though no doubt the landlord derived some financial benefit at the time, it being an ill wind that blows nobody good. Sarah Jane confirmed that Gill and Smith had called at her home on the evening of the excursion but she knew no more than that, explaining that she hadn't been speaking to her husband at the time. It was obvious that she was still antagonistic towards her late partner. Any feeling must have gone out of the marriage long since though it seemed doubtful if he had cared very much about that. The coroner was especially concerned to know just how drunk the deceased might have been on the night of the accident and if there had been any ill will between himself and his two companions, with obvious implications. But Gill and Smith stuck by their story; that they had been drinking earlier in the day but had stayed sober enough and had merely been looking for fish without result and had lost their way back, adding that 'Jimmy' as Bant liked to call himself on such expeditions, had been chatting normally about such things as his approaching court appearance, saying he expected to get off.

Did any of it really matter? In truth, the authorities might have been relieved to be so conveniently rid of such a nuisance. The jury soon returned with a verdict of accidental death, namely: 'deceased was killed while falling into a quarry'. A far cry from the old verdict of 'death due to a visitation from God'. Though who knows?

John 'Bant' Pattinson was given a decent burial, probably at the expense of his widowed father. And he was to merit one more public mention. The Assizes came soon enough and with them the case of highway robbery against the unfortunate cattle drover. Pattinson's two alleged accomplices were there, Joseph Thompson and Thomas Carlyle – but of course there was a vacant space where Bant Pattinson would have been. It was only necessary to confirm his death and the Chief Constable was swift to do this, advising pithily that while he hadn't seen the body, he had seen the funeral, speaking no doubt too with some satisfaction. From the public gallery came the sound of tittering.

At a time when crime had continued to drop in Cumberland with the average number of prisoners standing trial at the Quarter Sessions over the past five years having been two, and only five prisoners for trial on this occasion, there was ample time to devote to forty-six-year-old Thompson and thirty-two-year-old Carlyle, but they merited short shrift, going down for seven months apiece with no time off for time already spent on remand, even while the purse had been empty and the watch of poor quality. Bant might have livened the proceedings up but he was gone. The whole business seemed rather inconsequential now.

EPILOGUE

There we have it. Sixty years of crime of a selective kind in Cumberland over a period of slow but steady social change. Six whole decades separate the frenzied beating to death of a helpless woman in a hovel above Lanercost, from the ignominious death in Newbiggen Quarry of a criminal degenerate awaiting trial on a charge of mugging. And while the changes had at times been so slow to be scarcely noticeable, change there had been.

During our specific period of scrutiny, one thing has stood out in particular, the psychological make-up of certain of the major players: i.e. John Pearson with his bloodstained rake shank, William Charlton approaching his victim's lonely cottage stealthily through the darkness, Joseph Bell with his home-made bomb, Rudge, Martin and Baker coolly disposing of the policeman who challenged them and throwing his body over a wall. Their kind are still around today with their lack of conscience, their total disregard for the decent norms of everyday society. The functioning of the unruly brute or the scheming reprobate cannot be really said to have altered much at all, whether nor not it is inflamed by drink, motivated by cynicism, bitterness and greed, or by desperate infatuation and lust perhaps, as in the case of the black widow of Helton? Those kind of people will always be with us anywhere.

Nevertheless, there are invariably those unfortunate enough to end up in court who are not necessarily such serious criminals at all and there have been a fair proportion of those in our study too: the Reverend Smith, Catherine Simpson, Sarah Jane Lees, the controversial William Kerr, and the rather laughable Michael Crawley, whose case was somewhat different of course, to name but a few. There have also been several whose state of mind was very questionable such as James Dalgleish, Margaret Messenger and Joseph Wilson. With the addition of such thieving rogues as William Young and Fisher Ashton who would still have balked at murdering anyone, all in all, it has been quite a mixed bag.

So where did this leave the Cumbrian criminal scene in 1894? At first reckoning, in rather poor odour for there had still been capital crime to a fairly disturbing degree in the land of the lakes during our selected period, and other crime too. Yet it probably has to say something of itself that the best candidate available for our final case study was John 'Bant' Pattinson, a small-time rogue who could scarcely ever have aspired to a place amongst the bigger offenders. So things had to be getting better and statistics tell us they were. Not that Cumberland ever produced a Thurtell, a Palmer or a Mary Ann Cotton anyhow. Rudge, Martin and Baker did have a place in Madame Tussauds Chamber of Horrors for some years. But others such as Cass and Charlton have continued to be relegated to the pages of local publications. And one has to search hard amidst the dusty papers in Kew Public Records Office for any additional details at all of Hugh Grant or William Kerr.

But in any case, as has been remarked upon, things had already begun to change on the British penal and social scene. This was particularly true of Cumberland as anywhere in Britain. Most people in the county were now law-abiding, wishing to live as peaceably as possible and this had indeed been the case long before the nineteenth century. Consider too how many of those tried and executed at Carlisle during our sixty year study were even Cumbrians at all. Pearson, Thompson, Charlton, Dalgleish, Rudge, Martin, Baker, Hunter and Wilson. The majority of these had been born and grown up many miles distant. The same could be said for some of those before them. And as social conditions gradually improved locally, so many of the lesser criminals gradually fell away in numbers altogether until well into the twentieth century at least, despite the appalling poverty suffered again in the 1920s and 1930s in parts of the county. The courts too became still more reasonable in Cumberland as anywhere else.

Perhaps of additional importance, drunkenness had finally begun to decline nationwide, it having been the cause of more than its share of the violent crimes committed in Cumberland over very many years. It was still a problem but now it could be justifiably said, towards the end of Queen Victoria's reign, that there was certainly less drunkenness everywhere than there had been at the beginning of it, which all but encompasses the period of our local study. Indeed, in the Brampton area, thanks to the gradual efforts of the Countess of Carlisle and her temperance adherents, public houses were eventually closed for miles around.

Murder itself continued to diminish greatly in Cumberland and most of the more notorious killers over the seventy years proceeding 1894 were again outsiders: Chung Yo Miao, the Grange-in-Borrowdale honeymoon killer of 1928, tried at Carlisle but hanged in Strangeways Prison, Manchester, and Peter Allen the Preston dairyman, who along with Gwynne Evans, murdered John Alan West at Workington in 1964, he and Evans in fact sharing the doubtful honour of being the last two killers to be hanged in Britain. Any other local murders have been of a secondary kind over past decades aside perhaps for the Newton Arlosh and Calthwaite killings of 1977/78 and 1987 but the perpetrators of those were also from outside the county.

Thus most Cumbrians do appear to have simply continued averse to serious crime altogether despite the violent history their ancestors had known. To some extent at least, that trend does appear to have continued on many fronts, more or less to the present time. Over more recent years, violent crime and burglary has certainly increased again in the county, and drug abuse has became a problem as it is a problem anywhere. But we have been assured by the forces of law and order that the region still remains one of the safest in the country. That hopefully has still to speak very much for itself.

BIBLIOGRAPHY

This is not a comprehensive bibliography but covers the publications which have been most useful to me by way of providing additional background information as required.

Bailey B., Hangmen of England, W.H. Allen, 1989

Brown J.W., Round Carlisle Cross (Omnibus edition) Thurnam, 1951

Chesney K., The Victorian Underworld, Temple Smith, 1970

Cooper D., The Lesson of the Scaffold, Allen Lane, 1974

Ferguson R.S., History of Cumberland, 1890

Harrison B., Drink and the Victorians, Faber, 1971

Hughes R., The Fatal Shore – A History of the Transportation of Convicts to Australia: 1787-1868, Knopf, 1986

Jackson H & M., West Cumberland, Hirst-Jackson, 1991

Klontz C., The Embleton Murder

Pringle P., Hue and Cry – The Birth of the British Police, Museum Press, 1955

Richards D. & Hunt J.W., An Illustrated History of Modern Britain 1783-1964, Longmans, 1965

Roberts C., The Radical Countess, Steel Bros (Carlisle) Limited, 1962

Rose L., Massacre of the Innocents – Infanticide in Great Britain 1800-1939, RKP, 1986

Scull A.T., Museums of Madness – The Social Organisation of Insanity in Nineteenth Century England, Allen Lane, 1979

Stengel E., Suicide and Attempted Suicide, Pelican 1969

Topping G. & Potter J.J., Memories of Old Carlisle, Steel Bros, 1922

Towill S., A History of Carlisle, Phillmore, 1991

INDEX

INDEX

INDEX

INDEX